Genealogies of Identity
Interdisciplinary Readings on Sex and Sexuality

Edited by

Margaret Sönser Breen
and Fiona Peters

Amsterdam - New York, NY 2005

The paper on which this book is printed meets the requirements of "ISO
9706:1994, Information and documentation - Paper for documents -
Requirements for permanence".

ISBN: 90-420-1758-9
©Editions Rodopi B.V., Amsterdam - New York, NY 2005
Printed in the Netherlands

Ge   f ntit

Ir

Contents

List of Figures

Welcome to a *Critical Issues* Project

Genealogies of Identity appears within the *Critical Issues* project series of publications. These are inter- and multi-disciplinary research projects which are 'critical' in that the areas being developed are of vital and dominant concern in contemporary living and thinking and in relation to which rigorous and open questioning is required. The *Sex and Sexuality* research and publications project seeks to examine issues of sex and sexuality across a range of critical and cultural perspectives, and aims to explore the associated contexts of love, desire, intimacy, the erotic, betrayal and cheating. Key project themes are:

1. Sex, Sexuality, and Citizenship

> The political main streaming of lesbian and gay issues
> sexuality and health issues
> collective identities: race, class, gender and sexuality
> sexuality and work

2. Love, Desire, and Intimacy

> Psychoanalysis, cultural studies, interdisciplinary approaches
> What is love, what does it mean to desire, and what is intimacy?
> Cultural context and media representations
> Notions of friendship, acquaintance and trust.

3. Sexuality and the Erotic

> Understanding eroticism and the 'erotic'
> National and cultural histories of the erotic
> The erotic imagination
> Gender, bodies and the erotic

4. Love, Sexuality, Betrayal, and Cheating

> Cybersex, private sex and public sex
> Cheating and betrayal
> Marriage, the marriage 'contract', adultery, break-up, divorce

Dr Robert Fisher
Inter-Disciplinary.Net
http://www.inter-disciplinary.net

Preface

Margaret Sönser Breen

Genealogies of Identity: Interdisciplinary Readings of Sex and Sexuality consists of fifteen essays, versions of which were presented at the First Global Conference on Critical Issues in Sexuality, held in Salzburg, Austria, in October 2004. As its title suggests, this volume interrogates historically mediated narratives of the linkages among gender, sex, sexuality, and identity. The selected essays represent a variety of disciplinary approaches, including those of art history, cultural studies, government, history, human resource management, literature, social work, sociology, and theatre studies.

The volume's first section, "History, Sex, and Nation," is made up of four essays (the first two focusing on the nineteenth century and early twentieth century and the second two on the mid-to-late twentieth century) that analyse how discourses of "nation" construct and regulate gender, sex, and sexuality. The section begins with Robert D. Tobin's "Kertbeny's 'Homosexuality' and the Language of Nationalism," which considers the linkages between Karl Maria Kertbeny's participation in the Hungarian nationalist movement and his contributions to sexology. Born into a German family in the 1820s, Kertbeny was a member of the Hungarian expatriate community. Coining the term "homosexuality" in 1869, Kertbeny understood homosexuality in terms "not so much [of] the body as [of] a shared taste and aesthetic." This definition parallels the Hungarian nationalism of the nineteenth century, which "was not based in biology and race so much as in language in culture."

Following Tobin's essay is Julia Bruggemann's "Prostitution, Sexuality, and Gender Roles in Imperial Germany: Hamburg, A Case Study." This piece examines regulated prostitution in Hamburg between the unification of Germany and the start of World War I. During this time prostitution sparked heated public debates, which in turn became sites for the constitution and containment of female sexuality.

The third essay, Susanne Dodillet's "Cultural Clash on Prostitution: Debates on Prostitution in Germany and Sweden in the 1990s," sustains this focus on women and prostitution. Dodillet offers readers a comparative study of prostitution. Shifting attention from the early German state to the contemporary one, the paper contrasts Germany's definitions, state policies, and legislation of prostitution with Sweden's. Whereas Germany has consistently defined prostitution as an economic exchange, Sweden has understood it to be an act of female exploitation. This sharp distinction in definition has led to very different social and legislative responses to sex work. In Sweden, prostitutes are understood to be operating within a sexist [and heterosexist] system, whereby sex workers are only ever women and clients only ever men. The prostitutes are considered the victims of patriarchal oppression, with neither the resources nor opportunities to engage in other means of sustaining themselves. Accordingly, not the selling but rather the buying of sex has been made illegal. By contrast, Germany has legalised prostitution. This decision was informed by what might term an ironic combination of cultural forces – both early twentieth-century sexist social policies, which largely kept women within the domestic realm well into the 1960s, and queer grassroots activism of the 1980s and 1990s, which, predicated on the critical separation of gender and sex, pushed to destigmatise sex acts falling outside of hegemonic gender norms.

The final essay in this first section is Ed Green's "'Staying Bush' – The Influence of Place and Isolation in the Decision by Gay Men to Live in Rural Areas in Australia." In contrast to critics such as John D'Emilio and George Chauncey, who have considered how increased urbanisation has created the possibilities for the production of gay identities, Green explores how gay men have constructed their sexual identities with "little reference" to urban life. Drawing on interviews of gay men living in small towns and farms in Australia, Green argues that isolation actually proves key to gay men's fashioning of selfhood; isolation enhances the lives of gay men living in the bush

Part II of the collection, titled "Literature: Re-writing Desire," consists of four essays that span a range of interests: from the eighteenth-century novel, to contemporary British theatre, to post-colonial writings, to psychoanalytic theory. The first piece is Katerina Kitsi-Mitakou's "Whoring, Incest, Duplicity, or the 'Self-Polluting' Erotics of Daniel Defoe's *Moll Flanders*." Kitsi-Mitakou reads Moll as an embodiment of gender transgression. If on the surface the novel offers a cautionary tale of the importance of heterosexual family life, the very liveliness of the novel makes apparent that "a much more deviant model of sexuality" is at work (or play) here. For Kitsi-Mitakou, "[t]he book's double narrative both exposes and reflects the hypocrisy of early capitalist structures and undermines the harmonious union between the individual and society that it apparently promotes." Moreover, Defoe's *Moll* reveals how the emerging genre of the novel is ideally suited to explore "a new sexual pattern that prizes individualism and autonomy, is founded on the imagination, and engenders perpetual free pleasure."

Following Kitsi-Mitakou's essay is Karoline Gritzner's "Catastrophic Sexualities in Howard Baker's Theatre of Transgression." Gritzner examines the interrelation between erotic sexuality and death in contemporary English playwright and poet Howard Baker's "theatre of catastrophe." Drawing on the theories of Bataille, Baudrillard, and Adorno, Gritzner demonstrates how "erotic desire and the sexual encounter are theatrically articulated as the subversive and destructive effects of consciousness" in three dramas: *Gertrude the Cry*, *Snow White in Knowledge and A Girl*, and *Dead Hands*.

Desire is also a central concern for Shalmalee Palekar in "Unsacred Cows and Protean Beings: Suniti Namjoshi's Re-writing of Postcolonial Lesbian Bodies." In this piece, Palekar considers the work of Indian writer Suniti Namjoshi. Palekar is interested in how Namjoshi's "dense, dialogic, and multi-layered texts use ... protean animal/human bodies to examine questions of community and solidarity, and their implications for minority groups." The "raced" lesbian body is of especial interest here, for it functions as a politically charged doubled site of "otherness" and empowerment, which calls into question and destabilises conventions of literary genre and tradition.

With the final essay of this section, "Desire-less-ness," Fiona Peters interrogates the place of desire within analyses of sexuality. Peters asks "whether or not a concept of desire-less-ness might be useful as a means of understanding some contemporary manifestations of anxiety and cultural lethargy." Framing her inquiry in terms of the psychoanalytic work of Jacques Lacan, Julia Kristeva, and Slavoj Zizek, she offers a conception of desire-less-ness that she in turn applies to the desire-less protagonist of several of crime fiction writer Patricia Highsmith's novels, Tom Ripley.

Part III of this collection, titled "Bodies: Representations of Gender Identities," consists of three essays, the first of which is Barbara Wagner's "Underneath the Clothes – Transvestites without Vests: A Consideration in Art." Analysing works by Vito Acconci, Matthew Barney, Lynda Benglis, and Yasumasa Morimura, Wagner considers the issue of gender transgression in art from the 1970s through the 1990s. Wagner asserts that while "complete" gender transgression necessitates clearly defined gender boundaries, such boundaries, as her reading of the above examples indicates, do not exist.

Like Wagner's piece, Tovi Bibring's essay focuses on the body as the site of gender identity. "Of Swords and Rings: Genital Representation as Defining Sexual Identity and Sexual Liberation in Some Old French *Fabliaux* and *Lais*" examines medieval representations of gender, sex, and sexuality. Bibring demonstrates that "[l]earned, imagined, and desired genitals reflect social position and motivation of the individual as part of his quest for sexual liberation and sexual identity."

The final essay in this section is Serena Petrella's "Only with You – Maybe – *If* You Make Me Happy: A Genealogy of Serial Monogamy as Governance and Self-Governance." Petrella focuses on serial monogamy as a socio-economic ethically marked norm, against which individuals measure their personal fulfilment and success.

Finally, Part IV of the volume, "Legality, Bureaucracy, Religion, and Sexuality," is made up of four essays. The first two examine human rights in terms of positive sexual rights and children's sexual agency respectively. The third looks at gay men in the workplace, while the fourth discusses queer Christian social movements.

The first of these essays, "Alejandro Cervantes-Carson and Tracy Citeroni's "A Project for Sexual Rights: Sexuality, Power, and Human Rights," has as its goal "a political and normative project for the international establishment of sexual rights as human rights." Cervantes-Carson and Citeroni call for moving beyond a politics of tolerance toward a politics of recognition. Drawing on the debate between Foucault and Habermas, they advocate the development of positive sexual rights, designed to protect the individuals and groups historically marginalised because of their gender, sexuality, and/or sexual practices, and, accordingly, vulnerable to the violent disciplining of male hegemonic and heterosexist norms. For the authors, the ultimate goals of the political project of positive sexual rights are the loosening of male hegemony's hold over the discourse of sexuality and the decentring of heterosexuality altogether.

The next essay is Valerie D. Lehr's "International Law, Children's Rights, and Queer Youth." This piece challenges the notions that "youth are most appropriately not sexual and that parents should exercise control over important decision-making," and proposes instead that youth's exercise of agency, including sexual agency, is "particularly important for citizenship development in contemporary societies." Focusing primarily on U.S. discussions of youth, Lehr seeks to connect these discussions with an international human rights discourse.

Following Lehr's discussion of children's rights is Nick Rumens' analysis of gay men in the workplace, "Acting Like a Professional: Identity Dilemmas for Gay Men." Specifically, Rumens considers "how ten openly gay men working in one National Health Services (NHS) Trust in the U.K." avail themselves of contemporary discourses of normality, sexuality, and work in order to "to (re)interpret who they are and manage the tensions arising from how co-workers might seek to fix their identities in terms of sexuality." For Rumens, "professionalism especially articulates and reinforces specific gender conventional displays of masculinity among gay men."

Concluding this section and the volume is Jodi O'Brien's "How Big is Your God? Queer Christian Social Movements." Part of a larger ethnographic study, this essay examines the "emergence and proliferation of a uniquely queer Christianity … as a form of social movement taking place within the pews." O'Brien is particularly interested in the discursive strategies that congregations have developed in order both to recognise the presence of gay and lesbian members and to accommodate the contradictions in which their presence results.

The essays included in *Genealogies of Identity* examine issues of sex and sexuality across a range of critical and cultural perspectives. The essays consider historically specific discourses of sex and sexuality, their effect within public contexts such as the church and the workplace, and the link of those discourses to understandings of individual identity, citizenship, nation, and human rights. As well, the essays analyse representations of sexuality and desire in art, literature, theatre, and theory – representations that serve both to codify and to subvert social norms and aesthetic and theoretical traditions. Finally and more broadly, the essays taken together attest to the critical importance of inter- and multidisciplinary approaches to understanding constructions of gender, sex, and sexuality.

***

Editors' note:

We would like to thank the contributors to this volume, both for their essays and their willingness to answer our queries throughout the editing process. Series editor Robert Fisher has been absolutely central to this project. It was under his enthusiastic guidance that the First Global Conference on Critical Issues in Sexuality was organised. Stephen Morris, along with Margaret and Rob, was a member of the original organising committee. Finally, we would like to thank Eric van Broekhuizen of Rodopi for all his work in seeing this volume through its final publication phase. On a personal level, Fiona would like to thank Gary Peters for useful and incisive suggestions concerning the ordering of the chapters.

Margaret Sönser Breen   Fiona Peters
New London, CT, USA   Bristol, U.K.

PART I

History, Sex, and Nation

Kertbeny's "Homosexuality"
and the Language of Nationalism

Robert D. Tobin

Abstract

Karl Maria Kertbeny (1824-1882) coined the term "homosexuality" in 1869 in the midst of political discussions about the unification of Germany. Although medical discourses took up the vocabulary of "homosexuality," the discourses of liberal Hungarian nationalism affected Kertbeny in his thinking about sexuality. Nineteenth-century Hungarian nationalism was not based in biology and race so much as in language and culture. Similarly, Kertbeny's understanding of sexuality found homosexuality not so much in the body as in a shared taste and aesthetic. **Key Words:** Kertbeny, homosexuality, Germany, Hungary, Austria, liberalism, nationalism.

1.   Introduction

It is generally well known among historians of sexuality that in 1869 Karl Maria Kertbeny was the first person in any language to combine the Greek *homo* [same] with the Latin *sexus* [sex] in order to produce the word "homosexual." Scholarly research has scarcely ever gone beyond this fact, however, probably in part because Kertbeny's publications are difficult to find, not often collected by libraries or reprinted, and even more rarely translated into English. This lack of attention is unfortunate, because Kertbeny's writings reveal important aspects of the emergence of modern conceptions of sexuality. While much scholarship on nineteenth-century sexuality emphasises the growing authority of medicine in the sexual realm, Kertbeny's thinking shows how important liberal political notions of nationalism were in the development of the concept of the homosexual. Even more interestingly, Kertbeny's understanding of nationalism relies heavily on language, which perhaps explains why he found it so important to coin the term "homosexual."

Kertbeny's coinage appears in two open letters to the Prussian Minister of Justice, urging the decriminalisation of sodomy in the penal code that was to apply first to the North German Confederation and then to the unified German state that was to arrive in 1871. As Eve Kosofsky Sedgwick has adumbrated, the mere fact that the word emerged out of political discussion surrounding the creation of a modern nation-state is significant.[1] But it is just as interesting that Kertbeny was a passionate supporter of the Hungarian nationalist cause, which had been brutally crushed by the Habsburgs after the 1848 revolution. After a twenty-year freeze, though, the Hungarians had made significant progress in 1867 with the codification of the Habsburg dual monarchy and the creation of the entity known as Austria-Hungary or the Austro-Hungarian Empire. Kertbeny's deep involvement in Hungarian nationalism informed his thinking about civil rights and group identity and set the tone for the emergence of modern homosexual identity.

Karl Maria Kertbeny (1824-1882) was a quirky mid-nineteenth-century, central-European character. Born into a German family with the surname Benkert, he changed his name to Kertbeny because he wanted to adopt a Hungarian identity and he thought the new name sounded more authentic. Excepting only a few years in Budapest, he traveled through Europe from 1840 until the 1870s, part of the Hungarian expatriate community that became especially large after the failed 1848 revolution.[2] Although in his open letters, he called himself a physician, he tried to support himself as a man of letters, churning out volume after volume of essays and translations into German of Hungarian authors, as he traveled throughout Europe while agitating for social reform. Habsburg police reports give an instructive summary of Kertbeny's working life:

> Benkert, Karl Maria, also known as Kerbent and Remkhazy, writer from Pest, was a partisan for democracy and the Hungarian insurrection in 1848 and was sent as such by the leaders of the revolution to Germany, in order to awaken sympathy for the Hungarian cause and win interest for the Hungarians in the journals.[3]

The life of a man of letters abroad was not lucrative, and Herzer writes that Kertbeny's pattern seems to have been: (1) travel to a new European city, (2) seek out prominent authors, artists, and leftist political figures, (3) borrow money, and (4) run out of town. His financial state was such that, like many other Hungarian emigrés, he resorted to working as an informant to the Austrian secret police, a task that he apparently did not perform well.[4] Sadly, Kertbeny's literary efforts repaid as little in fame as they did in money: when his writings were noticed at all, they earned epithets such as "the most idle scribbling" and "repellent."[5]

Kertbeny was nothing if not highly connected in the world of the arts. While traveling, he frequently sought out creative people, such as Franz Liszt, Bettina von Arnim, George Sand, Alexander von Humboldt, Paul Heyse, and Max Stirner.[6] Many of his interlocuters were concerned – either personally or intellectually – with sexual desire between members of the same sex. With Charles Baudelaire, for instance, Kertbeny discussed the dark side of the passions of the author Eugène Sue. Henning Bech speculates that when Kertbeny met Hans Christian Andersen in 1860 in Geneva, the Danish author recoiled at Kertbeny's efforts to label him a "homosexual" – a thesis that Manfred Herzer derides.[7] Kertbeny himself insisted that his translations of the Hungarian national poet, Sander Petöfi, so impressed Andersen that the Danish author had them translated into Danish. In the 1860s, Kertbeny met and corresponded with Karl Heinrich Ulrichs, who worked publicly for the rights of urnings (his word for people with male bodies and female souls who sexually desired other men). Like Ulrichs, Kertbeny used the Serbe Verlag in Leipzig as a publisher to disseminate his work on sexuality. He also met with the liberal author Heinrich Zschokke, whose 1821 short story "Eros" is one of the first efforts in German prose to understand male-male desire. On his peregrinations throughout Europe, Kertbeny was excited and proud to meet with Heinrich Heine, who had castigated his fellow German poet, August von Platen, for his sexual interest in other men. In 1861, Kertbeny reported that in their discussions, Heine had called Platen "a ...," denying history the reward of knowing precisely what word was actually used.[8]

Kertbeny's claim to fame now is his combination of the Greek *homo* and the Latin *sexus* to describe someone who is inclined to have sex with a member of his or her own sex. Immanuel Kant had admittedly spoken of *homogen* and *heterogen* sexual choices, but it was Kertbeny who first employed the word "homosexual."[9] In two "open letters" to the Minister of Justice, each published in 1869, Kertbeny makes statements such as the following: "…. in addition to the normal sexual drive of humanity and the animal kingdom, nature, in her supreme whimsy over man and woman, has given certain masculine or feminine individuals a homosexual [*homosexualen*] drive."[10] He uses the term both to describe a person – the homosexual [*der Homosexuale*] – and to describe a sexuality – homosexuality [*der Homosexualismus*].[11] Kertbeny's publication merited a reference in an 1870 edition of a scholarly journal on Prussian law, but otherwise found little resonance.[12]

The word "homosexual," though, took on a life of its own. Herzer has discovered that just three years later, in 1872, another Hungarian translator actively involved in the Hungarian revolution, Daniel von Kaszony, who mentions Kertbeny's writings on homosexuality in his personal correspondence, uses the terms *homo sexualisme*, *homosexualiteit*, and *homosexuelle verkeering* in a publication that he translated into Dutch, which suggests that the term began to catch on at the time among radical Hungarians.[13] The word was adopted by the zoologist Gustav Jäger, who agreed to publish a number of Kertbeny's writings on homosexuality in his book *Die Entdeckung der Seele* [The Discovery of the Soul], which appeared in 1880. From there the term spread through sexological writings to the general public.

2.   Liberalism

Although the term "homosexual" attained prominence via medical circles, it is important to recognise that it first emerged in the context of a political discussion. Prussia's influence at this time was expanding; in 1869 it was unifying German law in the North German Confederation, which pointedly excluded Austria. The stakes were high: the single legal code that came out of this Confederation became the basis for the penal code of unified Germany in 1871. While many German principalities had adopted the Napoleonic code, with its liberal attitude toward consensual noncommercial sex between adults, Prussia had kept severe penalties for sodomy on the books, in part to distinguish itself from France and its lax moral ways. (In this respect, the country behaved like England, which also kept sodomy on the books in an effort to prove its moral superiority over the French.[14]) Kertbeny's intervention was an effort to encourage the Germans to use the opportunity that the rewriting and rethinking of the legal code provided to toss aside its old sodomy laws. "Homosexuality" as a term, then, was born in a political discussion, one, moreover, that took place at the birth of the German nation state.

The bureaucrats designing the new legal code understood which discourses had special interest in the regulation of sexuality. In his letter, Kertbeny quotes the astonishingly clear-sighted analysis of those committed to the continued criminalisation of sodomy. In proposing the application of the Prussian sodomy laws to the entire North German Confederation, the experts argued that although decriminalisation "can be justified from the standpoint of medicine, as well as through certain theories of law, the legal consciousness of the *Volk* judges these acts to be not merely a vice, but a crime."[15] A century before Foucault, German political figures were well aware of medicine's interest in asserting its responsibility for sexual matters and the liberal legal argument for the state to give up its interest in such arguably moral matters. Ultimately, Kertbeny's argument was to fail because the new German state was not prepared to accept such liberal scientific claims and took a stand on the sodomy laws.

As a liberal, Kertbeny argues for a strictly secular state. Kertbeny denounces sodomy laws as carry-overs from the days when canon law concerned itself with "original sin, the devil and witches."[16] Instead, Kertbeny hopes that the new German nation will be a "modern constitutional state" [*Rechtsstaat*], "the strict opposite of the theocratic-hierarchical autocratic state [*Pflichtstaat*] of feudalism."[17] A classical liberal, Kertbeny argues that the constitutional state's only duty is "to protect the rights of its citizens."[18] According to Kertbeny, "the constitutional state is only concerned with questions of sexuality insofar as the rights of others are infringed upon."[19] To back up his point, Kertbeny cites a series of liberal legal theorists including: Johann Jakob Cella, who had argued in 1787 that the law should only punish carnal crimes if they hurt others; Jean Jacques Régis de Cambacérès, who had moved forward Napoleon's liberal legal code; and Anselm von Feuerbach, who had attempted to distinguish between things that were immoral, like witchcraft, heresy, blasphemy and sodomy, and things that were illegal, like murder or rape, when he reworked Bavaria's penal code in 1813.[20]

In his liberal appeal to decriminalise sodomy, Kertbeny uses a language of human rights that draws equally upon the hypocrisy and the idealism of the human rights movement. In a dubiously emancipatory moment, he claims that sex is "one of the first of all human rights, which is not even denied to the Negro."[21] Despite assuming that Blacks normally have fewer rights than anyone else, he preaches a liberal gospel of "the ever more widespread consciousness of the equality of legal rights of life."[22] In the tradition of classical liberalism, Kertbeny generally envisions the right to sexuality negatively – that is to say, he argues that the state should stay out of the bedroom and should not impinge on the sexual freedom of his new category of homosexuals. As he remarks, the liberal state does not meddle uninvited in bad marriages, unless someone is being harmed – why should it interfere in "the possible relationship between man and man"?[23]

Behind Kertbeny's argument stands the ideal – cherished by many central European liberals – that the constitutional state should protect the rights of its minorities against the tyranny of the masses. Kertbeny's minority rights argument works because he insists that homosexuals are an identifiable group with immutable and fixed desires. Homosexuals are an identifiable type of person, not so much because of their bodily characteristics, but because of their shared tastes. "Anthropological observers" have noticed that male homosexuals are exclusively attracted to "the masculine *an sich* ... to its habitual atmosphere as well as its genital-erective particularity."[24] He also attributes an aesthetic sensibility to male homosexuals, because "from a purely anthropological perspective, the male body as an end in itself is uncontestably more beautiful."[25] All of this leads Kertbeny to conclude that the homosexual has a "fixed nature," which cannot be changed to desire women and which shouldn't be confused with a sexual attraction to children.

3.   Nationalism with a Twist: Magyarisation

Kertbeny's sense of human rights emerges from his belief in nationalism. Like most nineteenth-century liberals, Kertbeny believed that time was on his side, that history was progressing in a positive direction. As examples of steps forward in that progress, Kertbeny lists such well-known revolutionary years as 1789 and 1848, but he also adds historical developments that might seem more obscure, such as the Austro-Prussian War of 1866, in which Prussia forced Austria out of the German Confederation and paved the way for its own ascendancy first in the North German Confederation and then in the German Empire. Austria's loss in 1866 destabilised the Habsburgs so much that they were prepared to give in to the long-held aspirations of the Hungarians and divide their empire, creating the dual monarchy known as Austria-Hungary. The influence of central European nationalism on Kertbeny's thinking about sexuality is an untold aspect of the story of the emergence of the concept of homosexuality.

Kertbeny's profound commitment to Hungarian nationalism taught him the liberal rhetoric that he espouses in his open letter to the Minister of Justice. The spirit of liberalism permeated the Hungarian revolutionary cause. Among the demands of the 1848 revolutionaries were the abolition of serfdom, civic and religious equality before the law, universal taxes for all (including the nobility, who had been exempt from taxation), annual parliamentary meetings, freedom of the press, the release of political prisoners, trial by jury and a military oath of allegiance to the constitution.[26] Emancipation of the Jews was a consistent demand of the revolutionaries.[27] The revolutionary poet Petöfi had fought to bring Jews into the National Guard and denounced the government when it showed signs of backing away from emancipation.[28] The government that took over in 1867, when Hungary became autonomous, instituted many of the liberal reforms proposed twenty years before.

Despite his nationalism, Kertbeny places only a limited belief in the *Volk*. Commenting on the decision by the German authorities to ignore the medical and legal advice to decriminalise sodomy because of "the legal consciousness of the *Volk*," Kertbeny acidly notes that the *Volk* also used to believe in magic and witchcraft and that it can easily be misled.[29] "The legal consciousness of the *Volk*" is not something "against which all justice and logic must be silent!"[30] Although a sense of nationalism informs his notion of sexual identity, his nationalism is not the blind belief in the *Volk* that characterised some of the Romantics. Instead, Kertbeny's is a liberal nationalism based on the idea that the state should protect the rights of its minorities. Moreover, it is a nationalism based heavily on language rather than biology.

To understand this particular vision of nationalism, it is necessary to take a brief tour through Hungarian history. Once the Hungarians achieved their autonomous status within the Habsburg dual monarchy, they developed their own unique sense of nationalism, based on a linguistic sense of national identity. While many eastern and central European nationalist movements relied heavily on a belief in blood-based racial theory to prop up their identities, the Hungarians needed a different ideology. In 1867, only about 40% of the population of the Hungarian half of the Austro-Hungarian Empire was ethnically Hungarian. Romanians, South Slavs, Germans, and Slovaks each contributed as much as ten or fifteen percent of the population of Hungary, and there were numerous other smaller groups as well.[31] At times the national distinctions were blurry. At the beginning of the twentieth century, one Habsburg statistical officer wrote about an area along the border between Hungary and Slovakia,

> this population is on such an uncertain borderline between belonging to the Hungarian and Slovak national groups that it can be called Hungarian as justifiably as Slovak. It speaks and uses both languages alike, and it is practically up to the fancy of the census taker whether he lists them as Hungarians or Slovaks.[32]

As far as Hungarian nationalists were concerned, it was important for the success of the Hungarian half of the Habsburg Empire that national identity be an acquired characteristic.

For Hungarian nationalists, all the inhabitants of Hungary were Magyars, as was spelled out in legislation when the dual monarchy was established:

> in accordance with the fundamental principles of the constitution, all Hungarian citizens [constitute] a nation in the political sense, the one and indivisible Hungarian nation, in which every citizen of the fatherland is a member who enjoys equal rights, regardless of the national group to which he belongs.[33]

In order to promote a sense of national unity, the Hungarians embarked on an extensive program of Magyarisation, which relied heavily on the promotion of the Hungarian language. One historian reports that "the view prevailed that complete linguistic assimilation would also lead to total political integration, that is, allegiance to the Hungarian nation."[34] The schooling system was to help in the creation of a national identity: "One of the advocates of Magyarisation explained that the secondary schools were like machines: in went the Slovak boys at one end and out came the Hungarian men at the other."[35] While there was some concern about the population growth among the "sons of Árpád" (Hungarians by birth), there was much more exultation about the increasing population of Magyarised

Hungarian nationals.[36] Language and culture were the key elements in this sense of national identity.

The Magyar version of nationalism certainly had its repressive aspects, even though it was not biologically and racially based. While many German and Jewish Hungarians enthusiastically joined the Magyarisation programs, other ethnic groups resisted. Class played a role as well as ethnic background. In particular, the middle classes, including both the intelligenstia and the merchants, were prone to assimilate: "The higher up a citizen climbed on the social ladder, the more likely he was to change his national identity."[37] An initially liberal law on minorities within Hungary assured a variety of minority rights, largely based on language: petitions to the government could be delivered in the mother tongue, churches could hold services in whatever language they chose, schools could be taught in the language of the community, secondary education was supposed to be available in the language of minority groups.[38] However the administration of the nationalities law increasingly emphasised the effort to mold a Hungarian national identity out of the disparate peoples in the south-eastern half of the Habsburg Empire: "Over the years a nationalism which had been originally liberal in character began to identify itself wholly with the traditional Magyar sense of national mission, which viewed the Magyars' historic task in the second half of the nineteenth century as pioneering the new bourgeois economic, social and cultural progress in eastern Europe and the Balkans."[39] Clearly, concern for the rights of minorities began to dissipate, once the Hungarians no longer considered themselves a minority

Nonetheless, the Magyarisation program was surprisingly successful. One could read in 1896 that, "as far as the speed of Magyarisation is concerned, it is quite without parallel in the history of any nation."[40] Roughly two million people "converted" and became Hungarian in the final decades of the Austro-Hungarian Empire.[41] Putting it another way, "at the outbreak of World War I, one out of five persons who professed themselves Hungarians had turned Hungarian themselves or came from families that had become Hungarian during the previous two generations."[42] This includes up to 700,000 Jews, 500,000 Germans, 400,000 Slovaks, 150,000 Romanians and 150,000 South Slavs.[43]

A significant number of the political and cultural leaders of the Hungarian national movement were products of Magyarisation. Among the thirteen generals of the Hungarian revolutionary army whom the Austrians executed on October 6, 1849, there were Germans from Austria and Hungary, Hungarians from Armenia, as well as Croat and a Serbs.[44] Leading journalists, musicians and advocates of Magyarisation came from German, Jewish, and other backgrounds.[45] The poet Petöfi was the child of a Serbian father and a Slovak mother and actually changed his surname from Petrovics to the more Hungarian Petöfi.[46] Kertbeny himself, as we have seen, adopted a Hungarian identity, although born into a German family.

Even many people of ethnic Hungarian background underwent Magyarisation, because knowledge of Hungarian had declined precipitously – especially among the elites – at the beginning of the nineteenth century. Astonishingly, Latin had been the language of government well into the nineteenth century. The nobles spoke German. In fact, the Hungarian revolutionary army used German as a language of communication, because many of its officers did not speak Hungarian at all.[47] The great liberal Hungarian politician, Stephen Szechenyi, was not alone among the early revolutionaries in feeling more at home in German than Hungarian.[48] Ethnic Hungarians, as well as people from other ethnicities, went through Magyarisation in order to assume a Hungarian national identity.

4.   Sexuality

While Kertbeny claims to have had "a sharp eye for questions of race,"[49] it is significant that he and his fellow Hungarian nationalists understood nationality more as a linguistic and cultural phenomenon than as a racial one. For Kertbeny, sexuality too was a cultural construct, as well as a biological reality. Admittedly, Kertbeny frequently refers to homosexual desire as "inborn."[50] Nonetheless, he does not stress the innate aspect of sexuality as much as his fellow emancipationist Ulrichs. In fact, he cautioned Ulrichs from relying too heavily on the congenital nature of same-sex desire. As he observed in a letter to Ulrichs,

> there are people born with innate bloodthirstiness …
> One doesn't let these people do whatever they want or
> follow their desires. Even if one doesn't punish them for
> intentional acts if their constitution is proven medically,
> one does isolate them as much as possible and protect
> society from their excesses.

He concludes that "nothing would be won if the proof of innateness were successful."[51] (Kertbeny's example is not arbitrary – he argues, namely, that history shows no records of any "bloodthirsty" homosexuals.[52] That is to say, "bloodthirstiness" and "homosexuality" seem to be opposing qualities in his worldview.) Even though Kertbeny does publicly make use of the argument of innate sexual desire, it is clear that he privately harbored doubts on the subject.

Kertbeny believed that there were cultural differences in the expression of homosexuality. He argued that, whereas "in southern lands this inclination is directed at the beauty of mature youths,"

> the great majority of northerners in whom this inclination is innate [!] have a great horror of the boyish, the effeminate in their own sex and all the more passion, not for the "youth" [*Jüngling*], but for the "guy" [*Bursch*] (to which category soldiers usually belong), indeed for the man, even the mature man who has already passed 40.[53]

Later, Kertbeny would assert:

> in the Orient, in the South, among the Gypsies among us, and indeed often among the village Jews, a boy is already sexually active, indeed often married, at ten or twelve; in the North, however, the youth of the Indo-European race is not sexual, does not attract seduction and is not susceptible to seduction, until between 15 and 18.[54]

While revealing his "sharp eye for questions of race," Kertbeny is trying especially hard in these passages to disentangle homosexuality from any hint of pedophilia.

Despite this strain of biologised and racialised thinking about sexuality, Kertbeny remains in his later years a skeptical "opponent of all symptomological categorisations, which are too reminiscent of witch hunts."[55] Just as the Hungarian nationalists did not rely exclusively on race to construct the Hungarian, Kertbeny does not rely solely on biology to understand the homosexual. In his description of the homosexual, he does not attempt to locate difference in the body so much as in culture: a shared attraction to the masculine, an aesthetic sensibility are what unite the male homosexuals.

The linguistic basis of the Hungarian model of national identity sheds some light on the importance of literature in many of the writings of the early homosexual emancipation movement. In discussing Hungarian identity, Kertbeny emphasises the importance of poets like Petöfi because language and literature express "national character."[56] Similarly, those agitating for the rights of men who loved men rely heavily on literary productions in their arguments. Heinrich Hössli's two-volume apology for male-male love from the 1830s, *Eros*, consists in large part of citations from the literary traditions of the world. At the end of the century, Elisar von Kupffer's anthology of homoerotic poetry from around the world,

Lieblingminne und Freundesliebe [Ardor for Favorites and Love of Friends], continued to operate on the belief that the cultural products of language can help consolidate an identity based on same-sex love.

Kertbeny's model of sexual identity relies on an analogy with national identity that differs from a model that would become extremely popular in late-nineteenth-century central Europe and elsewhere: the model that compares homosexuals with Jews. Kertbeny is sympathetic to the plight of Jews, especially those in Austria:

> When one thinks of Austria and also knows how Jews have been treated there forever, then one will understand and confirm that the son of no other *Volk* in the Donau Monarchy may carry so much bitterness and contempt in the heart as precisely an Austrian Jew.[57]

Here it is worth recalling that while anti-Semitism was a virulent part of daily politics in Austria, the Hungarian government generally courted Jews, who were in turn enthusiastic supporters of the Magyarisation program.

Nonetheless, in his homage to Petöfi, Kertbeny distinguishes between the national poet, who "follows the inspirations and directions of his nationality" (even though he too was Magyarised) and the Jewish Heine, who as a "member of a cosmopolitan *Volk*," "feels the pains and misery of the entire world."[58] Despite the word "cosmopolitan," which often indicates anti-Semitic bias in central European writing on Jews, Kertbeny is not motivated by anti-Semitism – in fact, the entire collection in which this remark appears is dedicated to Heine, who is said to be a European, rather than a merely national, poet. Unlike writers such as Ulrichs, who compared homosexuals with Jews in order to gain for homosexuals the same minority rights that he wanted to see for Jews, Kertbeny distinguishes between Jews and national minorities. Whereas Kertbeny views Jewishness as transcending nationality, his cultural understanding of Hungarian identity emphasises its social construction through language and culture. The Hungarian national minority is the model that inspires his thinking on homosexuality.[59]

In concluding, it is important to remember that Kertbeny did not have a full-blown concept of gay identity when he coined the term "homosexual." Moreover, it is true that the assumptions associated with the word were heavily informed by the medical establishment that appropriated them. But it is nonetheless still significant that Kertbeny was operating in a climate that was thinking in complex ways about national identity and politics as he developed his sense of sexual identity. The connection between the coining of the term "homosexual" and the emergence of the German state is itself telling. Even more interesting is the effect on emergent conceptions of sexuality of the quite sophisticated thinking about minority groups and rights that was going on in the second half of the nineteenth century in the Austro-Hungarian Empire. Kertbeny, with his passion for Hungarian nationalism, was in the thick of such thinking. The understanding of Hungarian identity as determined and defined by language and culture colored his conceptualisation of homosexuality. Kertbeny is writing therefore before nationalism had become the reified and largely unexamined "central tool of liberal analysis" that Sedgwick argues needs deconstruction in her essay, "Nationalisms and Sexuality."[60]   In his writings, the argument that sexuality and nationality are analogous means that both are at least in part the products of social construction.

Notes

1. Eve Kosofsky Sedgwick, *The Epistemology of the Closet* (Berkeley: University of California Press, 1990), 133.

2. Manfred Herzer, "Kertbeny and the Nameless Love," *Journal of Homosexuality* 12.1 (Fall 1985), 3.

3. Cited by Manfred Herzer, "Kertbenys Leben und Sexualitätsstudien," in: Karl Maria Kertbeny, *Schriften zur Homosexualitätsforschung*, edited by Manfred Herzer (Berlin: Verlag rosa Winkel, 2000), 23. My translation.

4. The Habsburg secret police had heavily infiltrated the expatriate Hungarian community, according to Paul Lendvai, *The Hungarians: A Thousand Years of Victory in Defeat*, translated by Ann Major (Princeton: Princeton University Press, 2003), 254. On Kertbeny's work as an informant, see Ágnes Deák, "Translator, Editor, Publisher, Spy: The Informative Career of Károly Kertbeny (1824-1882)," *Hungarian Quarterly* 39.149 (1998), 26-33.

5. Herzer, "Kertbeny and the Nameless Love," 1-2.

6. Ibid., 3.

7. Henning Bech, "A Dung Beetle in Distress: Hans Christen Andersen meets Karl Maria Kertbeny, Geneva, 1860. Some Notes on the Archeology of Homosexuality and the Importance of Tuning," *Journal of Homosexuality* 34.3/4 (1998): 139-162. Herzer's response is in his essay "Kertbenys Leben und Sexualitätsstudien," 28.

8. This was in the first volume of Kertbeny's *Silhouetten und Reliquien*, p. 236. Cited by Herzer, "Kertbenys Leben und Sexualitätsstudien," 29.

9. In notes to the lectures from Kant's *Moralphilosophie* [Moral Philosophy] of 1785, he writes, "Secondly, belonging to the *criminus carnis contra naturam* [carnal crimes against nature] is the communion of

the *sexus homogenii*, when the object of the sexual inclination remains admittedly among people, but is changed such that the community of sex is not *heterogen*, but rather *homogen*, that is, when a woman satisfies her inclination with a woman or a man with a man." Kant's *Gesammelte Schriften*, vol. 27, section 4.1 (1974), 31; cited in Herzer, 50-51. My translation.

10. Kertbeny, *Schriften*, 110. All translations of Kertbeny are my own.

11. Ibid., 115, 142.

12. C. R. Sontag, "Drei Bemerkungen zu dem Entwurf eines Strafrechtes für den Norddeutschen Bund," *Archiv für preussisches Strafrecht* 18 (1870), 26. Cited by Herzer, "Kertbeny and the Nameless Love," 4.

13. Herzer, 45.

14. Louis Crompton, *Byron and Greek Love: Homophobia in 19ᵗʰ-Century England* (Berkeley: University of California Press, 1985).

15. Kertbeny, *Schriften*, 73.

16. Ibid., 99.

17. Ibid., 78.

18. Ibid., 79.

19. Ibid., 157.

20. For more on the legal history, see Isabel Hull, *Sexuality, State and Civil Society in Germany, 1700-1815* (Ithaca: Cornell University Press, 1996). See also Paul Derks, *Die Schande der heiligen Päderastie: Homosexualität und Öffentlichkeit in der deutschen Literatur, 1750-1850* (Berlin: Verlag rosa Winkel, 1990), 140-160.

21. Kertbeny, *Schriften*, 88.

22. Ibid., 83.

23. Ibid., 271.

24. Ibid., 113.

25. Ibid., 114.

26. Joerg K. Hoensch, *A History of Modern Hungary, 1867-1994*, second ed., translated by Kim Traynor (New York: Longman, 1966), 6.

27. Paul Lendvai, *The Hungarians: A Thousand Years of Victory in Defeat*, translated by Ann Major (Princeton: Princeton University Press, 2003), 231, 238.

28. Lendvai, 219.

29. Kertbeny, *Schriften*, 162, 166.

30. Ibid., 161.

31. Lendvai, 225.

32. Laszlo Katus, "Hungarians and National Minorities: A Demographic Survey (1850-1918)," *Hungarians and Their Neighbors in*

Modern Times, 1867-1950, edited by Ferenc Glatz (New York: Columbia University Press, 1995), 19-20.

33. Law XLIV of 1868; cited by Hoensch, 28.

34. Hoensch, 30.

35. Zoltan Szasz, "Government Policy and the Nationalities," *Hungarians and their Neighbors in Modern Times, 1867-1950*, edited by Ferenc Glatz (New York: Columbia University Press, 1995), 29.

36. Katus, 18.

37. Hoensch, 31.

38. Szasz, 25.

39. Hoensch, 29.

40. Katus, 18.

41. Hoensch, 31.

42. Katus, 17.

43. Ibid., 17; Hoensch 31.

44. Lendvai, 239-40.

45. Ferenc Glatz, "Bourgeois Transformation, Assimilation, and Nationalism," *Hungarians and Their Neighbors in Modern Times, 1867-1950*, edited by Ferenc Glatz (New York: Columbia University Press, 1995), 33.

46. Emil Niederhauser, "People and Nations in the Habsburg Monarchy," *Hungarians and Their Neighbors in Modern Times, 1867-1950*, edited by Ferenc Glatz (New York: Columbia University Press, 1995), 9.

47. Lendvai, 234.

48. Niederhauser, 9.

49. Kertbeny, *Schriften*, 261.

50. Ibid., 290.

51. "Ein Brief von Kertbeny in Hannover an Ulrichs in Würzburg," in *Capri* 1 (1987), 34. Cited by Manfred Herzer, "Einleitung," Heinrich Hössli, *Eros. Materialien* (Berlin: rosa Winkel, 1996), 11, footnote 11.

52. Kertbeny, *Schriften*, 212.

53. Ibid., 132-33.

54. Ibid., 300.

55. Ibid., 322.

56. Karl Maria Kertbeny, *Petöfi's Tod vor dreissig Jahren 1849* (Leipzig: Friedrich, 1880), 60.

57. Karl Maria Kertbeny, *Erinnerung an Charles Sealsfield* (Leipzig: Ahn, 1864), 29.

58. Karl Maria Kertbeny, "Einleitung," Alexander Petöfi, *Gedichte*, translated by K. M. Kertbeny (Frankfurt/M: Literarische Anstalt, 1849), xvi.

59. For a good review of studies of the comparison between Jews and homosexuals, see Daniel Boyarin, Daniel Itzkovitz and Ann Pellegrini, eds., *Queer Theory and the Jewish Question* (New York: Columbia University Press, 2003).

60. Eve Kosofsky Sedgwick, *Tendencies* (Durham, N.C.: Duke University Press, 1993), 147.

Select Bibliography

Bech, Henning. "A Dung Beetle in Distress: Hans Christen Andersen meets Karl Maria Kertbeny, Geneva, 1860. Some Notes on the Archeology of Homosexuality and the Importance of Tuning." *Journal of Homosexuality* 34.3/4 (1998): 139-162.

Boyarin, Daniel, Daniel Itzkovitz and Ann Pelgrini, eds. *Queer Theory and the Jewish Question.* New York: Columbia University Press, 2003.

Crompton, Louis. *Byron and Greek Love: Homophobia in 19th-Century England.* Berkeley: University of California Press, 1985.

Deák, Ágnes. "Translator, Editor, Publisher, Spy: The Informative Career of Károly Kertbeny (1824-1882)." *Hungarian Quarterly* 39.149 (1998): 26-33.

Derks, Paul. *Die Schande der heiligen Päderastie: Homosexualität und Öffentlichkeit in der deutschen Literatur, 1750-1850.* Berlin: Verlag rosa Winkel, 1990.

Glatz, Ferenc. "Bourgeois Transformation, Assimilation, and Nationalism." *Hungarians and Their Neighbors in Modern Times, 1867-1950*, edited by Ferenc Glatz, 33-43. New York: Columbia University Press, 1995.

Herzer, Manfred. "Einleitung." Heinrich Hössli. *Eros: Die Männerliebe der Griechen. Materialien*, 7-34. Berlin: Verlag rosa Winkel, 1996.

——. "Kertbeny and the Nameless Love," *Journal of Homosexuality* 12.1 (Fall 1985): 1-26.

——. "Kertbenys Leben und Sexualitätsstudien." Karl Maria Kertbeny. *Schriften zur Homosexualitätsforschung*, edited by Manfred Herzer, 7-61. Berlin: Verlag rosa Winkel, 2000.

Hoensch, Jörg K. *A History of Modern Hungary, 1867-1994.* Second edition. Translated by Kim Traynor. New York: Longman, 1966.

Hull, Isabel. *Sexuality, State and Civil Society in Germany, 1700-1815.* Ithaca: Cornell University Press, 1996.

Katus, László. "Hungarians and National Minorities: A Demographic Survey (1850-1918)." *Hungarians and Their Neighbors in Modern Times, 1867-1950*, edited by Ferenc Glatz, 13-21. New York: Columbia University Press, 1995.

Kertbeny, Karl Maria. "Einleitung." Sander Petöfi. *Gedichte*, translated by K. M. Kertbeny. Frankfurt/M: Literarische Anstalt, 1849.
——. *Erinnerung an Charles Sealsfield*. Leipzig: Ahn, 1864.
——. *Petöfi's Tod vor dreissig Jahren 1849*. Leipzig: Friedrich, 1880.
——. *Schriften zur Homosexualitätsforschung*, edited by Manfred Herzer. Berlin: Verlag rosa Winkel, 2000.
Lendvai, Paul. *The Hungarians: A Thousand Years of Victory in Defeat*. Trans. Ann Major. Princeton: Princeton University Press, 2003.
Niederhauser, Emil. "Peoples and Nations in the Habsburg Monarchy." *Hungarians and Their Neighbors in Modern Times, 1867-1950*. Edited by Ferenc Glatz, 7-13. New York: Columbia University Press, 1995.
Sedgwick, Eve Kosofsky. *The Epistemology of the Closet*. Berkeley: University of California Press, 1990.
——. *Tendencies*. Durham, N.C.: Duke University Press, 1993.
Szász, Zoltán. "Government Policy and the Nationalities." *Hungarians and Their Neighbors in Modern Times, 1867-1950*, edited by Ferenc Glatz, 23-32. New York: Columbia University Press, 1995.

Prostitution, Sexuality, and Gender Roles in Imperial Germany: Hamburg, A Case Study

Julia Bruggemann

Abstract
   This paper examines the system of regulated prostitution in Hamburg, its implementation, and the public debate it engendered between 1870 and 1914. Moreover, the paper addresses the construction of female sexuality and gender roles through the prism of prostitution. During this period, regulated prostitution was a contested issue and gave rise to intense public debates about its causes and implications. These discourses were sites where female sexuality was debated, controlled, contested, and historically constituted. **Key Words:** prostitution, Hamburg, sexuality, abolition, regulation.

1.   Introduction

   "I shall write down everything sincerely and honestly so that the whole world will be shocked to learn what the police have been capable of."[1] This bold indictment of police conduct was written in 1907 with the express purpose to expose illegal and immoral behavior in the police department in Hamburg. In the account that followed, the author alleged gross misconduct by several police officers in the second largest city in the German Empire and threatened to publish the text in form of a pamphlet in order to reach a wide audience. Yet the denunciation was not written by the office of the prosecutor or internal affairs. Nor was it the revenge of a disgruntled citizen of the port city. Surprisingly, it came from the pen of a prostitute. In spite of her marginalised position she felt entitled and indeed compelled to expose the transgressions of the local police. The accuser, Mathilde Schween, was a sixty-two-year old unmarried woman. According to her own narrative, she had been taken to a brothel in Hamburg by a corrupt police official when she was still a young girl and a virgin. As an officially registered prostitute in Hamburg and other German cities, she spent much of her adult life on the periphery of respectable society and amassed an intimate knowledge of the prostitution trade. Even after she was dismissed from police supervision in 1891, she did not leave the milieu. Instead she sold flowers and traded with tobacco and linens in those streets, which were populated by prostitutes, their procurers, and customers. At the end of her life Mathilde Schween wanted to publicise her experiences. In her manuscript she claimed to tell "all of the atrocities and abominations committed by the police [in Hamburg] since 1862 regarding the procurement of prostitution and trafficking in prostitutes."[2] According to her text, these included incidents of police corruption, the misconduct of specific officers, and the arbitrary enforcement of the official rules and regulations.

During her years as a "controlled girl" or "public girl" (*Kontrollmädchen* or *Öffentliches Mädchen*), as official prostitutes were called in Hamburg, Mathilde Schween suffered many humiliations. For example, like many other prostitutes, she was repeatedly incarcerated in the local workhouse, a quasi-prison for indigents and petty criminals. Moreover, she had an extensive criminal record including such offenses as assault, extortion, violations of the merchants code, as well as twenty-four convictions due to transgressions of the police regulations for registered prostitutes.[3] Indeed, Mathilde Schween led a life that was typical for a woman in her line of work, circumscribed by intrusive regulations and subject to repeated criminal prosecutions, although the fact that we know some personal information about her makes her unusual. Also atypical was Schween's willingness to stand up to public officials and allege unfair and corrupt treatment by the police. Most other prostitutes did not leave any traces in the public records.

In the end Mathilde was not successful in her efforts to publicise her allegations, because the police blocked her attempts by undermining her credibility. In a reply to Schween's accusations, one official argued:

> in light of these facts [her lifestyle and criminal record] and taking into consideration that women of such immoral conduct are notoriously unreliable and have lost all abilities to distinguish truth from untruth, the police department believes it best to ignore the letter of the woman, which lists without exception very general accusations and not to grant her an official hearing.[4]

The police thus used their power to discredit her and suppress her indictment of the prostitution milieu in favor of their own view, highlighting instead the city's alleged successful record in eliminating disease, public immorality, and public disorder.

Although Mathilde Schween's indictment was unique, the official response was not surprising. City officials had insisted for decades that the police played an important regulatory role in the prostitution business and Hamburg's municipal authorities consistently justified and explained their commitment to regulated and officially controlled prostitution and police intrusion by enumerating the potential problems that would befall the city in its absence. In a typical justification, a local official wrote:

> if the police are no longer able, through the localisation of prostitution, through unfettered supervision of their

establishments [brothels], and through the broad support
of their brothel-keepers, to contain these elements
[prostitutes] to some degree, murder, rape, and other
crimes and excesses of all kinds will increase to
unfathomable degrees.[5]

The assumptions are clear: the administration claimed the right and the
duty to create a system of regulation and control. Otherwise, they argued,
the city would sink into depravity and crime, because:

> incompleteness of control brings with it pimpery,
> elegant courtesans and the demi-monde. They are
> responsible for the ruin of the root of all morality, as
> they grow wild and imperceptibly confuse the sense of
> what is morally tolerable and intolerable. In their
> extreme degeneration they form a veritable nursery for
> crime and the subversion of public order.[6]

In other words, the local authorities were committed to a strenuous
regulatory system and rationalised it by promising the preservation of
public order and morality.

Another basis for regulation that was invoked regularly was its
alleged effectiveness in containing the threat prostitutes posed to public
health. The city employed three physicians to examine all registered
women several times a week. The doctors either declared the women to be
healthy and released them to the brothel or committed them to the
hospital, which had a ward set up for registered prostitutes in its section
for dermatology and venereal disease after 1877. As late as 1911, Dr.
Maes, the doctor in charge of the medical supervision explained,

> the regulation of prostitution to battle venereal disease is
> all the more necessary, because it is impossible to
> abolish prostitution. Prostitution is acknowledged as the
> main source for the spread of venereal disease and
> venereal diseases are no less dangerous and widespread
> than any of the other epidemics or other infectious
> diseases which threaten our public health.[7]

Again, the state claimed to have only the best interests of the city at heart.

Nevertheless, however carefully justified, defined, and enforced,
Hamburg's regulatory system did not deliver what it promised. Given the
increasing urbanisation and changing demographic, social, economic, and
moral realities at the end of the nineteenth century, the regulatory system

did not ensure public order, limit the spread of venereal disease, or protect Hamburg's society from vice and immorality, goals that were officially at the heart of the regulatory system. Instead, unregulated prostitution flourished, the incidence of venereal disease increased steadily, and rather than existing outside the view of the public, regulated prostitution became a topic of constant and intense public discussion. The municipal authorities were fully aware of the shortcomings of their regulatory system, yet they resisted any attempts to change it. This paradoxical behavior warrants explanation.[8]

This paper will take a look at the regulation of prostitution, its implementation, and the public debate it engendered in the late nineteenth century in order to develop an answer to the paradox outlined above. Moreover, this paper addresses the construction of female sexuality and gender roles through an exploration of the issues surrounding prostitution, more specifically, officially regulated female prostitution. Prostitution was at the heart of gender relations, because it involved the most intimate and private contact between two people in the most public setting and understanding it helps the historian deconstruct the factors governing the practices of socially acceptable male and female sexuality. Also, prostitution gave rise to at times intense public debates about its causes, social functions, and implications and these public discourses on prostitution were important sites where female sexuality was debated, controlled, contested, and historically constituted.

2.   Legal Background

In Imperial Germany, the new Imperial Criminal Code (*Reichsstrafgesetzbuch*) came into effect in 1871 and formed the legal basis for dealing with prostitution.[9] Two sections of the Code were particularly relevant. These were lifted almost verbatim from the Prussian Code of 1851. The most important section was the so-called "prostitution-paragraph," which set the legal definition of prostitution and determined that it was to be tolerated only within specific regulations:

> § 361,6: The following shall be liable on conviction to detention: Any common prostitute under Police supervision who acts contrary to the Police regulations for the preservation of health, public order and decency, as also any prostitute not under Police supervision.[10]

A second relevant paragraph dealt with the procurement and facilitation of prostitution and was therefore nicknamed "procurement-paragraph" [*Kuppeleiparagraph*] by contemporaries:

§ 180: Anyone who makes a practice of assisting or for his own benefit assists immorality by acting as an intermediary or providing opportunity therefore shall be guilty of Procuration and liable to Confinement.[11]

The tension between these paragraphs is immediately apparent. The "prostitution-paragraph" established that prostitution itself was to be tolerated – albeit within certain specific locally defined regulations. According to the "procurement-paragraph," however, any kind of facilitation of prostitution, pimpery, or procurement was to be prosecuted. This legal ambiguity created problems for local governments and police forces, because despite § 180, prostitution as a trade was dependent on pimps and procurers. Moreover, it created a discursive space for disagreement and contestation of the status quo. Standard legal interpretations of the relationship between the two sections in the code existed, but ambiguities remained and it was up to the local authorities to resolve them in their specific local regulations. Not surprisingly, local governments like the city state of Hamburg did so in light of their specific social and political circumstances, but often had to contend with opposing viewpoints that emerged in their communities.

3.   Local Background

What kind of city was Hamburg during the Imperial period? To contemporaries, Hamburg was known as a place where poverty coexisted with abundance, conservative political particularism with thriving Social Democracy, and proverbial north German stuffiness with notorious sexual promiscuity. In this context of multiple social realities, prostitution was no marginal phenomenon, practiced in alleys and corners and discovered only by the initiated. It was visible to anybody who lived in Hamburg or visited the city. Prostitutes walked the streets and leaned out of windows to attract customers. They were omnipresent, and by the turn of the century, prostitutes had become as much a part of Hamburg's urban landscape as ships in the port or the steeples of the five major parish churches.

Politically and economically, Hamburg was dominated by a small group of wealthy merchant families whose primary interest was the creation of a stable and profitable trade economy.[12] A predictable social environment at home, undisturbed by class or gender struggles, was essential for economic stability. Hamburg's ruling elites therefore attempted to control all aspects of life in the city and regulate all potentially destabilising influences including prostitution.

During the nineteenth century, Hamburg enforced a particular type of regulation which was known as "brothelisation" (*Bordellierung*). Women who worked as prostitutes had to register with the police and were assigned to live and work in specific brothels upon their registration. They were not allowed to choose their places of residence independently. Brothelkeepers received licenses from the police for running these profitable establishments and in return helped the police enforce their regulations.[13] The other system of regulation, which became customary elsewhere in Imperial Germany (most famously in Berlin) was called casernation (*Kasernierung*). Here, the police restricted registered prostitutes to specific streets or neighborhoods, but did not rely on brothelkeepers for control. In the latter regulatory system, prostitutes had a direct relationship with the police. Over time, casernation became the pre-eminent system of regulation in Imperial Germany, because it seemed to be in closer compliance with § 180 of the Criminal Code.

4.   Hamburg's Regulatory System

Brothelisation had a long history in Hamburg – going back to the thirteenth century – and thus was favored by the local authorities in spite of its potential incompatibility with the new Imperial Criminal Code. By working with brothel-keepers, the police in Hamburg and the leading municipal authorities were intimately involved in the prostitution milieu. Brothels, they believed, moved prostitution from secrecy into a public realm. A system of brothelised prostitution seemed controllable, hence less threatening. Moreover, the regulations were designed to control the negative side effects of prostitution, especially public immorality and disease. As we saw earlier, officials feared the former and the latter.

By defining what it meant to be a prostitute, subjecting women who fit the category to extensive and often intrusive and humiliating police regulations, and restricting them to brothels, the authorities created a group of marginalised women, who could "safely" perform sexual services without endangering the prevalent conception of bourgeois femininity which championed virginity and chastity outside marriage. The state created clear boundaries for their behavior and marked prostitutes, the sellers of extramarital sex, as a distinct category of women. The intentions of the political authorities are unmistakably revealed in their regulation and in the terminology deployed to describe the women. Brothelisation physically removed them from the rest of society and by calling prostitutes "public girls" (*öffentliche Mädchen*) the government drew a rhetorical boundary around them that separated them from all other women, who were private girls – or rather, women.

Typical for contemporary morality, Hamburg's administration did not condemn men who patronised prostitutes, but instead assumed the responsibility of providing a "clean" supply of women, who did not suffer from infectious diseases such as syphilis, which was still incurable at the time. Contemporary doctors supported this double standard claiming a scientific basis for both the male uncontrollable sex drive and natural sexual passivity for women.[14]

The city's determination to retain its traditional system of brothelisation was emphasised in new regulations that were promulgated in October 1871, some months after Hamburg had joined the new *Reich* and become subject to the new Imperial Criminal Code.[15] The new regulation emphasised that the official system of control continued to include not only the women, who had to register with the city in order to be legally able to work as prostitutes but also the men and women who profited from the trade as landlords or brothel-keepers.[16]

Registration was a complex process which was supposed to take place only under specific conditions. In previous centuries, women had presented themselves to the authorities to be registered as prostitutes. In 1869, the police began the practice of compulsory registration [*Zwangseinschreibung*]. After 1876, women were officially registered against their wills only if they had previously been registered in Hamburg or elsewhere. This restriction on involuntary registration was abandoned again in the 1880s, and by 1894 all women who were "obviously" engaged in prostitution were again registered mandatorily. By forcing "suspicious" women to register, the police drafted as many women as possible into the regulatory system. The police also asserted their right to determine who was to be considered a prostitute.

By 1902, five circumstances mandated the inscription of women in the official registry. Women had to be registered if they had been convicted of prostitution and were above the age of 18. Additionally, the police were supposed to register all women above 18 who continued to engage in illicit sex after warnings by the police. The police also had to register women who moved to Hamburg and had been registered prostitutes at their previous places of residence, unless they could prove that they were gainfully employed. Moreover, all women who were arrested for vagrancy and were found to have a venereal disease had to be registered. Lastly, women could still register themselves, although the regulations stipulated that the decision was voluntary and informed.

By decreeing which women were to be registered under which circumstances, the police defined and created prostitutes. Prostitutes were women who led so-called immoral lives, were homeless and sick, previously registered, or otherwise marginal to the bourgeois experience. The power to force women to register and submit to official controls granted the state the power to marginalise them and control their behavior. Moreover, it gave the state the power to define deviance and respectability more generally. The power of definition and control rested solely with the police and the institutions that protected and enforced the regulations.

Once inscribed in the official registry, women had to abide by minute regulations in order to remain free from prosecution. The regulations intruded significantly into their lives. Registered prostitutes had to submit to regularly scheduled – usually twice weekly – medical examinations, and a city physician had to declare them healthy before they could legally work again.[17] But the regulations went beyond precautions for health and hygiene. They intruded into all spheres of the prostitutes' personal lives. By demanding periodic medical exams and routine police inspections of women's ledger books, in which they recorded earnings and expenses, municipal authorities structured the women's lives and days.[18] Moreover, registered prostitutes were not allowed to live with children above the age of ten, even their own, nor meet up with them if they lived elsewhere, or go out with them.[19] Furthermore, neither the prostitutes nor the brothel-keepers were allowed to employ female servants below the age of thirty or twenty-five, at the risk of being persecuted for promoting secret prostitution.[20] Registration subjected not only a woman's time and body but also her residence to state regulation. The front doors were to be kept closed, the windows facing the street were to be kept shut and covered, unless they were opaque; the rooms on the first floor were to be kept dark at night and in the evenings, and the price lists for beverages and sexual services were to be posted visibly in all rooms.[21]

Professional conduct was proscribed as well. It was illegal for a prostitute to undress in front of someone else, unless she and her client were in a room other than the main guest room or lounge, nor was she allowed to perform so-called "unnatural" acts. The men who demanded and paid for such "unnatural acts" were, however, not troubled by the police. Additionally, music, dancing, and card- or other games were banned from the establishments.[22] The police regulations extended beyond the walls of the brothels as well and restricted the women's conduct in public.[23] A registered prostitute in Hamburg was, for example, not allowed to promenade on the *Jungfernstieg*, the local main boulevard or ride in an open carriage anywhere in town. She did not have the right to go to the theater (unless she was out of sight of the general public) or walk along the *Alster*, an inner-city lake with cafés and terraces on its banks. It was illegal for her to walk in public after 11 p.m. without an escort or address men in any way in the streets.[24] The official rationale for these intrusions, *Polizeiherr* Petersen argued in 1871, was to protect the women from exploitation, perpetuated and institutionalised in the women's continued fundamental financial dependence on their brothel-keepers. Additionally, they ensured that the political establishment retained a firm grasp on the definition and control of prostitutes. We do not know to what extent these regulations were enforced, but their existence gave the police the tools to prosecute prostitutes and other women at any time and thus strengthened their ability to exercise social control. As we saw with

Mathilde Schween, most registered prostitutes had a long record of transgressions.

The regulations bore out the city's longstanding commitment to brothelisation. In fact, when forced to justify its regulatory system to the federal government in Berlin, the authorities in Hamburg emphasised precisely the system's capacity for social control. Asked to determine whether the brothel-keepers should be charged with procuring, which was illegal, the *Obergericht* in Hamburg ruled in 1871 that the role of the brothel-keepers was not the facilitation of prostitution, but its control.[25] The state prosecutor argued that brothels in Hamburg had the "character … of official police-controlled [*sittenpolizeiliche*] establishments , … [they were] direct tools to control professional prostitution used by the morals police …" and the brothel-keepers were "a type of employed barrack wards of officially barracked prostitution."[26] The element of control thus remained primary.

Through the strict regulations and multiple layers of control, the government actively separated "public" women from all other aspects of middle-class sociability and amusement and restricted them to a life in the brothel milieu. As long as a woman was designated as a prostitute, she was not supposed to take part in mainstream Hamburg society and culture or even be tolerated in its vicinity. She was stigmatised and forced outside the boundaries of her contemporary world.

But not only prostitutes were restricted and victimised by the regulations aimed at them; by claiming the right to regulate prostitutes, Hamburg's government was able to control the behavior of other women as well. Female sexuality was only tolerated in the context and confines of marriage – otherwise it ran the risk of being defined as prostitution. For men, the regulatory system laid down a different standard. Their extra-marital sexuality was expected and protected. The profound influence the regulations had on women in general can be seen in the ill-treatment of non-prostitutes. In the most notorious cases, women, who aroused police suspicion by their clothes or general conduct were taken for prostitutes or even arrested and subjected to medical examinations.[27] Although these blatant cases of victimisation were isolated, the fact that the police could arrest women for prostitution simply because their clothing or behavior was deemed inappropriate or promiscuous shows how far-reaching the regulations were. They restricted all women, not just prostitutes. By defining a specific group of women who were available to all men for extramarital sex, the regulations for prostitutes made such behavior impossible for all other women. In this way the regulations delimited the boundaries of desirable general female sexuality: a "good and proper" German woman did not engage in extramarital and thus "public" sex.

It is my contention that this ability to exercise social control helps us understand why the local administration insisted on the continuation of a strict regulatory system, even in the face of its apparent failure to dam the spread of venereal disease and crime. Regulation may not have stopped the threats to public health and order, but they gave the local elites the power to enforce specific gender norms.

5.   Opposition to Regulation

But the story does not end here. Not all Hamburgers accepted the official view and supported the existence of regulated prostitution. In fact, many saw the regulatory system as a symbol of much that was wrong with their communities. Unlike the municipal authorities who wanted to control prostitution and preserve regulation, they strove to abolish the regulation of prostitution or even the phenomenon itself. By articulating different ideas about gender roles and morality, the responsibilities of police and state etc., they presented a potential threat to the status quo that went far beyond the importance of prostitution.

In fact, regulated female prostitution was one of a number of issues that generated a broad-based reaction in Hamburg and Imperial German society generally as it fired up many different people to share their views and opinions in public ways in the decades leading up to World War One. These discourses about prostitution connected to other issues which also held great currency at that time, such as the role and legal status of women in German society, the emerging discipline of sexology, the threats posed by pornography etc. Like many of these other contemporary public discourses, the one about regulated prostitution cannot simply be understood along class or gender lines. Certainly the class identity and interest of the speaker was often important, but not the only indication of a person's opinion about regulated prostitution. Many members of the middle classes disagreed with each other and official policies while some members of the working classes may have felt protected by Hamburg's insistence on strict control. Similarly, gender identity also functioned in unpredictable ways. While some women were strong supporters of state-regulated prostitution, others were bitter opponents of the same rules. In other words, what emerges is a picture of an often messy and unpredictable, yet always dynamic, vibrant, and increasingly self-confident society – one that stood in contrast with the traditional political and economic elites of the port city.

In the early 1870s, Hamburg's municipal government successfully resisted challenges from the German federal government to change the local system of regulation to one resembling casernation which would bring it into closer compliance with national law. In a protracted legal battle, Hamburg's political elites were able to stake out and defend their position regarding regulated prostitution.[28] The successful defense of Hamburg's regulatory practices did not, however, eliminate public debate on the issue. In fact, the last decades of the nineteenth century saw growing public interest in the regulation of prostitution. Its merits and side effects became a topic of intense public debate in Hamburg and elsewhere in Imperial Germany. Participants in these public debates challenged the regulation of prostitution for a variety of often contradictory reasons. In doing so, they questioned and – sometimes inadvertently – helped destabilise or blur the definition of prostitution and by extension female sexuality more generally. By the turn of the century organised groups, such as Social Democrats, activists from the bourgeois women's movement and the Protestant morality movement, and private individuals, had entered the public debates about the regulation of prostitution to articulate their dissatisfaction with the status quo.

Although the following sections do not claim to be exhaustive, they give an indication of the wide-ranging and sometimes contradictory concerns that motivated people and associations to get involved in the debate over regulated prostitution; a debate that helped question and challenge the contemporary notion of gender relations.

6.   Early Opposition

Already in the 1870s and 1880s private individuals approached the municipal government in Hamburg with complaints about the regulation of prostitution and its enforcement by the local police. Most of the time, these petitioners were not primarily concerned with issues of morality or the enforcement of a specific definition of female sexuality, but rather they advanced economic arguments or articulated concerns about public security to back up their demands. Many of the pleas and petitions that survived in the archives came from artisans, homeowners, or shopkeepers, who argued that they were negatively affected by the brothels in their neighborhoods and hoped to convince city officials to close them, move them to other areas of the city, increase police supervision, or to amend current practices in some other way.[29] Most of these individual petitioners did not explicitly address the merits or implications of the official regulation of prostitution nor did their petitions sanction of challenge a particular vision of gender roles. But by questioning aspects of the enforcement of regulated prostitution they forced the government repeatedly to re-evaluate and reinforce its own position on these matters. Many of these petitions were unsuccessful, but they strengthened the government's commitment to regulated prostitution and ensured that the issue was never forgotten or marginalised.

7.   Protestant Morality Groups

Protestant morality groups of which there were a growing number in Hamburg and elsewhere in Imperial Germany by the turn of the century, used the emerging public discussion about the regulation of prostitution very differently and with other goals in mind. They specifically addressed the connection between the official regulation of public immorality and the loss of public authority. They acknowledged the importance of absolute values and clear-cut boundaries between what was desirable sexual behavior and what was not, but these conservative moralists went further than Hamburg's regulationist politicians. They believed that prostitution was a negative outgrowth of the modern urban experience and that the government should not be complicit in this evil by regulating and tolerating it. Instead, the government and the police should put all their strength and ability into fighting prostitution and its negative side effects such as procurement or pornography, which the moralists perceived as threats to the survival of the traditional order of German society. A German and Christian state could not, they argued, tolerate and regulate organised immorality without losing its moral authority and credibility itself.[30] Therefore they hoped to eradicate prostitution entirely through a network of philanthropic institutions and public education/awareness campaigns.

Theirs was a different understanding of gender relations than that of the municipal authorities. Protestant moralists did not endorse the sexual double standard that formed the basis of the regulation of prostitution. They did not accept that prostitution was a necessary evil. To them regulated prostitution was merely evil and should be eradicated. But, protestant conservatives did want to protect traditional gender roles based on bourgeois marriage. They argued that male extra-marital sexuality – especially if it was sanctioned by the state in the form of regulated prostitution – undermined the very fabric of German life. Without solid marriages and traditional families to buttress morality, all of society would unravel. One German pastor explained his position:

> We fight so that men enter marriage in a state of moral purity [*sittlich rein*]; we want to prohibit that men become intellectually dulled and physically ill during their youths, under which women will ultimately suffer. We want to prohibit men from having sexual contact with those women, who have the lowest morality, and from using this swamp to develop their opinions about women. ... Our work stands in the service of German women and benefits the German people. ...No sexual

double standard, but also no lax morality for both partners, but serious morality for both![31]

Their reaction to regulated prostitution thus proffered a distinct vision of gender relations in Imperial Germany.

8.   Social Democrats

Not surprisingly, activists from the other side of the political spectrum argued quite a different case. Social Democrats who were coming into their own at the turn of the century participated passionately in and often initiated public debates about the regulation of prostitution in Hamburg as well as on the national stage. For Social Democratic politicians, regulated prostitution was a powerful image of the exploitation of working class women by middle class men. They objected to the intrusion of the police into working class lives and the concentration of officially sanctioned brothels in working-class districts offended their sense of morality.[32] Moreover, they also offered a different vision of gender relations. They condemned prostitution as an outgrowth of the capitalist system and advocated a different kind of morality based on compassion for the women who were trapped in the prostitution milieu. To emphasise their distance from the prostitution milieu, leading Social Democrats tended not to stress their solidarity with the exploited women, but emphasised instead the moral outrageousness of the institution, even if this position sometimes meant that they had to borrow their arguments from other discourses. In one instance, a Socialist leader in the *Reichstag* used religious vocabulary, which anticipated the subsequent co-operation of Socialists with Protestant moralists in the fight against regulated prostitution. He argued: "Because it is impossible for us to tolerate and perpetuate such a condition [regulated prostitution] in a *Kulturstaat*, what is more, in a "Christian" state, we have to intervene."[33]

In socialist theory, the "women's question" was secondary to the "social question." It did not need to be addressed separately, as bourgeois women demanded, and it would be solved only under socialism. The oppression of women would end as the classless state ended all oppression. Social Democrats dealt similarly with the contemporary sexual double standard. They argued that prostitution, too, was associated primarily, if not exclusively with bourgeois capitalism, and it, too, would disappear after a successful revolution and the establishment of socialism. The most important, influential, and widely read book on the subject was August Bebel's *Women and Socialism*.[34] His view of prostitution, its causes, and potential remedies, was related to the revolutionary socialist project and opposed to the status quo.[35] In his book, Bebel characterised prostitution as a complement to bourgeois marriage, an inevitable feature of bourgeois capitalism. "Marriage represents one side of sexual life in the bourgeois world. Prostitution is the other. Marriage is the front, prostitution the back of the same coin."[36] He concluded, "prostitution therefore becomes a necessary social institution in bourgeois society, like the police, the standing army, the church, and capitalists."[37]

On the surface his assertions sounded similar to the official position, which also deemed prostitution a "necessary evil." Some of his other ideas also echoed those of contemporary experts on prostitution, some of whom he cited in his book. He agreed that the unchecked spread of prostitution had negative moral consequences, but argued that registration often pulled women further from respectable lifestyles than prostitution alone did. He wrote that "a further consequence of these police regulations is that they make it excessively hard, if not impossible [for a woman] to return to a respectable living. A woman who has become subject to police control is lost for society; she often wretchedly perishes within a few years."[38] Bebel echoed contemporary concerns over declining public moral standards. However, unlike other experts on the subject, he accused the men, who frequented prostitutes, from students to prominent politicians and business leaders, for this decline in public morality.[39] Bebel reminded his readers of the negative health risks associated with prostitution. Venereal diseases compromised the health of families and regulated prostitution did not, he argued, stem the growing tide of venereal disease, but lured unsuspecting men into false security.[40]

Although many of his evaluations of prostitution sounded familiar, Bebel drew different conclusions. Like the Protestant moralists, he argued that the state had become complicit in the evil of prostitution by tolerating and regulating it. But he insisted that the real reason for the perpetuation of prostitution was the economic situation of women and the sexual double standard enforced by bourgeois capitalism. Rather than locating the cause for prostitution in the women's moral weakness as did the Protestant activists, or in their psychological deficiencies, or biological abnormalities – all prevalent explanations at the time – he argued that it was the economic system which caused the increase in prostitution. Accordingly, his solution to the "prostitution problem," as a part of the women's problem and the "social problem" more generally, called not for the imprisonment or regulation of prostitutes, or even their "moral improvement" but for the end of the entire social system.

9.   Feminists/Abolitionists

Perhaps the most important participant in the growing public discussion about the regulation of prostitution for our context was the International Abolitionist Federation, a radical bourgeois women's group dedicated to the abolition of regulated prostitution. The organisation advocated better conditions for working women and sexual education so that brothels could no longer benefit from a steady stream of women who were forced into the profession by bad employment opportunities or ignorance, but primarily, the organisation worked for the abolition of all regulation. The organisation's first German chapter was founded in Hamburg on January 18, 1899 under the leadership of Lida Gustava Heymann and quickly gained momentum and enjoyed local exposure and notoriety. In subsequent years, the organisers fought aggressively for the abolition of all regulation of prostitution in Hamburg and Germany. While their struggle was not successful in the pre-war period, it ensured that the debate about the official regulation of prostitution remained in the public consciousness. These women specifically used the public sphere by inviting guest speakers to large public meetings that were covered in the mainstream daily press. These public meetings called into question traditional notions of public and private female sexuality. With their slogan "The same morality for men and women" (*"Gleiche Moral für Mann und Frau"*), they began to stretch the boundaries of acceptable female behavior by advocating equal treatment of prostitute and client, thus undermining the socially stigmatised position of the prostitute.[41]

Heymann and the other abolitionists in Hamburg regarded regulated prostitution to be a "medical error, a social injustice, and a veritable crime against all law," and their association sought to eradicate the institution.[42] The abolitionists argued that the individual right of self-determination should take the place of government regulations. They believed that only responsible individuals could provide the foundation for a sound state and "the state that enforces regulations that provide security and responsibility for men in vice destroys responsibility, which is the foundation for morality. By charging only the woman with the consequences of a joint [sexual] act, the state perpetuates the ominous idea that there exists a different morality for both genders."[43]

Abolitionists were feminists. They believed that the same morality should exist for men and women. To many contemporaries such notions were anathema because they called into question the sexual double standard that provided the foundation for contemporary gender roles. Contrary to some contemporary claims, Heymann and her associates, however, did not promote free love, but simply insisted that men and women be treated equally. If men could enjoy sexual freedoms outside marriage, the same rights should be made available to women, or rather, men should be held to the same high moral standards as women. By offering a radically different conception of gender roles, feminist activists such as Heymann's abolitionists forced the government to re-evaluate and defend the official regulation of prostitution and their definition of desirable female sexuality.

10.   Conclusions

Of course, these were not the only groups that became involved in the public debate about the regulation of prostitution, but they provide an overview over the kinds of issues that motivated citizens of Hamburg. The increasingly lively and loud public discourse about prostitution and its regulation may help us understand the policies of the municipal authorities. The power to establish and enforce the regulation of prostitution allowed Hamburg's officials to define and control gender roles and female sexuality in the early part of the Imperial period. This power became increasingly embattled and rather than giving in to public pressures, the municipal authorities stubbornly held on to their commitment to social control. Whatever their other shortcomings, the regulations helped maintain the municipal authorities' power of definition. The rules created clear boundaries for the behavior of official prostitutes. The state defined prostitutes and consequently had the authority to define morality, sexuality, and respectability, especially as these related to female sexuality and gender relations. By officially regulating prostitution, the state asserted its power to control and punish those who defied its standards, in word and deed, even if it did not manage to do so every time.

As I have tried to show, the state's power to define prostitution did not go unchallenged. In addition to Mathilde Schween, whose attempt to publish her opinions was so easily averted, there were others who had something to say about prostitution and its regulation and whose voices could not be suppressed as easily as hers. In fact, in the decades leading up to World War One, Hamburg was the site of many lively, sometimes polemic, and often contentious discussions about the merits and shortcomings of regulated female prostitution. Women and men of different backgrounds and with often antagonistic agendas became involved public debates about regulated prostitution through articles, rallies, and sermons, and were active in political parties, philanthropic and voluntary organisations, clubs, and as individuals. By challenging the official regulations these individuals and groups also questioned the state's monopoly of definition and offered up their own views as alternatives.

I have tried to examine the background, details, and meaning of Hamburg's system of regulated female prostitution as well as the public discussions it engendered during the decades before World War One.[44] Different concepts of gender, morality, and politics emerged and revealed the stubbornness of the political authorities as well as the vibrancy and assertiveness of the emerging public. Prostitution itself may not have been an agent for change, but official decisions about its regulation and the reactions to these decisions facilitated the emergence of a confident population willing to question its government − often leading to unlikely alliances − and paving the way for changes in the post-WW1 period.

Notes

1. All the documents pertaining to Mathilde Schween's letter can be found in Staatsarchiv Hamburg (hereafter StA HH) 111-1 Senat; Cl VII Lit. Lb Nr, 28a 2 Vol 136 Fasc 9. Unless otherwise noted, here and elsewhere, all translations are my own.

2. StA HH 111-1 Senat; Cl VII Lit. Lb Nr, 28a 2 Vol 136 Fasc 9; copy of the letter of Frau Schween.

3. StA HH 111-1 Senat; Cl VII Lit. Lb Nr, 28a 2 Vol 136 Fasc 9.

4. StA HH 111-1 Senat; Cl VII Lit. Lb Nr, 28a 2 Vol 136 Fasc 9; Letter of chief of police Roscher to Senator Schröder of 10 February 1909.

5. Bundesrath Session 1874 No 12, Bericht des Ausschusses für Justizwesen, 5.

6. StaHH 352-3 Medinzinalkollegium II P 1 Band 1 "Prostitution Allgemeines," 1847-1907, S. 108-112 Appraisal of the chief of police, 6 May 1873.

7. StaHH 352-3 Medzinalkollegium II P 1 Band 2 "Prostitution Allgemeines," 1908-1920, Appraisal of Maes, 7 February 1911.

8. Hamburg's insistence on a policy that did not work and in fact seemed to be designed in such a way that it could never work has been called a "paradoxical ideology." See also Frank Hatje, "Money makes the world go round. Prostitution in Hamburg (1780-1870), *Hamburger Wirtschafts-Chronik*, Neue Folge, 2 (2001/02) 59-94, 81.

9. See Michael Bargon, *Prostitution und Zuhälterei; Zur kriminologischen und strafrechtlichen Problematik mit einem geschichtlichen und rechtsvergeleichenden Überblick* (Lübeck: Verlag Max Schmidt-Röhmhild, 1982).

10. *Imperial German Criminal Code*; translated into English by Captain R.H. Gage and A.J. Waters (Johannesburg: W.E. Horton & Co, 1917), 93-94.

11. Ibid, 47.

12. For the primacy of trade and economic interest in domestic policy decisions see Richard J. Evans. *Death in Hamburg: Society and Politics in the Cholera Years 1830-1910.* (Oxford: Oxford University Press, 1987), passim, but esp., 105.

13. This system was amended in 1876 to rely less overtly on the brothel-keepers and come into closer compliance with § 180, but its tenor remained essentially the same throughout the period.

14. Among others, Andreas Hill. "'May the doctor advise extramarital intercourse?' Medical debates on sexual abstinence in Germany c. 1900." In *Sexual Knowledge, Sexual Science; The History of Attitudes to Sexuality*, eds. Roy Porter and Mikulas Teich, 284-302 (Cambridge: Cambridge University Press, 1994), 288.

15. Hamburg had been a member of the North German Confederation since 1867 and thus subject to its Criminal Code, which also included a paragraph outlawing procurement. The new regulations were issued in the context of a new local law (*Gesetzsammlung der freien und Hansestadt Hamburg*, Amtliche Ausgabe, 5. Band , Jahrgang 1869, 199; Gesetz betreffend das Verhältnis der Verwaltung zur Strafrechtspflege und die Competenz der Polizeibehörde, 30. April 1869 § 17) which stipulated that the police could adjudicate all matters regarding sexual offenses without recourse to the courts. The police became the arbiter in all cases dealing with prostitution or illicit sexuality. Their stake and collusion in the prostitution system was now officially sanctioned.

16. Cited in Urban, Alfred. *Staat und Prostitution in Hamburg vom Beginn der Reglementierung bis zur Aufhebung der Kasernierung (1807-1922).* (Hamburg: Verlag Conrad Behre, 1927), 99, § 1. These regulations were reissued several times during the Imperial period albeit only with marginal changes.

17. Ibid, § 7 and § 18.

18. Ibid, § 6.

19. StaHH 111-1 Senat; Cl VII Lit. Lb Nr 23 a Vol 54; "Polizeiliche Vorschriften die Bordelle und öffentlichen Mädchen betreffend, Hamburg 1852" §11.

20. Cited in Urban, *Staat*, 99ff § 10.

21. Ibid, § 8 .

22. Ibid, § 10.

23. Ibid, § 12.

24. StaHH 241-1 I Justizverwaltung II D b 2 Vol. 1 [4]; "Polizeiliche Vorschriften für unter Controlle der Sittenpolizei stehende Frauenzimmer," 1 April 1889.

25. *Das Deutsche Strafgesetzbuch und polizeilich concessionierte Bordelle. Aktenstücke einer Meinungsverschiedenheit zwischen dem Deutschen Reichskanzleramt und dem Senat von Hamburg mit Rechtsgutachten von 16 deutschen Universitäten.* Hamburg, 1877, 28 as cited in Urban, Staat, 41.

26. Ibid.

27. Lyda Heymann und Anita Augspurg. *Erlebtes - Erschautes: Deutsche Frauen kämpfen für Freiheit, Recht und Frieden 1850-1940.* (Meisenheim am Glan: Anton Hain, 1977), 42.

28. See my dissertation for a more detailed account of this legal and political struggle: Julia Bruggemann, "Through the Prism of Prostitution: State and Society in Hamburg, 1800-1914," Georgetown University, 1999.

29. Bundesarchiv Potsdam, Reichsjustizamt/-ministerium, R 3001, 5779 Band 1, Blatt 230 - 270; StaHH, 241-1 I Justizverwaltung; I II

D b 2 Vol. 1; StaHH, 111-1 Senat; Cl. VII Lit. L b Nr. 28 a Vol. 106b Fasc 2; StaHH, 111-1 Senat; Cl. VII Lit. L b Nr. 28 a Vol. 136 Fasc. 6.

30. Kampf wider die Prostitution. Eine Denkschrift des Central-Ausschusses für die Innere Mission der deutschen evangelischen Kirche, Berlin 1885, 20.

31. "Der Kampf um das christliche Sittlichkeitsideal." Referate gehalten von Pastor Mahling, und Lehrer Sydow in der Protestversammlung des Hamburger Vereins zur Hebung der öffentlichen Sittlichkeit am Mittwoch, den 20. März 1901, Hamburg 1901, 3.

32. Richard J. Evans. *Tales from the German Underworld; Crime and Punishment in the Nineteenth Century.* (New Haven and London: Yale University Press, 1998), 200-201.

33. *Stenographische Berichte des Reichstags*, 42. Sitzung 6 February 1894, 1026. August Bebel.

34. August Bebel, *Die Frau und der Sozialismus.* Originally published in 1879.

35. Frevert, Ute. *Women in German History, From Bourgeois Emancipation to Sexual Liberation.* (Oxford and New York, 1989), 140.

36. Bebel, *Die Frau und der Sozialismus*, 207.

37. Ibid, 208.

38. Ibid, 216.

39. Ibid, 222.

40. Ibid, 214 ff.

41. On the activities of the abolitionists in Hamburg, see StaHH 331-3 Politische Polizei; SA593, Band 1, 2, specifically, StaHH 331-3 Politische Polizei; SA593, Band 1, 22.

42. StaHH 331-3 Politische Polizei; SA 593 Band 1, "Satzungen des Hamburger Zweigvereins der britischen, kontinentalen und allgemeinen Föderation. Angenommen, den 18 Januar 1899."

43. Ibid.

44. Male prostitution also existed, but it was not regulated and did not become a topic of much public debate at the time.

Select Bibliography

Bargon, Michael. *Prostitution und Zuhälterei; Zur kriminologischen und strafrechtlichen Problematik mit einem geschichtlichen und rechtsvergleichenden Überblick.* Lübeck: Verlag Max Schmidt-Röhmhild, 1982.

Bebel, August. *Die Frau und der Sozialismus.* Stuttgart: Dietz, 1879.

Evans, Richard. *Death in Hamburg: Society and Politics in the Cholera Years 1830-1910.* Oxford: Oxford University Press, 1987.

——. *Tales from the German Underworld; Crime and Punishment in the Nineteenth Century*. New Haven and London: Yale University Press, 1998.

Frevert, Ute. *Women in German History, From Bourgeois Emancipation to Sexual Liberation*. Oxford: Oxford University Press, 1989.

Heymann, Lyda und Anita Augspurg. *Erlebtes – Erschautes: Deutsche Frauen kämpfen für Freiheit, Recht, und Frieden 1850-1940*. Meisenheim am Glan: Anton Hain, 1977.

Urban, Alfred. *Staat und Prostitution in Hamburg vom Beginn der Reglementierung bis zur Aufhebung der Kasernierung (1807 – 1922)*. Hamburg: Verlag Conrad Behre, 1927.

Cultural Clash on Prostitution:
Debates on Prostitution in Germany and Sweden in the 1990s

Susanne Dodillet[1]

Abstract

At the end of the twentieth century, both Germany and Sweden engaged in extensive discussions of prostitution – discussions that resulted in two very different prostitution policies. Whereas prostitution was made a legal profession in Germany, the purchase (but not the selling) of sexual favours was forbidden in Sweden. This paper examines the debates that preceded this legislation. Different women's organisations were active as lobby groups to speed up prostitution laws in both countries. As I will show, even the countries' traditions of policies of gender equality may have influenced how lawmakers decided to cope with the phenomenon of prostitution. **Key Words:** prostitution, Germany, Sweden, legislation.

1.   Introduction: Swedish and German Legislation on Prostitution

In 1999 it became illegal to buy sexual favours in Sweden. This new law marked clearly that prostitution is not accepted by the Swedish society. Two years later, in October 2001, the German parliament passed a law that approved prostitution as a legitimate profession. The purpose of this law was to counteract the stigmatisation and discrimination of prostitutes.

While the German majority celebrated its law as a big improvement, it was (and still is) a thorn in the side of many Swedish politicians: "I deeply dislike what's going on in Germany. It is a strike against equality. It is a strike against brotherhood," was how the Swedish minister for the equality between women and men, Margareta Winberg, commented on the German legislation.[2] "The whole parliament should go out and tell that we are strongly against this type of legalisation on prostitution which Germany is advocating," Ulla-Britt Hagström from the Conservative Party suggested.[3] Hagström's idea was refined by Ewa Larsson from the Green Party, who recommended to use Sweden's "good reputation on issues concerning equality" to counteract the German policy.[4] Yet, the Swedish law was not much noticed in Germany.

The disagreement between Sweden and Germany about how to answer the question of prostitution can be explained by the fact that German and Swedish politicians do not speak about the same issues when they discuss the question. Both sides define prostitution differently. The first part of this article deals with these different definitions. The second part tries to explain why the legislators in Sweden and Germany choose such different ways to define and treat this subject.

2.   What is Prostitution?
A. Sex Slavery or Professional Prostitution?

Most Swedish politicians who are engaged in the debate on prostitution assume that prostitution is unacceptable and must be combated. Everybody agrees that prostitution can cause damage to those directly involved as well as to society at large. Prostitution is being compared to slavery, and it is described as a tragic trap, as an occupation no parents would want for their children and as an extreme variant of commercialism. "Prostitution serves no positive purpose at all. On the contrary, it gives rise to suffering, degradation, spreading of sexually transmitted diseases, compulsion, and danger of outrage," as the Social Democratic Party described it in a bill from 1991.[5] Gudrun Schyman, at that time the leader of the Left Party, held the opinion that "prostitution is a variant of rape and abuse,"[6] an opinion that is shared by many members of the Swedish parliament. Further, the debaters mean that internal prostitution and international trafficking are connected: "Trafficking can never be separated from prostitution. If we have no prostitution, or if there is no market for it, there is no trafficking," Ulla-Britt Hagström, a member of the conservative Christian Democratic Party, explained.[7] Other politicians in the Swedish parliament consider that there are close connections between drug abuse and prostitution, and stress that these connections not only concern drug addicts who try to finance their abuse by selling sex, but also the fact that the environment prostitutes are exposed to can lead to drug abuse.

In Germany the discussion is quite different. Most people do not think of prostitution as harmful in itself. Problems like incest, drug abuse, and trafficking, which are very central in the Swedish debate, are rarely mentioned by those involved in the discussion in Germany. One explanation of why the German opinion differs may be that prostitution is not seen as a one-sided issue. In Germany prostitutes are divided into groups with differing grades of involvement. Besides professional prostitutes who seem to work voluntarily, trafficking and prostitution, which is carried out by people who finance their drug habits, are considered to have strong connections to coercion, violence, and sexual abuse. Prostitution that is carried out by people who need money to finance their addiction is called *Beschaffungsprostitution* (procurement prostitution). This is similar to the German word *Beschaffungskriminalität,* which describes crimes that are committed by people who need money to buy drugs. German officials and the public agree that trafficking and

Beschaffungsprostitution are problems that have to be fought fiercely. However, they also stress that these types of prostitution cannot be compared to the work of professional prostitutes and therefore have to be discussed in different terms. Irmingard Schewe-Gerigk from the Green Party belongs to those who analysed the different concepts of prostitution:

> *Beschaffungsprostitution*, which is carried out due to drug abuse, is a dramatic problem. These women are addicted to drugs and do not work as prostitutes professionally. Their occupation works according to other laws. To be able to help here, a principal change of the drug policy is needed.
>
> Even the problems of trafficking need other solutions, like an international cooperation, effective criminal law directions, and the enforcement of alien rights to guarantee effective victim protection.[8]

The division of prostitution into different categories is one explanation for the fact that several problems that are associated with prostitution in Sweden are excluded from the German discussion. The apprehension that trafficking and drug abuse are topics that must not intermix with professional prostitution is criticised a lot by Swedish politicians, who do not distinguish between different motivations for prostitution.

B. Johns and Their Victims or Sex Workers and Their Customers?

In the Swedish debate people assume that all prostitutes are victims of the sex industry; they are abused by others who want to satisfy their sexual needs. Furthermore, it is indicated that prostitutes are often unemployed, homeless, diseased, and/or drug addicts and that the majority of them has been exposed to abuse, incest, and/or oppression during their childhood. Karin Pilsäter from the Swedish Liberal Party represents the major opinion on the subject:

> We know that the majority of the women who are prostitutes have been subject to sexual abuse of some kind during their childhood. Prostitution is often connected to drug abuse in the form of tobacco, alcohol, or narcotics.[9]

Prostitutes are described as belonging to a very exposed group and it is emphasised that these women are in need of help.

The German debate on the other side is about professional prostitutes who are described as emancipated women, as independent mercantilists, or self-confident employees who constitute a representative average of the population, who are in control of their own decisions. Petra Pau, along with the Socialist Party, voices the following opinion in a proposed bill of 2000:

> New criminological research has shown that, over the past few years, the image of the oppressed woman, who has been driven into this profession, can no longer be maintained. Prostitutes today resemble average businesswomen. ...People understand more and more that at least the predominant number of the prostitutes make a conscious decision to start and to go on with their activity.[10]

Another disparity between the Swedish and German opinion concerns the definition of the commodity of sex trade. While the assumption that prostitutes' customers buy sexual favours dominates in the German debate, most of the Swedish experts argue that prostitution implies men buying women. Inger Segelström from the Swedish Social Democrats expressed in a statement to the parliament: "We Social Democratic women in the world's most emancipated parliament cannot allow that men buy women for money."[11] In Sweden the assumption that prostituted women sell themselves leads to the notion that prostitutes embody their occupation. Prostitution is not only regarded as pertaining the prostitutes' business but seems to assert a totalising claim on the prostitute's identity. Prostitutes are regarded as unable to keep their personality, their feelings, and their body out of prostitution. It is important to stress that the customers of sexual services are considered to buy prostitutes, not to consult them. Prostitution seems to affect the prostitutes' lives even after they have had a client. The man has bought a part of the woman that she cannot get back. The conviction that prostitutes are bought leads to the notion that they lose the right to rule over their own bodies as a result. The abolishment of prostitution seems to be the only way to give back that democratic right to the women.

In the German dispute nobody questions that prostitutes have control over their bodies both when they have a client and when they do not. The view that prostitutes sell sexual services, and not themselves, supports the interpretation that the German majority distinguishes among the personality, the private life, and the occupation of the prostitutes. Prostitutes are viewed as people who have privacy and leisure time. The dominant German opinion that prostitutes decide on their own which services they want to provide finds an expression in the choice of the German word *Freier* as the term for the sex customer. *Freier* is an old-fashioned term for a man who is courting (*freien*) a woman. The term thus has a positive connotation. (By contrast, in Sweden sex customers are often called *torsk* (cod), which is a clearly negative term.) The description *Freier* implies furthermore that the clients cannot be sure to get what they want, but have to exert themselves to win the prostitute's favour. In addition, the term *Freier* arouses associations with love affairs and encourages a romanticised image of prostitution.

C. Feminism or Liberalism?

The Swedish legislators base their work on a feminist analysis of the society that shows that women do not have the same access to work, money, and power as men. In this patriarchal society the socially powerful – in other words, men (in Sweden it is assumed that the clients of prostitutes are male, while prostitutes are female) – have the possibility of buying sexual objects, or as the Swedish Social Democrat Ulla Pettersson puts it: "By accepting prostitution society tolerates a humiliating perception of women. The view that women can be bought for money expresses a disdain for women as human beings."[12] Independent of why a woman starts to prostitute herself, her status is defined by the dominating analysis of the patriarchy in the Swedish point of view. The distinction between enforced and unsolicited prostitution, which is very important in the German debate, is regarded as absurd by most of the Swedish experts. Prostitution cannot be a personal choice as it is a part of the contempt for women in our society. As prostitution seems to be contrary to the norms and values of an emancipated society, the eradication of prostitution is regarded as an important milestone on the way towards more emancipation. The founders of the Swedish anti-prostitution law consider their law to be a result of the feminist policy of the country.

Instead of regarding prostitution as socially created and instead of discussing, like their Swedish colleagues, the interests and power structures behind sex trade, most German debaters assume that prostitution is a natural phenomenon. Prostitution is not called into question, but it is considered to be indispensable for satisfying the constant demand for sexual services. Horst Eylmann, a German Christian Democrat, explained in the *Bundestag*:

> Already Solon established brothels and the religion built
> up brothels in the form of temple prostitution in
> churches. Prostitution is ineradicable. Even the Christian
> sexual morality that condemns every kind of sexuality
> that does not serve reproduction has allowed it.[13]

While Swedish politicians emphasise that the long history of prostitution does not have to mean that prostitution will have just as long a future, the argument that "prostitution is the world's oldest profession" is considered as evidence for its eternal existence in Germany. The interceders of the German legislation think that prostitution will not disappear due to a prohibition of sexual trades. They are against criminalising prostitution and demand to fight only those aspects of sex trade that are an expression for oppression. The prostitutes' biggest problem is considered to be the discrimination they undergo due to their occupation. This disregard of the prostitutes' work is to be counteracted by the acknowledgement of their work as a regular profession. In Germany prostitutes have gained access to unemployment benefits, health insurance, and pension schemes, which will lead to their integration into society. The gender perspective, which is so important in Sweden, does not play a major role in the German prostitution debate. On the contrary, it is underlined that sexual satisfaction is not gender-related and that therefore both men and women can be interested in buying sex. The German legislators understand their prostitution law as an expression of their liberal attitude towards different sexual behaviours.

D. Vision or Status Quo?

The Swedish prostitution policy is based on a vision: Society without prostitution. Legislators regard it as their duty to establish directives for the achievement of this future society. In the Swedish debate it is continually emphasised that the state has the main responsibility for the establishment of norms and values of the society. The prostitution law, which first of all signals that prostitution is not accepted in Sweden, is one example of this practice. Gudrun Schyman, when leader of the Swedish Left Party, described the signal function of legislation in the following way:

> Legislation aims not only at getting hold of criminals and the affectivity of laws cannot only be judged by counting how many delinquents have been adjudged. Legislation is also about the norms and values of society. When beating children was outlawed there were many who argued that this was a meaningless law because it was difficult to control whether it was followed. But this law had standardizing effects, and in the same way a law that criminalizes the purchase of sexual services will mark how the society shall look on unequal distribution of power between men and women.[14]

A visionary standpoint like this does not seem to exist within the German debate. Instead, politicians try to adapt law to the changing sense of justice within the German society. When arguing for their prostitution law German legislators usually refer to public opinion surveys that show that prostitution is considered a legitimate occupation by the German majority. What is accepted cannot be *sittenwidrig* (immoral) and therefore can also not be forbidden. The German Social Democrat Anni Brandt-Elsweiler declared in the *Bundestag*:

> Norms aren't permanent values, but exposed to constant changes. Today a large part of the German population no longer considers prostitution immoral [*sittenwidrig*]. Even courts join more and more often in this opinion. ...With our proposal we haven't done anything but adapted legislation to the changed awareness of the population.[15]

Sittenwidrigkeit (immorality) is a term with a long tradition within the German judiciary, where a legal act is defined as *sittenwidrig* (immoral) when through its content, motive, and purpose it conflicts with the tactfulness of the average opinion. The question to what extent prostitution is *sittenwidrig* or not was a pivotal point for the German debate. The great importance that was attached to *Sittenwidrigkeit* as a juridical term, led to the following reasoning: When prostitution becomes more and more a part of the society and people start to get used to it and accept it, prostitution no longer strikes against conventions and cannot be forbidden. In Germany *Sittenwidrigkeit* – or in other words the view that dominates in the country – is the benchmark for prohibition or permission. In Sweden, by contrast, the question is answered depending on how it affects the vision of an equal society.

The analysis of the Swedish and German prostitution arguments shows that the laws of these countries were not created spontaneously, crudely, or mistakenly, but were instead based on intensive discussions. The arguments that those involved in this discussion apply are logical from their point of view, and they are respectively more or less consistent, which makes it impossible to say which of these strategies is the better or more rational. Both Swedish and German politicians think of their prostitution law as a humanitarian way to cope with the phenomenon of prostitution. The fact that their decisions nevertheless are so harshly criticised by their respective counterparts is a result of both sides acting on the assumption of different norms and values when discussing the question of prostitution.

The following retrospective on the background of the debates implies an attempt to find the origins of the different approaches. A comparison between Swedish and German strategies concerning other gender related issues, such as family and labour market policy, will finally illustrate the prostitution debate in a larger political context.

3.   The Background of the Discussions

Of course, political debates do not take place in a vacuum. Politicians are influenced by their surroundings, different opinion leaders, and lobby groups. This becomes clear when analysing the documents on which politicians in Sweden and German base their arguments.

Before a law is proposed and debated in the Swedish parliament, the government commissions an inquiry on the particular question. The prohibition on buying sex was thus preceded by two investigations that submitted three reports: *Prostitution: Description, Analysis, Solutions* from 1980,[16] *Prostitution in Sweden: Background and Solutions* from 1981,[17] and *Sex Trade* from 1995.[18] The investigators of these studies were mainly social workers and researchers with working experiences from aid organisations that aim to help prostitutes to stop selling their bodies and start a life outside prostitution. All three studies are written from a feminist perspective and come to the conclusion that prostitution reduces women to sex objects, which in turn opposes the pursuit of an equal society. It is important to notice that none of the reports suggests criminalising only the customers of sexual services, as was later done in Sweden. While the first inquiry recommended not victimising any of the parties, as both sides must be regarded as victims of the patriarchal society, the second wanted to criminalise both parties as both a buyer and a seller are needed for prostitution to take place. Both propositions were harshly criticised by several organisations of the women's movement that called for criminalizing buyers only. Women's organisations like the association of crisis centres for women *ROKS*,[19] the *Fredrika Bremerförbundet (FBF)*, and the women's organisations of the political parties held the opinion that the power relation between the parties involved in the sex trade should be made clear and stressed the powerlessness of the sellers, their drug and alcohol addiction, and the sexual cruelty these women may have been exposed to during their childhood. Prostitutes were described as belonging to a risk group, and it was underlined that these women should not be punished. In its statement *Fredrika Bremerförbundet* criticised the *Sex Trade*-report with the following words:

> For the FBF it is hard to understand the investigation's motive for criminalizing both the seller and the buyer of sexual services. In addition to the abasement it means for a woman to sell her body she will be punished even as a criminal due to the proposal. This double punishment is both inhuman and obsolete.[20]

The protests of the women's organisations had a great impact on the debate on prostitution in the Swedish parliament. More and more participants in this debate appeared as advocates in the prostitutes' names. The opinion that prostitutes are victims and the consequent stressing of their exposed and vulnerable social position is also an explanation for why prostitutes themselves never played an active role in the Swedish debate, in contrast to the German debate where – as we will see – the sex workers themselves started the discussion about a new prostitution law.

In February 1998, Prime Minister Göran Persson's Social Democratic government followed the line of criminalising the buyers. In their proposal bill the government declared that it is "unacceptable" in an equal society "that men buy temporary sexual relations with women for money."[21]

In the German *Bundestag*, in turn, the Green Party was the first to bring forward a legislation proposal concerning prostitution in 1990. Even this initiative was influenced by an intensive lobbying. In Germany several independent prostitution organisations were working to halt the discrimination against prostitutes and sex workers, and for the acceptance of their occupation as a legal profession. These groups offered meeting places and counselling bureaus where prostitutes could get advice and help from other prostitutes as well as non-prostituted women. Apart from this the organisations ran and still run PR-campaigns that serve to decrease prejudice against prostitution by throwing light on the prostitutes' real working and living situations. *Hydra*, the biggest and most famous of the German prostitution organisations, was in contact with the Green Party when it was working out its proposal bill, and it is also named in the Party's law proposal from 1990.[22] The impact prostitution organisations like *Hydra* had on the German prostitution policy cannot be overestimated. However, there is one aspect of the groups' argument that never gained a broader recognition in the *Bundestag*: their pro-sex feminist critique of the patriarchy.

In their magazine *Nachtexpress*, the *Hydra*-women write that "it is not prostitution as an occupation but prostitution as an institution of the patriarchy that must be antagonised."[23] Sex work is thus not seen as something bad in itself, but becomes so, according to *Hydra*, in a patriarchal society. Therefore *Hydra*'s position may best be understood as a queer-feminist or pro-sex feminist position: the organisation advocates a radical change in the social power structure, at the same time fighting for the prostitutes' right to carry out their work. In her book *"Wir sind Frauen wie andere auch!"* ("We are women like the rest!"), Pieke Biermann, one of the prostitutes who were involved in *Hydra* during the 1980s, stresses that the discrimination of prostitutes is one of many examples for the disparaging treatment of women's employment in general. As a measure against the oppression of prostitutes and other women in working life, Pieke Biermann demands higher wages for all women. "The battle against slavery starts with the fight for wages, as slavery stops with pay."[24] Women will work as prostitutes even in the future, but they will do it under better conditions than today. Pieke Biermann's book is even quoted in the law proposal of the Green Party from 1990.[25]

The notion that prostitution could not be abolished was shared by all politicians who took part in the prostitution debate in the *Bundestag*. *Hydra*'s notion that prostitution, as it looks today, is an expression for a patriarchal society can only be found in the Green Party's 1990 proposal. In all later proposals, movements, and all other contributions to the debate, that aspect was toned down by all parties, and it was underlined that not only women but also men are affected by the legal discrimination.

Recapitulating, one can say that the lobbying of the prostitution projects had a determining influence on German legislators. However, feminist analyses of the distribution of power in the society could never gain ground in the German debate. In October 2001, the prostitution law was passed with the votes of the Social Democrats, the Green Party, the Liberals, and the Socialist Party. Only the Christian Democrats voted against the German prostitution law that was established to defend the human right to carry out a profession without being discriminated against. Through the prostitution law German politicians could express their liberal attitude towards the role of sexuality in society.

A comparison of the backgrounds of the legislations in Germany and in Sweden shows that feminist organisations like *ROKS* and *Fredrika Bremerförbundet* were initiators of the Swedish prostitution debate and that they succeeded in influencing the legislation. The Swedish parliament inherited the arguments of these organisations and established a gender perspective into their analyses. In Germany, on the other hand, none of the parliamentary parties regarded, and still regard, prostitution as an example for unequal distribution of power between men and women. Not even the Green Party, which was influenced by *Hydra*'s work, used the analysis that women do not have the same access to work, money, and power as men as an argument for their proposed legislation. While the Swedish prostitution law in many respects is based on feminist arguments, human rights generally and sexual liberty especially are emphasised in the

German debate. Now one can ask why German politicians – unlike their Swedish colleagues – did not and still do not regard prostitution as a gender question. An answer could be that the countries' prostitution policies must be seen in relation to different traditions concerning the gender politic and the parliaments' ways of dealing with other questions that are relevant to women. An overview on these traditions will therefore conclude this article.

4.   Equality Policy 1970-1990

When the women's-rights movement of the 1970s spread its demands for equal rights for men and women on the labour market, the challenge of the traditional division of labour between men and women, in the home and at the workplace, was a quite untried thought in Germany – but it was not in Sweden. Already in the 1930s the Social Democrat Alva Myrdal, among others, had started to work for social reforms that aimed at women's social and political integration. Myrdal's vision was a family, with both mother and father at work eight hours a day and the children being well cared for at the kindergarten.[26] This vision was partly fulfilled already in the 1930s by the founding of day-care centres and other social services. In Germany, meanwhile, the Nazis carried out a women oppressing fertility policy in the name of motherhood with medals for women with more than one child. Hitler considered women's emancipation to be an outcome of Jewish intellectualism.[27]

The German notion of the woman as a mother was not abandoned after World War II, but strengthened by a new constitution that emphasised the role of the family as the foundation of the society. The principle was built on Otto von Bismarck's social laws from the 1880s, due to which the state's task on the social field was defined as subsidiary. This means that the state constitutes an addition to the family, which represents the foundation for society. Due to this strategy the principal duty of the state came to be the support of the family and not the individual as in Sweden.[28] While the idea of equality of opportunity between women and men under the influence of Alva Myrdal and others had been introduced to Swedish family- and labour market policy, the Western German society model of the 1960s was still based on the image of women as housewives and men as breadwinners. These differing strategies manifested themselves, for example, in the strategies these countries chose to solve the huge lack of manpower that both suffered from in the end of the 1950s and in the beginning of the 1960s. While women during that time were more than welcomed into the labour market in Sweden, German politicians solved the problem by recruiting male workers, so-called *Gastarbeiter*, from Southern Europe.

During the 1970s the view that antiquated gender roles and sex discrimination should be counteracted resulted in several reforms of family legislation in Sweden. In 1971 joint taxation was replaced by separate assessment, which made it more profitable for women to be employed outside the home. In addition, the extension of day care centres started and Sweden developed a child-care system even for children under two years of age. As opposed to parents in other European countries, Swedish families were able to use full-time childcare, which made it possible to combine parenthood and full-time work. Parents' insurance, the right to work six hours a day for parents of younger children, and the right to take a leave of absence for up to sixty days a year in order to care for an ill child are examples of reforms from the 1970s that stimulated parents to share the responsibility for their children. The rise of the number of women gainfully employed from 53% in 1970 to 83% in 1990 shows that these law reforms led to an increase in equality.[29]

In Western Germany the development of equality has been and still is much slower. Until 1976 family laws that allowed men to keep their wives from working outside the house if they had left their housework undone remained in effect. It was not only the Conservative Parties that tried to keep the traditional division of labour between men and women. During the 1970s a trend came about inside the German women's liberation movement, which claimed a *neue Mütterlichkeit* (new motherhood). This trend did not seek to abolish a division of society into male and female working spaces, but contented itself with emphasising that women's properties and tasks are as important and as worthy as those of men. The campaign "*Lohn für Hausarbeit*" (salary for housework), with the goal to make either the state or the gainfully employed partner in the marriage pay wages to the one working in the household, was the most famous action of this new motherhood movement.[30] One of the women engaged in the campaign was Pieke Biermann, who later became a spokeswoman for the prostitutes' project *Hydra* (see above). Biermann's book on unpaid housework is called *Das Herz der Familie* (The Heart of the Family) and was first published in 1977. Many within the women's movement regarded the *Lohn für Hausarbeit* campaign as a chance for women, especially mothers and housewives, to experience that their unpaid, but socially necessary work, finally would be acknowledged. Others, however, feared the preservation of the traditional and gendered division of labour. The opinions within the German women's movement, then, were differing. Particular big discussions were started by the so-called *Müttermanifest* (Mothers' Manifesto), which some women from the Green Party propounded in 1987. This manifesto promised women a particular social status and a possibility for self-fulfilment through their role as mothers. The Green Party's proposal was particularly supported by the conservative parties.

Ideas that sustain the traditional female role are reflected in many German laws. Joint taxation, for instance, is still applied in Germany. Attempts to reform this form of taxation were postponed, utilising the argument that the neutral position of joint taxation towards different forms of living together is not consonant with the constitution that gives prominence to the family as a foundation of society. Instead of extending childcare supply, Germany chose to extend the parental leave that was introduced in 1979. Since 1996 every child has the right to attend kindergarten according to German law. However, in practice the extension of child-care services has been delayed due to the competition for public funds after the German Unification, and far from every child can go to kindergarten today. In contrast to Sweden, Germany has neither kindergartens nor schools open in the afternoon, which requires that someone be at home when the children come home for lunch. In 1990 only 56% of the Western German women were gainfully employed, most of them in half-time jobs.[31]

In East Germany women's role in society developed in a totally different way than it did in the west. According to Marxist ideology, women's exclusion from the labour market was regarded as an origin of women's oppression in the GDR, which is one reason why the integration of women into the labour market moved much more quickly there. Especially during the 1970s several measures were taken to make it easier for women to combine family and work, including the reduction of working hours for mothers, the increase in child benefits and aid for studying mothers, as well as an expansion of child care and nursery schools. Day care and gainful occupation were self-evident for women in the East. Before the German Unification, 91% of the women in East Germany were working outside their homes. The fact that women in the GDR were financially independent does, however, not signify that they really were on a par with men. As in most other communist countries, the labour-market in the GDR was gendered, and politically and socially important positions were held by men. This one-sided distribution of power between men and women was hardly noticed in the GDR, which can be explained by the fact that women because of their (apparent) equality on the labour-market might have considered the question of women's rights as solved. Even the suppression of opposing voices by the sole socialist political party's dogmatic policy might have hindered the spread of feminist thoughts. After the German unification, East German women lost their position as employees. Public childcare was cut down, and schools were adapted to the West German system. The Christian Democratic government under Helmut Kohl combined – with incisive wording – the modernization of the East German economy with the implementation of a conservative view of the female role based on the West German model.[32]

The examination of the Swedish and the German labour markets and family policies shows that the strategies of these countries as well as their norms and values not only differ in legislation regarding prostitution. Prostitution policy rather seems to be one example of different basic settings towards women and family, sexuality and cohabitation. The German policy is to a great extent shaped by conservative Christian norms. These values not only find an expression in the Christian Democratic view of prostitution as something immoral (*sittenwidrig*), but also in the notion of the family as the foundation of society, a notion that is dominant in Germany. Even if there are contradictory voices in the parliament, ideas are particularly acknowledged in the *Bundestag* that can be combined with the traditional social system that is advocated by the conservative parties. The example of the Mother's Manifesto of the Green Party from 1987 makes clear that these ideas not only descend from the Christian Democratic policy, but have turned into the norm even in other political camps. The manifesto shows that political parties like the Greens, who are associated with the feminist movement, do not naturally oppose a traditional treatment of gender in society. The prostitution law that consolidates the ruling society's structures is another example. Debaters who analyse the mechanisms of the patriarchy are marginalized in the German debate. In the Swedish parliament, in contrast, thoughts that are based on an analysis of the distribution of power between women and men in the patriarchy establish confidence and bridge divides between the parties. Feminist ideas that challenge effective distributions of power are regarded as radical in Germany, while they have become mainstream in Sweden. The replacement of joint taxation by separate assessment and the extension of childcare services, which makes it easier for women to work outside the home under the same conditions as men, are examples of Swedish laws that are based on a critique of patriarchal society structures. Sweden's decision to criminalise the buying – but not the selling – of sexual favours is another expression of this policy.

Finally, one can state that the disagreement about prostitution legislation between Germany and Sweden rests on the fact that the countries are marked by different traditions, and their arguments start from different norms and values when they discuss the question. This is the reason why neither statements like Margareta Winberg's "I deeply dislike what's going on in Germany. It is a strike against equality. It is a strike against brotherhood,"[33] nor the German valuation of the Swedish standpoint as prudish, unrealistic, and naïve contributes to a rapprochement between the countries' prostitution policies. To be able to understand each other the debaters have to acquaint themselves with the social courses and traditions in which the opposing view has its origin. Whether this can lead to an overcoming of the dissention between the debaters is a question that remains to be answered.

Notes

1. Thanks to Catherina Centanni for proofreading.

2. Sveriges Riksdag, *Svar på interpellation 2000/01:229 om legalisering av prostitution*, Snabbprotokoll 2000/01:67, Anf. 4, 15 February 2001. This and all subsequent translations are my own.

3. Sveriges Riksdag, *Svar på interpellation 2000/01:229 om legalisering av prostitution*, Snabbprotokoll 2000/01:67, Anf. 6, 15 February 2001.

4. Sveriges Riksdag, *Svar på interpellation 2000/01:264 om sexköpslagen*, Snabbprotokoll 2000/01:78, Anf. 106, 13 March 2001.

5. Sveriges Riksdag, Justitieutskottet, *Prostitution*, Motion 1990/91:Ju625, 23 January 1991.

6. Sveriges Riksdag, Justitieutskottet, *Med anledning av prop. 1997/98:55 Kvinnofrid*, Motion 1997/98:Ju28, 4 March 1998.

7. Sveriges Riksdag, *Svar på interpellation 2000/01:229 om legalisering av prostitution*, Snabbprotokoll 2000/01:67, Anf. 3, 15 February 2001.

8. Deutscher Bundestag, *Erste Beratung eines Gesetzes zur Beseitigung der Diskriminierung von Prostituierten*, Drs 13/169, 17 April 1997, 15354-15355.

9. Sveriges Riksdag, Justitieutskottet, *Kvinnofrid*, Motion 1997/98:Ju933, 6 October 1997.

10. Deutscher Bundestag, *Entwurf eines Gesetzes zur beruflichen Gleichstellung von Prostituierten und anderer sexuell Dienstleistender*, Drs 14/4456, 1 November 2000, 8.

11. Sveriges Riksdag, *Kvinnofrid*, Snabbprotokoll 2000/01:114, Anf. 139, 28 May 1998.

12. Sveriges Riksdag, Justitieutskottet, *Prostitution*, Motion 1990/91:Ju625, 23 January 1991.

13. Deutscher Bundestag, *Erste Beratung eines Gesetzes zur Beseitigung der Diskriminierung von Prostituierten*, Drs 13/169, 17 April 1997, 15359.

14. Sveriges Riksdag, Justitieutskottet, *Med anledning av prop.1997/98:55 Kvinnofrid*, Motion 1997/98:Ju28, 4 March 1998.

15. Deutscher Bundestag, *Zweite und dritte Beratung Entwurfs eines Gesetzes zur Verbesserung der rechtlichen und sozialen Situation der Prostituierten*, Drs 14/196, 19 October 2001, 19194.

16. Borg, Arne et al., *Prostitution. Beskrivning analys förslag till åtgärder*, (Stockholm: LiberFörlag, 1981).

17. Inger Lindqvist, *Prostitution i Sverige. Bakgrund och åtgärde: betänkande av prostitutionsutredningen*, (Stockholm: LiberFörlag, 1981).

18. Inga-Britt Törnell, *Könshandeln: betänkande av 1993 års prostitutionsutredning*, (Stockholm: Fritz, 1995).

19. Kvinnojourernas Riksorganisation.

20. Fredrika Bremerförbundet, *Remissvar*, (Stockholm: Regeringskansliets arkiv- och dokumentationscenter i Stockholm, 1995)

21. Sveriges Riksdag, Regeringen, *Kvinnofrid*, prop. 1997/98:55, 5 February 1998, 22.

22. Deutscher Bundestag, *Entwurf eines Gesetzes zur Beseitigung der rechtlichen Diskriminierung von Prostituierten*, Drs 11/7140, 16 May 1990.

23. Quoted according to Petra Schmackpfeffer, *Frauenbewegung und Prostitution* (Oldenburg: Bibliotheks- und Informationszentrum der Universität Oldenburg, 1989), 120.

24. Pieke Biermann, *"Wir sind Frauen wie andere auch!"* (Reinbek bei Hamburg: Rowohlt, 1982), 20.

25. Deutscher Bundestag, *Entwurf eines Gesetzes zur Beseitigung der rechtlichen Diskriminierung von Prostituierten*, Drs 11/7140, 16 May 1990, 10 and 12.

26. Yvonne Hirdman, „Kvinnor - från möjlighet till problem? Genuskonflikten i välfärdsstaten - den svenska modellen", in *Kjønn og velferdsstat*, ed. Anne-Hilde Nagel (Bergen: Alma Mater Forlag, 1998), 126-130.

27. Rosemarie Nave-Herz, *Die Geschichte der Frauenbewegung in Deutschland* (Hannover: Niedersächsische Landeszentrale für politische Bildung, 1997), 42-46.

28. Ewa Hedlund, *Kvinnornas Europa* (Borås: Dagens Nyheters Förlag, 1993), 128.

29. Ibid, 113-114.

30. Nave-Herz, 70-75.

31. Hedlund, 126.

32. Ibid, 128-132. Nave-Herz, 86-99.

33. Sveriges Riksdag, *Svar på interpellation 2000/01:229 om legalisering av prostitution*, Snabbprotokoll 2000/01:67, Anf. 4, 15 February 2001.

Select Bibliography

Biermann, Pieke. *"Wir sind Frauen wie andere auch!"* Reinbek bei Hamburg: Rowohlt, 1982.

Borg, Arne, Folke Elwien, Michael Frühling, Lars Grönwall, Rita Liljeström, Sven-Axel Månsson, Anders Nelin, Hanna Olsson, Tage Sjöberg. *Prostitution. Beskrivning analys förslag till åtgärder*, Stockholm: LiberFörlag, 1981.

Deutscher Bundestag. *Entwurf eines Gesetzes zur Beseitigung der rechtlichen Diskriminierung von Prostituierten*, Drs 11/7140, 16 May 1990.

——. *Erste Beratung eines Gesetzes zur Beseitigung der Diskriminierung von Prostituierten*, Drs 13/169, 17 April 1997.

——. *Entwurf eines Gesetzes zur beruflichen Gleichstellung von Prostituierten und anderer sexuell Dienstleistender*, Drs 14/4456, 1 November 2000.

——. *Zweite und dritte Beratung Entwurfs eines Gesetzes zur Verbesserung der rechtlichen und sozialen Situation der Prostituierten*, Drs 14/196, 19 October 2001.

Fredrika Bremerförbundet. *Remissvar*. Stockholm: Regeringskansliets arkiv- och dokumentationscenter i Stockholm, 1995.

Hedlund, Ewa. *Kvinnornas Europa*. Borås: Dagens Nyheters Förlag, 1993.

Lindqvist, Inger. *Prostitution i Sverige. Bakgrund och åtgärde: betänkande av prostitutionsutredningen*. Stockholm: LiberFörlag, 1981

Nave-Herz, Rosemarie. *Die Geschichte der Frauenbewegung in Deutschland*. Hannover: Niedersächsische Landeszentrale für politische Bildung, 1997.

Hirdman, Yvonne. "Kvinnor - från möjlighet till problem? Genuskonflikten i välfärdsstaten - den svenska modellen." In *Kjønn og velferdsstat*, edited by Anne-Hilde Nagel, 126-130. Bergen: Alma Mater Forlag, 1998.

Schmackpfeffer, Petra. *Frauenbewegung und Prostitution*. Oldenburg: Bibliotheks- und Informationszentrum der Universität Oldenburg, 1989.

Sveriges Riksdag, Justitieutskottet, *Prostitution*, Motion 1990/91:Ju625, 23 January 1991.

——. Justitieutskottet. *Kvinnofrid*. Motion 1997/98:Ju933, 6 October 1997.

——. Regeringen. *Kvinnofrid*. Prop. 1997/98:55, 5 February 1998.

——. Justitieutskottet. *Med anledning av prop. 1997/98:55 Kvinnofrid*. Motion 1997/98:Ju28, 4 March 1998.

——. *Kvinnofrid*. Snabbprotokoll 2000/01:114, Anf. 139, 28 May 1998.

——. *Svar på interpellation 2000/01:229 om legalisering av prostitution*. Snabbprotokoll 2000/01:67, Anf. 3, 15 February 2001.

——. *Svar på interpellation 2000/01:229 om legalisering av prostitution*. Snabbprotokoll 2000/01:67, Anf. 4, 15 February 2001.

――. *Svar på interpellation 2000/01:229 om legalisering av prostitution.* Snabbprotokoll 2000/01:67, Anf. 6, 15 February 2001.

――. *Svar på interpellation 2000/01:264 om Sexköpslagen.* Snabbprotokoll 2000/01:78, Anf. 106, 13 March 2001.

Törnell, Inga-Britt. *Könshandeln: betänkande av 1993 års prostitutionsutredning.* Stockholm: Fritz, 1995.

"Staying Bush" – The Influence of Place and Isolation in the Decision by Gay Men to Live in Rural Areas in Australia

Ed Green

Abstract

There have been few studies of gay men living in rural areas, but those studies have generally argued that most rural-born gay men have had to migrate to the city in order to find acceptance and a sense of selfhood. This paper contests that supposition. Using interview data gathered from gay men living in small towns and on farms in Australia, it argues that these gay men have created a sense of place and space and a self-identity for themselves with little reference to the city. This paper, part of a larger work, uses the issue of isolation to illustrate how gay men living in rural areas use and adapt features of the bush to enhance their own lives. Paradoxically, isolation has been cited as the very factor of rural life that has been instrumental in forcing the decampment of many gay men from the bush. In contrast, this paper suggests that gay men living in the bush see the isolation in their lives as an asset on which to build the way of life that they want to live. It argues that they use the natural geographical isolation to create a social isolation that enhances their lives. Far from forcing them to leave the rural environment that they know and like so much, isolation allows them to stay in the bush. **Key Words:** isolation, rural, gay, place, homosexuality, male, Australian bush.

1.   Introduction

Rural areas the world over are often portrayed as conservative, intolerant places where acceptance of difference is low and a fierce conformity and parochialism, if not abject bigotry, are the queens [sic] of a hierarchy of values. For gay men in Australia, "the bush" was depicted as a place where they were "stigmatised or marginalised."[1] "The bush" had, for gay men, acquired a reputation of being a place of social isolation and rejection.[2] It was branded, for gay men, a place of never-ending emotional drought and heartbreak.[3] Yet gay men, arguably still the most marginalised and maligned of minority groups in our society, live in rural areas.

The predominant social construction of homosexuality and of gay identity is as an urban (and urbane) phenomenon. George Chauncey,[4] and even the Australian academic Dennis Altman,[5] writes that gay men have flocked to the cities in order to be gay and to find others like themselves. This construction of the sociology of homosexuality concurs with Preston's view that rural gay men usually thought they had only two choices: "...they could either sublimate their erotic identities and remain in their hometown,"[6] or "...they could move to a larger centre of population and lose themselves in its anonymity."[7]

In 1994, Adele Horin, writing in a Sydney newspaper about a gay man recalled that,

> He'd left his hometown in rural NSW twenty-six years earlier to find himself in Sydney. He was gay. That's what gay boys from the country did then. They slipped away from family, farm [and] community to find out why they were different.[8]

Accepted wisdom has it that small towns have a reputation for being so hostile to gay people that it is difficult to believe that any gay man would willingly choose to live there. This, and the geographical isolation of the bush, it is assumed, made it imperative for gay men to move to the city in order to find identity, community, desire and love.[9] Gay men in Australia, as elsewhere in the world, are said to have raised clouds of dust as they left the bush and headed for the cities.[10] They came to the cities to "lose themselves"[11] – and to "find themselves"[12] – in the "gay world of overlapping social networks."[13]

Horin's article goes on to contend that gay men have begun to return to rural communities. In describing those men who were now returning to their rural roots as "prodigal sons," she implies that they may not have originally left the bush entirely of their own volition. Horin implies that had gay men not had to "slip away" from family and farm, many may well not have done so. Fellows, in his study of rural gay men in the U.S., observes that,

> If the prospect of staying in their rural communities had not appeared to be so incompatible with leading honest,

unconstricted lives, more of these men might have made their home in farm communities.[14]

Those gay men who remained in the bush and those who decided, for whatever reason, to return to their rural origins have been largely ignored in this dialogue. It has been, for too long, argued that gay men have deserted "the bush." It has been, for too long, unquestioningly accepted that a gay identity and lifestyle, and all that that means, can only be attained in the metropolis. It has been, for too long, assumed that "the bush," by its very nature, prevents the formation of a strong personal identity among gay men and the living of authentic gay lives.

Using personal interview data gathered from gay men living in small towns and on farms in Australia, this paper argues that rural gay men have used a sense of place and space to create a self-identity for themselves with little reference to the city. This paper, part of a larger work, uses the issue of isolation to illustrate how gay men use and adapt features of the bush to enhance their own lives. Isolation has been cited as the very factor of rural life that has been instrumental in forcing the decampment of many gay men from the bush.[15] In contrast, this paper argues that gay men living in the bush use the natural geographical isolation to create a social isolation that enhances and enriches their lives. It suggests that these gay men see the isolation in their lives as an asset on which to build the lives that they want to live. Far from forcing them to leave the rural environment that they know and like so much, isolation allows them to stay in the bush. And just as a sense of community and belonging may give urban gay men a sense of selfhood, gay men in rural areas can also find a sense of selfhood in living in the bush itself and belonging to the dispersed gay community there.

2.   Place

For the rural gay men in this study, "place" was a major influence in their lives. Their affinity with the bush allowed them to use place and space to improve their lives and, in fact, construct the lives that they wanted to live. In one of the early interviews, an informant commented that he did not think that too many unhappy gay men would be found living in the bush. At that stage of the research, this was a surprising and challenging comment. He said the "...[gay] people that live in the bush ... are quite happy to stay in the bush."[16] The implication of his comment was that gay men living in the bush were generally there by choice, they were happy with that choice and they intended to stay in the bush. The most common reasons these men gave for wanting to stay in the bush was that they liked rural living and they were happy where they were. Rural places gave these gay men the important cornerstones of a lifestyle which itself was closely related to the nature of the bush. Space and seclusion, quiet, tranquility, communing with nature, and the unhurried pace of life were elements of bush life valued by these men. So, too, was the chance for some to live out of town on a farm and to be away from people.

These men described the bush – the "where I live" – in glowing terms. One man enthused,

> It's just beautiful. And there's, you know, the Canola – acres and acres and acres...of Canola plant and all this golden bright yellow covering, you know, hill after hill and that. That is just wonderful, you know. I find it just incredible for me.[17]

While one might think of Rudy's description of the countryside as a little too "over the top" and a little too "camp," it is obvious that he really did like the bush as a place and he liked living in that place. His testimony indicates a real and genuine appreciation of the physical attractiveness of the bush. This physical attractiveness of where these men live contributes to their appreciation of place and the importance of it in their lives.

But it was somewhat surprising to find that these gay men, in speaking about the salient and appealing aspects of the bush, also accentuated those very aspects that are often quoted as being the major disadvantages of rural life. The bush was, for them, an attractive place because, as one man said, "It's rugged, it's ahm...rough country.... 'pretty' is the wrong word."[18] But all of these words were inextricably linked to the "beauty" of the bush.[19] For some of the men, the severity of the bush was attractive. The floods, the impassable roads and the physicality of their work had an attractive edge. Those aspects of the bush normally regarded with some disdain, even by country people, were not spoken of by any of the gay men in this study. The heat and the dust and the flies, for example, did not rate a mention. These are not the comments that might have been expected from gay men describing the rural places where they live.

For these gay men, deciding to live in the bush was based on much more than simply liking the place. Their reasons for "staying bush" echo the words of Simon – "...it's [the bush] part of my make-up."[20] He was referring to the fact that the bush was not only part of his life, but it was part of his being. The bush played a part not only in these men's happiness and their satisfaction in life, but it was part of who they were. The men in this study saw the country as providing exactly the opportunity they wanted and needed to have the space to be themselves and to have the lifestyle they wanted – rural and gay.

3.   Isolation

Isolation is often cited as the main disadvantage of rural life, especially for gay men. This aspect of rural life, though part and parcel of the bush, is perennially paraded as being the issue that drives gay men in droves away from the bush.[21] But the testimony of these gay men emphasised that isolation was one of the real attractions of the bush. In fact, the physical and social isolation they could create in their lives by using the geography of the bush was the factor these gay men most often cited as to why they liked living in the bush. Isolation was a feature of the bush that they were able to use with great effect to enhance their lives.

These men also linked the beauty of the bush that they saw with the isolation that the bush allowed them to feel. As these men talked about the splendor of place, almost in the same breath and thought, there was a mention or implication of geographical isolation. One man expressed it this way: "...I love the country. ... you know, the quiet and the peace of the countryside. I love the beauty of the countryside..."[22] and then went on to describe the bush as "...a very isolated...isolated area."[23] It was as if these men equated the beauty of the landscape with its ruggedness and its isolation.

One man said that,

> I love our farm. It's beautiful. ... gorgeous [Laughs]....
> Our farm...our cows have the best view in the whole
> district...beautiful.[24]

The view that Rodney's cattle enjoyed, "... the best in the district," was so beautiful precisely because it was a view from the isolation of the farm. For these gay men, the isolation and the ruggedness of the landscape only added to the beauty of the place in which they lived which, in turn, reinforced their reasons for living there.

These gay men not only liked the isolation that was fundamental to the rural landscape in which they lived, but they included the isolation as part of their lifestyle. Yet, this deliberate imposition of elements of isolation in their lives did not, paradoxically, make them feel isolated. In fact, it had the opposite effect. The natural isolation and beauty they so valued and enjoyed bound them to the bush. It increased these men's sense of connectedness to the bush. It increased their sense of belonging "to" and belonging "in" the bush. It underpinned their desire to stay where they felt they belonged and where they knew they wanted to be. The isolation of the bush was inextricably linked to why these gay men chose to stay (in the) bush and worked so determinedly to do so.

4.   Using the Isolation of the Bush

The isolation of which these gay men spoke was a multifaceted issue just as the effects it had on their lives in the bush were also various and complex. This theme of liking the isolation of the bush, the geographical as well as the social that flowed on from it, was a surprising and common feature of the testimonies of the men in this study. Their testimonies made it clear that they expected and accepted an element of isolation and aloneness to be part of their lives. It was a factor that they appreciated and welcomed in their lives. For these gay men, isolation and aloneness was not a source of loneliness but was, in fact, a source of personal space and, in some ways, something of a blessing and a joy. One man admitted that "…yeah, I like the isolation. I like the…ahm… freedom to do what I want."[25] Another emphasised that, for him, the whole point of living in a rural community was "…[the] isolation, I suppose."[26] Yet another commented, "I even like having to drive the two or three hours to get to another town."[27]

These gay men not only appreciated the isolation that was part of the nature and essence of the rural landscape in which they lived, but they were intent on incorporating it into their lifestyle. For them, it was about choice and the way they wanted to live. Isolation was an aspect of their lives that they often sought out and even brought about. Some men created it by living out of town. Others created it by withdrawing from the community and not participating in communal life to the extent that might have been expected of them. And some did it by doing both and so blending the social isolation in their lives with the nature of the geographical landscape. These men's lives often involved disengagement with the community in order to lead a "gayer" life. Country living enabled them to be by themselves and thereby to be themselves. They were able, all in their own way, to fuse the rural and gay components of their respective identities into their lives and lifestyles.

An important avenue by which these men created a sense of isolation in their lives was to not disclose their homosexuality to the wider community. These men believed that if their sexuality was to become public knowledge, they would face the possibility of rejection and ostracism and their family would also pay a price. But, contrary to expectations, their non-disclosure was not to achieve inclusion with the community, but, in fact, to facilitate some disconnection from the community. While these men did not disclose their homosexuality to the general community, this did not mean that the community was unaware or had few suspicions of their homosexuality. Non-disclosure was a deliberate strategy to keep suspicions as suspicions and not confirm them. This was a very incisive means to silence the community. Not allowing the community the opportunity to know something to which they could adversely react was an effective mechanism to avert that reaction. Non-disclosure became a device that these men used not to deny knowledge of their homosexuality to the community but to deny the community the opportunity to take a hostile stance. It was an act of socially isolating themselves. The act of not disclosing their homosexuality, while on the pretext that it was none of the community's business, was used to quietly pre-empt and silence adverse comment and so create a level of social isolation in their lives to complement the geographical isolation of the bush. This allowed them to keep some distance between themselves and the community and it allowed these men to have the lower profile in the town that they wanted.

It should be noted in passing, however, that these rural gay men were not reluctant to tell the people most important to them — their families and friends — that they were gay. In this study, only two men had not disclosed their homosexuality to their family. All the men in this study had local friends who knew they were gay. Again, contrary to expectations, disclosure was used to find support and inclusion. So, the self-imposed isolation arising from non-disclosure of their sexuality was selective and did not apply to those among whom these men found acceptance. Selective disclosure of their homosexuality allowed these men to position themselves within the social milieu to their advantage. Just as non-disclosure kept them away from the community's scrutiny and reach, disclosure brought them within the scrutiny and reach of those with whom they wanted contact — family, friends, potential friends… and sex buddies.

Another of the ways in which isolation impacted on these rural gay men was in regard to the extent and nature of their friendships. Though they reported a degree of aloneness in their lives, they were not friendless. The satisfaction of being "alone" and restricting their socialising to a small circle of friends was, for them, one of the delights and charms of living in the bush. It appears as if the geographical isolation of the place and the socially isolated nature of these men's lives enhanced and strengthened the limited friendships they formed. Rodney implied that his friendships in Gunnawere were close and accepting,

> …and I've got all my friends around me. I've got beautiful friends. I've got the best friends. They all live here as well, you know. That's why I'm really lucky….I'd be really sad if any of them left, but they don't leave.[28]

Rex said that his friends were small in number, but close and that the relationships go back a long way,

> I have...ohhhh...five or ten close friends...mainly gay.
> Long term. Comfortable....most of them know each
> other....[29]

That these men had their own small and intimate circles of friends was clear evidence that they could establish and sustain significant friendships despite the isolated nature of their lives. For many of the men in this study, friendship with others was a longstanding and enduring aspect of their lives. The fact that most such friendships were local, or close by, added to the advantages of living in the bush. These close bonds of friendship were among the reasons these men were happy to stay in the bush.

However, a desire to establish and sustain wider circles of friends within the mainstream community was not on these men's agenda. Whether this was because they disconnected themselves from the community in order to live their lives beyond the reach of its curious gaze, or whether the community was essentially unwelcoming to them was not always easy to pinpoint, though both factors appeared to be at play. Regardless of the reasons, it is clear that these men had no wish and no need to maintain close friendships in the mainstream community in which they lived.

But this lack of a wider friendship network within the community was something that these gay men had experienced all their lives. Izak's words about what friends and friendships involve are revealing. A friend is "someone to talk [to]" about anything anytime.[30] A friend is someone "you can just open up [to]."[31] These kinds of friends were not to be found in the general community, especially if one was gay and knowledge of that aspect of one's life was not in the community domain. Many of the men implied that the lack of friendships beyond the small and longstanding circle was simply one of the tolerable consequences of rural life. To live in semi-isolation in both a geographical and social sense was these men's desire and the need for friends beyond what they had was unnecessary and a hindrance to the life they wanted to lead.

The element of isolation that these gay men were able to infuse into their rural lives also gave them a sense of freedom. Bobby spoke of in these terms,

> ...ahm...yeah, I like the isolation. I like the...ahm
> ...freedom to do what I want.[32]

For Bobby, freedom and isolation were co-related. Similarly, Izak said that one of the things he liked about Geriffi was "...I guess, it's my freedom here. I just feel so free here."[33] For these men, freedom was more than the space to do as one pleased. Freedom had another dimension that revolved around being free to be gay. Living out of town, and with little connection to it, and away from prying eyes provided some men in this study with one avenue of being free. Additionally, there were men who lived in rural towns who also embraced with some gusto this feeling and sense of freedom that "out-of-towners" said living in a rural environment gave them. As was said earlier, the isolation in these men's lives, whether natural or created, allowed them, paradoxically, greater freedom to lead "gayer" lives.

The act of distancing themselves from the community, or the act of not becoming too involved in it, gave them a freedom to be who they were and to live their lives largely as they wished. These men fused the natural geographical isolation of the bush with a self-imposed social isolation to give themselves a freedom from community involvement, local scrutiny and social constraint. In living unobtrusively and quietly and somewhat removed from the mainstream community, these men had the lifestyle they sought — rural and gay.

This sense of freedom, like the isolation these men prized so much, was achieved by disconnecting from the community in which they lived. It was achieved by distancing themselves from insignificant others. This paper has already remarked on these gay men's ability to use the non-disclosure of their homosexuality to not only prevent unpleasant criticism of themselves by the community, but to facilitate a detachment from it. Their friendships were not drawn from the wider community in which they lived. These men seemed to have little meaningful engagement with the community, and, from their point of view, there was little enticement or invitation from the community for them to interact with it. These men rarely involved themselves in community affairs or events. From these men's testimony, it appeared that they were rarely invited. Paradoxically, they were contented with that situation and did not want to be part of the community if that meant being unaccepted because they were gay.

The bush was where these gay men could realize the possibility of a rounded and fulfilled life. One man described this as a "...lifestyle of space,"[34] and another said that it was the "...space to be by yourself."[35] This isolation of the bush allowed them to experience and enjoy their rurality and to accommodate their homosexuality as well. Isolation was the major factor in their decision to live in the bush.

5.   Interpreting Isolation – Creating A Latter Day Arcadia?

How might these men's use of geographical isolation and their deliberate creation of social isolation be interpreted? One way to read it is through their subconscious attempt to envisage the bush as a latter day Arcadia, though none of them referred to this directly.

Gay theorist Bryne Fone believes that the homosexual imagination employs the Arcadian landscape as a place "…where it is safe to be gay."[36] Kellogg argues that "The universal desire to be free, but safe, … has given birth to a literature of Arcadia…."[37] The centrepiece of that literary tradition is that the rural landscape was imagined as an idyllic place. It was also a place of freedom (and liberation), of self-discovery, chosen isolation, naturalism…and of homoerotic desire.

In this study of gay men living in rural areas, these Arcadian literary metaphors are reflected in their testimonies. This is not to say that these twenty-one men were avid readers of Whitman, or of the pastoral idylls of medieval Europe or of the classical texts of Virgil. These men were not aware of this long literary tradition and they did not consciously invoke it to explain their lives or their image of the Australian bush. It is not intended in this paper to indulge in what Shuttleton calls the "crass canonisation" of the rural.[38] Certainly, the pastoral idyll has been used on occasion to vehemently denigrate and exclude homoerotic desire.[39] Nevertheless, the way these men expressed their desire and will to live in the bush can be partly explained and understood in terms of these Arcadian places of fantasy.

Those interviewed said that one of the reasons they decided to live in the bush and to make their lives there was because of their sense of belonging and affinity with it. That affinity is displayed in a number of ways, one of which is the depiction of the bush as a place of rugged beauty. The men emphasised that the isolation of the bush allowed them the space to be gay. The bush gave them privacy, seclusion, and a "shut-offedness," not only from the inquisitive and interfering eyes of others, but also to explore and to be who they were. They described the bush as a place where they could escape the scrutiny of the communities in which they lived and the social constraints imposed on their lives. The mythical Arcadia, too, was a place of isolation and aloneness. It was a place of freedom,

> …freedom from the prying eyes of others, a freedom to
> be oneself and a place endowed with a freedom that
> open space can give and a freedom to be oneself.[40]

For the men in this study, isolation and freedom went together. The country provided the isolation in which they found the freedom and opportunity to find themselves. This has strong resonances with the representation of that idyllic Arcadia. The bush, for these gay men, encompassed all the attributes of that Edenesque place and their decision to live there can, in part, be understood through this paradigm.

The other aspect of this Arcadian fantasy that finds reflection in this study is that Arcadia was a place to which men retreated. The mythical Arcadia was not only a place in which men could be themselves and by themselves, but a place in which they could be with others like themselves. This, too, is reflected in the testimony of these men. This paper has shown that these men not only retreated and withdrew from an involvement with the wider community in which they lived, but they also retreated to the intimacy of a small circle of close and accepting friends. They dreamed of finding a special friend with whom they could spend their lives together by themselves. It was Sam's dream to find a man who would live with him on his cattle farm. It was the life of splendid isolation together that appealed to Jack and to Nick in their respective lives. It was living together in an isolated village that Petro missed most when he broke up with his boyfriend. Bobby loved living on the farm with his lover (and their horses). Together alone was what Cleever and Gerry appreciated most about their partnership and their lives on the outskirts of town.

The men in this study have, in a way, created their own retreat from the real world. They made lives for themselves in, but apart from, isolated towns and environments. They lived on properties away from the community and in places and spaces they considered beautiful, peaceful and where they could be who they were and wanted to be. They isolated themselves both geographically and socially in the bush to get way from the claustrophobia and potential hostility of the small-town environment.

The rural has usually been depicted as a man's world, and this was certainly so in the Arcadian mythology. For example, Whitman, Auden, Forster, Hopkins, Vidal, Carpenter and, to name some Australians, Donald Friend,[41] as well as Jeffrey Smart,[42] all spoke of an "idyllized" "manly-love" (that could only be) realised in isolated rural settings.[43] For the men in this study, being a man and loving a man was an important aspect of their lives. And more than anything, they dreamt of opportunities of living together in a relationship with their own white knight in their own Garden of Eden.

These gay men did see the bush as a place in which they could find happiness and contentment with another man. They did see the bush as a place in which they could be with another man away from the intrusive gaze of the community in which they lived. They did see the bush as a place in which they could live a gay life of their own making. The bush was, for these men, a beautiful place in which they had decided to live, all the more so because of its isolation. Though these men have not necessarily claimed that they led totally fulfilled lives, they did insist that, for them, living in the bush held out the (only) promise and possibility of just that.

6.   Conclusion

This is a far cry from the usual depiction of the lot of most rural gay men. For example, Bell and Valentine's conclusion to their study of "queer country" is that "For many with same-sex feelings...the country-side offers nothing but isolation and loathing..."[44] Such sentiments find little support here. This paper rejects unequivocally the postmodern idea of social theory being rooted, and only able to be rooted, in the city. It rejects the argument of Soja that

> ...the population beyond the reach of the urban is comprised of *idiotes,* from the Greek root *idios,* meaning "one's own," "a private person," unlearned in the ways of the *polis*...[45]

whereby the urban is the only place learned and urban(e) enough to be worthy of critical intellectual consideration. Under Soja's model, the rustic, and those who live there, are, and will remain, "...justifiably marginal and vestigial."[46] This study demonstrates that gay men choose to, and do, live fulfilled lives in rural communities. And while academic "outsiders" might, in their urban(e)-centric ideas about the lives of gay men in rural areas, see and term such lives as "unlearned" and "vestigial," this study also rejects such conclusions.

Gay men in Australia are increasingly deciding to make their lives in rural environments because of the attractions they see in such places. And those attractions include those very attributes that have previously been considered instrumental in driving masses of gay men away from rural places. Some gay men in Australia are deciding to stay (in the) bush and make their homes and lives there precisely because of the isolation rather than being forced to leave because of it.

Notes

1. Richard Roberts, "Factors Influencing the Formation of Gay and Lesbian Communities in Rural Areas," *National AIDS Bulletin* (April 1993), 14-17.

See also, Lorene Gottschalk and Janice Newton, "Not So Gay In The Bush: 'Coming Out' In Regional and Rural Victoria" (Ballarat: University of Ballarat, 2003), 14-15.

2. Lynne Hillier, Deborah Warr and Ben Haste, *The Rural Mural: Sexuality and Diversity in Rural Youth – Research Report* (Melbourne: Centre for the Study of Sexually Transmissible Diseases, La Trobe University, 1996), 40.

3. Rachael Hogge, *"Working it Out": A Needs Analysis for Sexual Minority Youth in North West Tasmania* (Devenport: Devenport Youth Accommodation Services Inc., 1998), 49.

4. George Chauncey, *Gay New York: Gender, Urban Culture and the Making of the Gay Male World, 1890-1940* (New York: Basic Books, 1994), 2.

5. Dennis Altman, "Marginality on the Tropic," in *De-Centering Sexualities: Politics and Representations Beyond the Metropolis*, ed. Richard Phillips, Dianne Watt and David Shuttleton (London: Routledge, 2000), 46-47.

6. John Preston, *Hometowns: Gay Men Write About Where They Belong* (New York: Plume Books, 1991), xvi.

7. Ibid.

8. Adele Horin, "Prodigal Gays are Reclaiming the Country," *Sydney Morning Herald*, 22 June 1994.

9. Hillier, Warr and Haste, 1.

10. Garry Wotherspoon, *City of the Plain* (Sydney: Hale and Iremonger, 1991), 15.

11. Preston, xvi.

12. Horin.

13. Chauncey, 2.

14. Will Fellows, *Farm Boys: Lives of Gay Men from the Rural Midwest* (Madison: University of Wisconsin Press, 1996), 314.

15. Gottschalk and Newton, 94-98.

16. Interview Data. [5/p. 42]. These bracketed references are to the transcripts of the interviews, the first number being the interview and the second number being the page of the original transcript.

17. Interview Data. [2/p. 49].

18. Interview Data. [20/p. 5].

19. Interview Data. [20/p. 5].

20. Interview Data. [10/p. 40].

21. Every Australian study cited in this paper, like many other international papers, cited "isolation" as a factor that is always detrimental to the well-being of gay men living in rural areas.

22. Interview Data. [2/p.29].

23. Interview Data. [2/p.29].

24. Interview Data. [13/p.4-5].

25. Interview Data. [20/p.10].

26. Interview Data. [6/p.97].

27. Interview Data. [20/p. 53].

28. Interview Data. [13/p.6].

29. Interview Data. [21/p.30-31].

30. Interview Data. [12/p.20-21].

31. Interview Data. [12/p.20-21].

32. Interview Data. [20/p.10].

33. Interview Data. [12/p.23].

34. Interview Data. [20/p.9].

35. Interview Data. [6/p.117].

36. Bryne Fone, "This Other Eden: Arcadia and the Homosexual Imagination," *Journal of Homosexuality* 8.3-4 (1983): 13.

37. Stuart Kellogg, ed., *Literary Visions of Homosexuality* (New York: Haworth Press, 1983), 4.

38. David Shuttleton, "The Queer Politics of Gay Pastoral," in *De-Centering Sexualities: Politics and Representations Beyond the Metropolis*, ed. Richard Phillips, Dianne Watt and David Shuttleton (London, Routledge, 2000), 125 -146.

39. Ibid., 129. Shuttleton cites but one example of where this Arcadian tradition was given a more sinister twist. The early German homosexual emancipation journal *Der Eigene* (1896-1931) was often illustrated with photographs of athletic youths posing naked in rural-like settings. But the text that accompanied such Arcadian photographs was "... distinctly anti-feminist and often supportive of a nationalist, masculinist supremacism approaching Nazism."

40. Bryne Fone, *Homophobia: A History* (New York: Picador, 2000), 281.

41. See his move from Sydney to Hill End. Paul Heatherington ed., *The Diaries of Donald Friend*, Volume 2 (Canberra: National Library of Australia, 2003), 338-339.

42. Note Smart and his boyfriend's move from Rome to the Tuscan country-side. See Jeffrey Smart, *Not Quite Straight - A Memoir* (London: William Heinemann, 1996), 414-415.

43. Fone, 1983, 13-34. "Manly-love" comes from the writings of John Addinton Symonds (1840-1893) who used it to denote a difference between effeminate homosexual men and homosexual men exhibiting more masculine behaviour. Walt Whitman (1819-1892) also took up the theme and coined the phrase "manly friendship" to counter what Fone says was "the widespread assumption that men who loved men were effeminate." See also Fone, 2000, 280-297 and 338-341.

44. David Bell and Gill Valentine, "Queer Country: Rural Lesbian and Gay Lives," *Journal of Rural Studies* 11.2 (1995): 113-122.

45. Edward W. Soja, *Postmodern Geographies: The Reassertion of Space in Critical Social Theory* (London: W. W. Norton & Co. Inc., 1989), 235.

46. Barbara Ching and Gerald W. Creed, "Introduction," in *Knowing Your Place: Rural Identity and Cultural Hierarchy*, eds. Barbara Ching and Gerald W. Creed (New York: Routledge, 1997), 8.

Select Bibliography

Altman, Dennis. "Marginality on the Tropic." In *De-Centering Sexualities: Politics and Representations Beyond the Metropolis*, edited by Richard Phillips, Dianne Watt, and David Shuttleton, 37-48. London: Routledge, 2000.

Bech, Henning. *When Men Meet: Homosexuality and Modernity*. Cambridge: Polity Press, 1997.

Beemyn, Brett, ed. *Creating a Place for Ourselves: Lesbian, Gay and Bisexual Community Histories*. New York: Routledge, 1997.

Bell, David and Gill Valentine. "Queer Country: Rural Lesbian and Gay Lives." *Journal of Rural Studies* 11.2 (1995): 113-122.

——. "Farm Boys and Wild Men: Rurality, Masculinity and Homosexuality." *Rural Sociology* 65.4 (2000): 547-561.

Bishop, Andrew. "A Wagga Boy's Own Story." *Talkabout* (July 1994): 30-31.

Boulden, Walter T. "How Can You Be Gay and Live In Wyoming? What is the Experience of Being a White Middle-Aged, Gay Man Living in Wyoming?" Ph.D. Thesis. Cincinnati: The Union Institute. Unpublished. 1999.

Broad, Lucy. "Being Gay in Rural Australia." *Transcript of Heywire – An On-Line Discussion.* 19 August 1999, <http://www2.abc.net.au/heywire.august/posts/21.shtm>.

Broderick, Erin et al. *Bush Talks*. Syndey: Human Rights and Equal Opportunity Commission's National Inquiry into Rural and Remote Education, 1998.

Browning, Frank. *The Culture of Desire: Paradox and Perversity in Gay Lives Today*. New York: Crown Publishers, 1993.

——. *A Queer Geography: Journeys Towards A Sexual Self*. New York: Crown Publishers, 1996.

Carrington, Nigel. "Country NSW - There's More Than Ever Before." *Talkabout* (July 1991): 12-13.

Chauncey, George. *Gay New York: Gender, Urban Culture and the Making of the Gay Male World. 1890-1940*. New York: Basic Books, 1994.

Cheers, Brain. *Welfare Bushed: Social Care in Rural Australia*. Aldershot, U.K.: Ashgate Publishing Ltd., 1998.

Ching, Barbara and Gerald W. Creed, eds. *Knowing Your Place: Rural Identity and Cultural Hierarchy*. New York: Routledge, 1997.

Chris, "Waking Up Gay in the Country." *Rural Gaze* 3 (1993): 1 and 13.

Cody, Paul and Peter Welch. "Rural Gay Men in Northern New England: Life Experiences and Coping Styles." *Journal of Homosexuality* 33.1 (1997): 51-67.

Connell, Robert W. "Live Fast and Die Young: The Construction of Masculinity Among Young Working-Class Men on the Margin of the Labor Market." *Australian and New Zealand Journal of Sociology* 27.2 (1991): 141-171.

——. Mark D. Davis, and Gary W. Dowsett. "A Bastard of a Life: Homosexual Desire and Practice Among Men in a Working-Class Milieu." *Australian and New Zealand Journal of Sociology* 29.1 (1993): 112-135.

D'Augelli, Anthony R. and Mary M. Hart. "Gay Women, Men, and Families in Rural Settings: Toward the Development of Helping Communities." *American Journal of Community Psychology* 15.1 (1987): 79-93.

Davila, Robert D. "Many Gays are Opting for a Country Lifestyle: Trend Reflects Key Changes in Society." In *Sacramento Bee*, 1 June 1999. <http://www.ruralgay.com/Press/sacbee.htm>.

Davis, Thomas B. "Perceptions and Experiences of Growing Up Gay in Rural Louisiana: A Reflexive Ethnography of Six Gay Men." Ph.D. Thesis, University of Louisiana at Monroe. Unpublished. 2003.

Dempsey, Deb. *A Report on Discrimination and Abuse Experienced by Lesbians, Gay Men, Bisexuals and Transgender People in Victoria*. Melbourne: Victorian Gay and Lesbian Rights Lobby, 2000.

Editor. "Pride Across America: Life of Gays and Lesbians in Small Towns - A Special Advocate Report." *The Advocate*. 20 June 2000. <http://www.findarticles.com/cf_0/m1589/2000_June_20/627417 91/print.jhtml>.

Fellows, Will. *Farm Boys: Lives of Gay Men from the Rural Midwest*. Madison: University of Wisconsin Press, 1996.

Fone, Bryne. "This Other Eden: Arcadia and the Homosexual Imagination." *Journal of Homosexuality* 8.3-4 (1983): 13-34.

——. *Homophobia: A History*, New York: Picador, 2000.

Heatherington, Paul, ed. *The Diaries of Donald Friend*. Volume 2. Canberra: National Library of Australia, 2003.

Hillier, Lynne, Deborah Warr and Ben Haste. *The Rural Mural: Sexuality and Diversity in Rural Youth – Research Report*. Melbourne: Centre for the Study of Sexually Transmissible Diseases, La Trobe University, 1996.

Hodge, Stephen. "No Fags Out There: Gay Men, Identity and Suburbia." *Journal of Interdisciplinary Gender Studies* 1.1 (1995): 41-48.

Horin, Adele. "Prodigal Gays Are Reclaiming the Country." *The Sydney Morning Herald*. 22 June 1994.

Howard, John. "Place and Movement in Gay American History." In *Creating a Place for Ourselves: Lesbian, Gay and Bisexual Community Histories*, edited by Brett Beemyn, 211-226. New York: Routledge, 1998.

——. *Men Like That: A Southern Queer History*. Chicago: The University of Chicago Press, 1999.

Kellogg, Stuart, ed. *Literary Visions of Homosexuality*. New York: Haworth Press, 1983.

Kramer, Jerry L. "Bachelor Farmers and Spinsters: Gay and Lesbian Identities and Communities in Rural North Dakota." In *Mapping Desire: Geographies of Sexualities,* edited by David Bell, 201-213. London: Routledge, 1995.

Lynch, Frederick R. "Non-Ghetto Gays: A Sociological Study of Suburban Homosexuals." *Journal of Homosexuality* 13.4 (1987): 13-42.

McCarthy, Linda. "Poppies in the Wheatfield: Exploring the Lives of Rural Lesbians." *Journal of Homosexuality* 39.1 (2000): 75-94.

McDermott, Quentin. "Hitting Material." Four Corners: TV Program Transcript. *Australian Broadcasting Commission*. 17 July 2000. <http://www.abc.net.au/4corners/s152974.htm>.

Miller, Kenton Penley and Mahamati, *"Not Round Here": Affirming Diversity, Challenging Homophobia – Rural Service Providers Training Manual*. Sydney: Human Rights and Equal Opportunity Commission, 2000.

Parvin, Paige. "Gay in the Small-Town South." *Southern Voice*. 10 August 2000.<http://www.southernvoice.com/southernvoice/news/record/.html?record=9302>.

Philips, Richard, Dianne Watt and David Shuttleton, eds. *De-centering Sexualities: Politics and Representation Beyond the Metropolis*. London: Routledge, 2000.

Plummer, David. *One of the Boys - Masculinity, Homophobia and Modern Manhood*. New York: Harrington Press, 1999.

Poetschka, Neil and Jeff Linnach. "Rural Men and Beats – Report on Men Who Use Beats in the Macquarie and Central West Area Health Service Regions." Dubbo: Central West Area Health Service and Macquarie Area Health Service. Unpublished. 1995.

Precker, Michael. "Out in the Country." *The Dallas Morning News*. 16 May 1999. <http://www.dallasnews.com/lifestyles/0516life3rural.htm>.

Preston, John. *Hometowns: Gay Men Write About Where They Belong*. New York: Plume Books, 1991.

Probst, Rad. "Small Montana Town Great Place for Gay Community."
    Daily Trojan. 18 March 1998. <http://www.usc.edu/student-
    affairs/dt/V133/N39/03-uber.39d.html>.
Riorden, Michael. *Out Our Way: Gay and Lesbian Life in the Country*,
    Toronto: Between the Lines Press, 1996.
Rist, Darrel Y. *Heartlands: A Gay Man's Odyssey Across America*. New
    York: Penguin Books, 1992.
Roberts, Richard. "A 'Fair Go For All'? Discrimination and the
    Experiences of Some Men Who Have Sex With Men in the
    Bush." In *Communication and Culture in Rural Areas*, edited by
    P. Share, 151-173. Key Papers Series 4. Bathurst: Centre for
    Rural Research, Charles Stuart University, 1995.
——. "Factors Influencing the Formation of Gay and Lesbian Communities
    in Rural Areas." *National AIDS Bulletin* (1993): 14 -17.
——. "Men Who Have Sex With Men In The Bush: Impediments to the
    Formation of Gay Communities in Some Rural Areas." *Rural
    Society* 2-3, (1992): 13-14.
——. "School Experiences of Some Rural Gay Men Coping With
    'Countrymindedness.'" In *Gay and Lesbian Perspectives III*,
    edited by Wotherspoon, Garry, 45-69. Sydney: University of
    Sydney, 1996.
Sears, James. "Rebels, Rubyfruit, and Rhinestones: An Introduction."
    2000. <http://www.jsears.com/blueintro.htm>.
Shuttleton, David. "The Queer Politics of Gay Pastoral." In *De-centering
    Sexualities: Politics and Representation Beyond the Metropolis*,
    edited by Richard Philips, Dianne Watt and David Shuttleton,
    125-146. London: Routledge, 2000.
Silverstein, Charles. *Man to Man: Gay Couples in America*. New York:
    William Morrow and Company, Inc., 1981.
Smart, Jeffery. *Not Quite Straight – A Memoir*. London: William
    Heinemann, 1996.
Smith, James D. and Ronald J. Manskoske. *Rural Gays and Lesbians:
    Building on the Strengths of Communities*. New York: Harrington
    Park Press, 1997.
Soja, Edward W. *Postmodern Geographies: The Reassertion of Space in
    Critical Social Theory*. London: W. W. Norton & Co Inc., 1989.
Stevenson, Warwick. "This is My Home." *DNA Magazine* (January 2002):
    62-65.
Thorpe, Alan. "Sexualities and Straightjackets: Issues Affecting Gay Men
    in Rural Communities – An Exploratory Investigation of
    Homosexuality in Rural Areas." M.Ed. Thesis. Unpublished.
    Canberra: University of Canberra, 1996.

Wafer, Jim, Erica Southgate and Lyndall Coon, eds. *Out in the Valley: Hunter Gay and Lesbian Histories*. Newcastle: Newcastle Regional Library, 2000.

Weston, Kath. "Get Thee To A Big City: Sexual Imaginary and the Great Gay Migration." *GLQ* 2 (1995): 253-277.

Whittier, David K. "Social Conflict Among 'Gay' Men in a Small(er) Southern Town." In *Rural Gays and Lesbians: Building on the Strengths of Communities*, edited by James D. Smith and Ronald J. Manskoske, 53-72. New York: Harrington Park Press, 1997.

Wotherspoon, Garry. *City of the Plain*. Sydney: Hale and Iremonger, 1991.

PART II

Literature: Re-writing Desire

Whoring, Incest, Duplicity, or The "Self-Polluting" Erotics of Daniel Defoe's *Moll Flanders*

Katerina Kitsi-Mitakou

Abstract
The aim of this essay is to explore the sexual politics of Defoe's *Moll Flanders*, a novel that seems to instruct towards heterosexuality and family life, but in fact advocates a much more deviant model of sexuality: marketable, incestuous, and autoerotic. Moll's mercenary and predatory nature transgresses her gender limits and allows her to escape from feminine reproduction to social production by trading her only capital, her flesh, while her insatiable desire for wealth operates according to eighteenth-century beliefs in human nature as nakedly selfish, and economic affluence as the route to happiness. The book's double narrative both exposes and reflects the hypocrisy of early capitalist structures and undermines the harmonious union between the individual and society that it apparently promotes. Moreover, the novel as a genre that encompasses the notions of secrecy, fictionality, and imaginary increase that consumes the self is the ideal form to express such deceptive politics. Far from being independent categories, whoring, thievery, and writing, I wish to argue, converge as the new credit economy and the fledgling genre of the novel are attuned to a new sexual pattern that prizes individualism and autonomy, is founded on the imagination, and engenders perpetual free pleasure. **Key Words:** capitalists, eighteenth-century sexuality, incest, lying, novel, "self-pollution," thievery, whoring.

1.   Introduction

Published in 1722, *Moll Flanders* is an exemplary exposition of the instability surrounding the concept of sexuality at the time, or rather its inevitably duplicitous nature. If one considers sexual desire not as a natural given, but as a cultural construction shaped by socio-historical impetus, Defoe's novel can be read as a reflection of the eighteenth-century anxiety for a peaceful symbiosis of self and society. And if the eighteenth century claimed to have found the answer to this most puzzling dilemma, by justifying the pursuit of personal profit and proposing it as a means to social prosperity, then Daniel Defoe's novel suggests that such assertions are illusory. Neither in the new individualistic economy, nor in the dominant bourgeois pattern of heterosexuality and patriarchal marriage can the individual and society coexist harmoniously.

Although the main heroine of the novel operates within the borders of heterosexual union and marriage, she never denounces her ultimate desire for the cell of the same, the self – whether this be the actual cell at Newgate, that is, her birthplace, to which she eventually returns, or even the body cells of her kin, with whom she is incestuously coupled, and with whom she never stops fantasising further union. The discourse of sexuality in *Moll Flanders*, I wish to argue, along with the discourse of trade (for sexual fulfillment is always inextricably bound with wealth accumulation and profit in the book), as well as the genre of the novel, conflate in that they follow the autoerotic, masturbatory politics of secrecy, duplicity, imagination, insatiability, and autarchy. The novel is a celebration of self-satisfaction, or, in eighteenth-century terminology, "self-pollution,"[1] in spite of Defoe's public defense of the patriarchal family (in his pamphlet *The Family Instructor* 1715),[2] his public attack on masturbatory practices,[3] and the general early eighteenth-century banning of onanism as aberrant and highly dangerous.

2.   Novel: A New Genre "Paving the Way to Solitary Vice"

> The World is so taken up of late with Novels and Romances, that it will be hard for a private History to be taken for Genuine, where the Names and other Circumstances of the Person are concealed, and on this Account we must be content to leave the Reader to pass his own Opinion upon the ensuing Sheets, and take it just as he pleases.[4]

In a world polluted by the lies of the newly born genre of the novel, Defoe's pseudo-editor in *Moll Flanders* promises his readers the pleasures of romping within the "sheets" of a "private history." This introductory remark is, of course, nothing but a lie, as the reader – the modern reader at least – knows, despite *Moll's* generic indeterminacy, that the book "he" is enjoying in privacy *is* a novel.[5] Still, there remains in such lies a fleeting trace of truth: names and circumstances *do* lie concealed in the "ensuing sheets," whereas the reader's pleasure lies in discovering them. Furthermore, the above claim succeeds in announcing *Moll Flanders'* central themes: the eroticisation of secrecy and lies, as well as the insidious and unbridled nature of bourgeois sexuality. And if sexuality and the novel are siblings in that they share the same parentage – the Enlightenment and capitalism or the bourgeoisie – their union then is incestuous by nature. What better mode could there be in such a case for disclosing the truth about sexuality but the novel?

Why does Moll's pseudo-editor need to justify the publishing of her story by pronouncing it a piece of autobiography, and insisting on its historical veracity as well as on its instructive and moral content? If the novel is a literary form that excites the imagination, offers solitary pleasure, transforms reading into a secretive activity, and presupposes an autonomous reader, then the dangers that novels pose are evident. In his recent study on *Solitary Sex*, Thomas Laqueur interestingly argues that "Novels, the imagination, and modern solitary sex took a major turn together."[6] In an age that celebrated the individual and considered personal freedom and the ability to imagine as fundamental faculties of modern society, excessive imagination and the self-governing self were simultaneously attacked. Foucault's thesis that new forms of subjectivity and desire were created merely in order to be controlled and repressed is once again verified.

It is not only the theme of Defoe's novel that constitutes danger by projecting the image of a self-made woman in *Moll Flanders* standing alone and free from social and moral constraint.[7] Being a novel, and so, meant to be read in privacy, *Moll Flanders* was supposedly potentially "pav[ing] the way to solitary vice,"[8] entrapping the reader with pleasures analogous to those of the masturbator, offering "the pleasure of fictionality itself: the frisson of absorption in a reality that was known to be artifice," in other words, "the seductiveness of "nobody's story.""[9] "Novelism," in Laqueur's words, "like onanism was dangerous because its protagonists were not really there and were all the more stimulating for their absence."[10]

In an effort to circumvent negative responses, Moll's spicy tale is dressed up by a modest editor, who warns the reader to make good use of "the abundance of delightful incidents" in the book. As for his part, he takes care "to give no lewd Ideas, no immodest Turns" and makes sure that all shocking details are "usefully apply'd."[11] The pleasure which the life, "Brightness and Beauty" that the "criminal Part"[12] of the story offers us, the editor contends, is purged by the "penitent Part" that accompanies it. As the "I" persona goes back to the beginnings of her life in an introspective and also retrospective mode, the private world of the individual shifts into the public realm.[13] The private is exposed to the eye of the reader for his benefit in an effort to instruct and teach him a moral lesson: "…the Book is recommended to the Reader, as a Work from every part of which something may be learned, and some just and religious Inference is drawn, by which the Reader will have something of Instruction, if he pleases to make use of it."[14] And so, although this is the story of a whore, adulteress and thief, who is also the offspring of debauchery and vice, every part of it is wrapped up "so clean as not to give room, especially for vicious Readers, to turn it to his Disadvantage."[15] Textual striptease is meant to educate on virtue and guide the autonomous self to its proper place back in society.

3.   Marriage, Deception, Incest

In the late seventeenth and early eighteenth centuries, two main factors determined the formation of the new norms of heterosexuality and the patriarchal family. The first was the breakdown of domestic economy in the seventeenth century, a result of capitalist formations. In the lower strata, as farmers lost access to land, there was a decrease in their wives' agricultural employment, whereas in the newly emerging bourgeois class, women's idleness was encouraged, and their work was oriented towards female accomplishments.[16] Consequently, labour, especially in the middle and upper classes, was sexually divided into female inside work (reproduction) and male outside work (production). Secondly, the two sexes were discovered to be distinct — female bodies were no longer thought to be distorted versions of male unitary bodies, but began to be considered as naturally and physically different than men's.[17] This emergence of gender difference imposed the pattern of cross-sex genital intercourse consummated within marriage. In a universe, however, which was pronounced by Hobbes to be in constant motion and where no stable or fixed ideas prevailed, such newly established norms were not unproblematically absorbed. Mandeville's or Hobbes' *man*, a machine motivated to pursue pleasure and driven by lusts and avarice, strived for the satisfaction of *his* selfish needs, and often disregarded the standards.[18]

It has been argued by several critics that the character of Moll Flanders repeatedly transgresses both gender roles as well as the code of normative sexual behaviour.[19] Quite early in her life she becomes aware of the exclusion of women from the sphere of production. Young Moll's desire to earn her bread by her own work, mending lace and washing ladies' laced-heads, and win the title of a "gentlewoman" is shattered when her meager income can hardly provide the bare essentials for her. Soon Moll discovers that it is not through honest labour, but through the exploitation of her sexual potential that she can finally win the title she craves for. Moll eventually does become a gentlewoman, only not in the sense she had originally intended, i.e., that of a woman who attends or waits on a lady, but in the sense of a kept woman or prostitute.

Through her first lover, the elder son of her foster family, Moll learns that the only product she has to sell is her body and that the only market open for her is that of marriage.[20] Yet, although Moll can offer no resistance when she is pushed by the elder son into marrying his younger brother, in the marriage contracts that are to follow, she changes from a passive object of exchange into an active dealer. If "Marriages were...the Consequences of politick Schemes for forming Interests, and carrying on Business," Moll reasons, and if this "Market run very Unhappily on the Mens side,"[21] still, she asserts to her female companions, women have the power to turn the tables upon men, and play their own game back upon them.[22] The book projects a female support network, Swaminanthan contends, as Mother Midnight, Moll's first nurse, even her actual mother are all independent, self-made women, involved in a "triumphant matriarchal system that transcends circumstances of sexual and financial transaction."[23] They "manipulate patriarchal restrictions on their gender *in solidarity*" and "exercise covert power by forming mutually beneficial unions that physically and emotionally shelter them from a male-dominated system."[24]

Moll's success is indeed due to her excellence in this art of "Deceiv[ing] the Deceiver."[25] She hides her true identity, her income, her intentions, her former life, and husbands; she hides any part of her story that could prove disadvantageous to her. Even in moments that are supposed to be highly emotional, such as Moll's reunion with Jemy, her fourth husband, in prison, she is careful to tell him only so much of her story as she thinks is convenient.[26] But *lying to* a man is not a mere survival tactic. As Moll's obsession with secrets displays, it can be as stimulating and as pleasurable as *lying with* a man — even more perhaps. Her frolicsome repartee with Humphrey, her third husband-to-be, is a perfect example of the fraudulent nature of love and desire, enhanced by and reflected in their highly ambiguous language. Moll's answer to his avowal, "*Be mine, with all your Poverty*," epitomises the lovers' ultimate desire: "*Yet secretly you hope I lie*."[27] The apparent meaning of Moll's words — that despite his declaration that he could love her in all her poverty, he secretly wishes her to be rich — is undermined by the double meaning of "lying." Their aim is to postpone, or even cancel the exposure of truth, for the game can arouse only as long as there are secrets to hide. Moll is desirable only as long as she remains a self-ruling, self-pleasing woman.

But Moll and Humphrey's first linguistic exchange hides more secrets than they think they conceal: the secret desire to lie within the cell of the self which materialises in their incestuous union, when later on in the story they are discovered to be brother and sister. Incest has been pronounced to be after all the ultimate, "dreadful secret" and "indispensable pivot" of every family.[28] And since family is, in Foucault's words, "a hotbed of constant sexual incitement," incest is the "object of obsession and attraction," constantly "solicited and refused."[29] It is indeed in its refusal that civilisation has built its foundations. And if prohibition of incest is the "threshold of all culture,"[30] then return to it would signify the most extreme contravention, especially when it is committed by a woman, in which case there is a violation of the gender role system as well. For, while Moll's whoring and thieving practices are "already constituted within an androcentric ordering of female desire," as Ellen

Pollak has argued, her incestuous acts signify the dissolution of the patriarchal family and its structures.

No other crime disgusts Moll more than that of her having been the wife of her own brother. "Bedding with him" is nauseous, abhorring, "unnatural in the highest degree in the world," "the worst sort of Whoredom."[31] Despite her mother's advice that they continue to "lie [both *with* and *to* each other] as [they] us'd to do together, and so let the whole matter remain a secret as close as Death,"[32] Moll would rather embrace a dog than come between the sheets with her brother/husband.[33] It is exactly this renouncing of her incest, the only crime for which Moll truly repents, that makes her a redeemable character. Still, despite Moll's re-entry into the system of patriarchal heterosexual exchange (when she withdraws from her brother/husband in Virginia, she becomes the whore of a gentleman in Bath, and later the wife of a Lancaster gentleman/highway man, Jemy, and also the wife of a clerk), the novel's subtext reveals that her incestuous fantasies have never really come to an end. "I was," Moll confesses upon her return to Virginia, "as if I had been in a new World, and began secretly now to wish that I had not brought my *Lancashire* Husband from *England* at all."[34] She is, however, quick in correcting herself: "that wish was not hearty neither, for I loved my *Lancashire* husband entirely, as indeed I had ever done from the beginning."[35]

Such cases of double narrative are perhaps the novel's distinctive mark, whereas the inconsistencies in the portrayal of unwitting sibling incest manifest the general uncertainty of the time regarding this concept.[36] Furthermore, although aversion to incest is unquestionable, at the same time, Defoe allows the reader to partake in Moll and Humphrey's matrimonial bliss before their true kinship is discovered, and Moll to state freely that inheriting her mother's plantation in the New World is the culmination of her desires. Incest is both banned and condoned, as Moll's marriage to her brother/husband was what actually united her with her mother. One might venture to say at this point that the object of Moll's desire is the mother, or even the "self," for Moll is, after all, a replica of her mother, copying her in almost all crucial acts of her life. They are both convicted of a felony for stealing drapery; they both end up in Newgate[37] and escape death by being transported to America; they are both self-made; they are both associates in incest.

4.   Capitalists, Whores, Masturbators

The fusion of Moll's sexual and trading politics confirms that the spheres of the market and that of the flesh are not unattached. In Moll's various encounters with her lovers or husbands, financial gain becomes indistinguishable from sexual pleasure, as it has been stressed by various critics.[38] While seduced by the elder Brother at the age of eighteen, for example, Moll is sincere enough to confess (as he puts five guineas into her hand) that his gold fires her blood more than his words: "I was more confounded with the Money than I was before with the Love."[39] Later on in Moll's life, when she has grown into an ingenious manager of sexual exchanges, there is a total transference of body parts to money-boxes or coins in the narrative. Peeping into purses, drawing out secret keys, breaking into and fumbling about in private drawers, or pouring money into her lap,[40] all seem to be the consummation of her relationship with her Gentleman Lover in Bath. As Kibbie has suggested, sexual intercourse is nearly redundant and anticlimactic when it actually happens after two years of them lying in each other's bed without making any further advances.[41]

The eroticisation of money, however, takes a different turn when in her fifties, past her prime, and "bleeding to death" (a metaphor that has been interpreted as indicative of her menopausal state),[42] Moll is unable to exploit her body any more in order to increase her scant capital, and so, turns from whoring to thievery. Stealing for Moll becomes soon more than mere means of support; it is a "trade" only she knows best how to excel in, being a master of lies, secrecy and disguise, an "art" that elevates her "to a height beyond the common Rate."[43] And, like her years of "Matrimonial Whoredom," the criminal part of Moll's autobiography is governed by desires that cannot be moderated. While Moll's turn to theft halfway through her story is initially her only way out in an economic system that denies women any access to production, later, even when she has acquired enough to live an easy life, Moll finds it impossible to put an end to her illegal and immoral activities, and becomes a robber of luxury commodities.

Her incurable self-love and insatiable lust for luxuries — indubitably the motive power in Moll's constantly moving universe[44] — render, of course, Defoe's Moll a product distilled from eighteenth-century political science and economy. More than anything else, she is the human enfleshment of Mandeville's avaricious and Machiavellian bees. In the spirit of Hobbes' assertion that "All society ... is either for gain or for glory; that is, not so much for the love of our fellows, as for the love of ourselves,"[45] Bernard Mandeville, a Dutch émigré physician in England, pronounces vice and egoism the motive powers of the universe. In *The Fable of the Bees: Or, Private Vices, Publick Benefits* (1714), a moral poem accompanied by lengthy prose commentaries, Mandeville scandalously exposes the hypocrisy of any virtuous act and argues that individualism is the foundation of national prosperity and happiness. In his unorthodox beehive metaphor, what makes the hive a paradise for bees is fraud and thievery: "All Trades and Places knew some Cheat, / No

Calling was without Deceit."[46] Envy and Vanity, Pride and Luxury are indispensable to a successful industry, while "Sharpers, Parasites, Pimps, Players, Pick-pockets, Coiners, Quacks, South-sayers"[47] guarantee a healthy economy.[48] Mandeville's paradoxical society seems to have stimulated Defoe, who although set against Mandeville's proposals of the exploitation of the labourers, prostitutes and poor children for the benefit of the state, agreed with his basic thesis that self-interest is the motivating force in human nature.[49]

As gold watches, rings, plate, lace, even periwigs, silver-fringed gloves, swords, and snuff-boxes accumulate in her hands and are exchanged for money, Moll diligently registers the growth of her capital with exceptional candour, allowing the reader the pleasure of a full view of her most intimate financial condition (for sexuality and economics have by this point in the narrative completely converged). "I was the richest of the Trade in *England*...for I had 700 *l* by me in Money, besides Clothes, Rings, some Plate and two gold Watches,"[50] she declares, but she is never able, however, to quench the satisfaction of multiplying her wealth, and put an end to her innumerable acts of public mischief before she is caught. For once the distinction between necessity and luxury has been eliminated, every new item Moll may potentially possess becomes a necessity. Is this blurring between need and superfluity not, after all – the inflation of desire, in other words – the basis of the new economy, as well as the route to success?[51] We might as well recall at this point that Moll's (and Jemy's) transformation from convicted felon to indentured servant to free citizen materialises thanks to the money and goods she has saved and left in the care of Mother Midnight. This dramatic change of status is affirmed in the narrative through detailed lists of commodities in her possession that increase in correspondence to her rising position. Moll's money can "buy" her not only a private cell in Newgate or a private cabin on the ship to America, it supplies her with "an abundance of good things for [their] Comfort in the Voyage, as Brandy, Sugar, Lemons, etc. ...and abundance of things for eating and drinking in the Voyage; also a larger Bed and Bedding proportion'd to it," and also "with a Stock of Tools and Materials for the Business of Planting."[52]

If insatiable sexuality has been gendered female throughout history, unbridled consumerism has, not accidentally perhaps, also been associated with femininity in (or since) the eighteenth century. Since the sixteenth century women have been chosen to symbolise the destructive forces of capitalism. The capitalist is compared to a whore in Thomas Wilson's *Discourse Upon Usury* (1572),[53] for capitalists, like whores, could not quench their passions; they both created and fed on capital, and made use of their bodies/capitals for the best profit. Moreover, in *The Fable*, as Laura Mandell has observed, the passion for commodities is explicitly dichotomised in its abject female form, vicious consumerism, and its ideal male form, virtuous mercantilism: "a considerable Portion of what the Prosperity of *London* and Trade in general, and consequently the Honour, Strength, Safety, and all the worldly Interest of the Nation consist in, depends entirely on the Deceit and Vile Stratagems of Women."[54]

Both for Mandeville and Defoe female avarice is a necessary evil sustaining a prosperous economy. Yet, while for Mandeville whores are the reservoir of all filthy and revolting passions, "a piece of 'blown' or spoiled meat that 'a Modern Butcher ... hang[s] up for a Cure' to attract the flies away from his fresh meat," as he argues in *A Modest Defence of Publick STEWS*,[55] Defoe's treatment of whoring expunges it of its abject qualities.[56] So, Moll's acquisitiveness and greed are punished with her imprisonment at Newgate, but Moll the capitalist is neither revolting nor contaminating; she is actually redeemed. Both whoring and thieving in particular, which resembles the much-debated practices of usury and credit, that is, money's infinite capacity for an anomalous, sterile, and incestuous form of self-generation,[57] are indispensable stages to success.[58]

Success, like the new economy, or the new genre of the novel, is founded on the imagination, that is, giving trust to lies,[59] placing credit in paper money,[60] or being transported to a land of unlimited possibilities. Moll's dream of infinite wealth and liberal citizenship materialises in the utopian land of the colonies, which against the background of the seventeenth century generously offered itself for reaping – even to indentured servants.[61] Moreover, the idea of new credit has always been inherent in the process of transportation. Moll's emigration to Virginia and Maryland both times is her means of acquiring a name, a past, property, citizenship, all given on credit. At the same time, Moll has achieved the impossible and is, according to Novak, the perfect colonist, adding to England's wealth and prosperity: she has "created new wealth by growing tobacco," "increased the population by importing slaves," "employed the poor in the form of indentured servants and convicts," and "imported products from England to use on their plantation."[62] It is a dream *almost* too good to be true.

Secrecy, lies, insatiability and autarchy are the principles that run the new economy and reflect the politics of a masturbatory sexuality: unlimited free pleasure. Can sociability survive the delirium of self-satisfaction and material gain? Can heterosexual marriage sustain the complexities of the sexual body? Although Moll's successful ending appears to answer both questions affirmatively, Defoe's model of sexuality in *Moll Flanders* undermines such hasty solutions. Moll and Jemy's marriage that ends up as a perfect union, a symbiosis "with the greatest Kindness and Comfort imaginable," "in good Heart and Health" and "sincere Penitence"[63] is Moll's final superb lie. The desire to maximise profit, the ability to engender capital out of nothing, the vile stratagems employed, and the impossibility of civilising and socialising an endlessly desiring self make capitalists, thieves, whores follow the tracks of solitary masturbators. The self remains eternal prisoner to its own cell, a cell that is dark, private, and isolated.

Notes

1. Thomas Laqueur traces the birth of modern masturbation, or else, the invention of "self-pollution" as a new disease, in the publication of *Onania* by John Marten in 1712. See Thomas Laquer, *Solitary Sex: A Cultural History of Masturbation* (New York: Zone Books, 2003).

2. John Richetti contends that Defoe's fiction moves beyond the didacticism of his non-literary works, and often "generates an institutional form of its own that tends toward a subversive anti-institutionalism." See John Richetti, "The Family, Sex and Marriage in Defoe's *Moll Flanders* and *Roxana*," *Studies in the Literary Imagination* 15 (1982): 19-35, p.23.

3. Replying to a question in his *Review*, Defoe asserted that "self-pollution was a mortal sin but that the problem ought no more to be discussed in public 'than to be acted in private'" (quoted in Laqueur, 2003, 178).

4. Daniel Defoe, *Moll Flanders,* ed. and Introduction by David Blewett (Harmondsworth: Penguin, 1989), 37.

5. There has been a long controversy among critics over whether *Moll* is closer to confessional/spiritual autobiography or the picaresque tradition and criminal biography. For more on this see Blewett's "Introduction" in the Penguin edition of *Moll*.

6. Laqueur, 2003, 320.

7. The mere name of Moll Flanders, with its connotations of prostitution, illegal trade and criminality, predisposed the reader of Defoe's time to expect a tantalising story. For more on Moll's name and its implications see Gerald Howson, "Who Was Moll Flanders?" *The Times Literary Supplement,* 3438 (January 18, 1968): 63-64; Jina Politi, "Moll's True Name and the Mechanics of Motion," in *The Novel and its Presuppositions* (Amsterdam: A. M. Hakkert, 1976), 114-35; and Ellen Pollak, "*Moll Flanders*, Incest, and the Structure of Exchange," *The Eighteenth Century* 30 (1989): 3-21.

8. Laqueur, 2003, 269.

9. Ibid., 320.

10. Ibid., 324 .

11. Defoe, 38, 39. Thomas Grant Olsen, in "Reading and Righting *Moll Flanders*," *Studies in English Literature 1500-1900* 41 (2001): 467-81, has interestingly argued that the narrator's circuitous

method of storytelling, the links on the narrative and the figurative chain that lead to repetition without difference (or the "circular pattern of fatality and necessity" that accompanies the lineal sequentiality of Moll's chronicle, according to John Richetti) resemble the pattern of incest, an issue which will be discussed in the following section of this essay. See John Richetti, "Defoe: Mapping Social Totality," in *The English Novel in History, 1700-1780* (London and New York: Routledge, 1999), 52-83, p.59.

12. Defoe, 38.

13. Early eighteenth-century novels are an interesting amalgam of autobiography and history, as in their largest part they revolve around the life of an individual who is going back to his beginnings, and who is in constant "tension with social and interactive values" (Paul J. Hunter, *Before Novels: The Cultural Contexts of Eighteenth-Century English Fiction* (New York: Norton, 1990, 341)). In as far as the novel "attempts to incorporate a larger social and cultural view," "a comprehensive context for individual lives, a perspective in both time and space" (ibid., 341), it is a successful combination of the private with the public.

14. Defoe, 40.

15. Ibid., 38.

16. Michael McKeon, "Historicizing Patriarchy: The Emergence of Gender Difference in England, 1660-1760," *Eighteenth-Century Studies* 28 (1995): 295-322, p.299.

17. For an extensive study on the one-sex model that dominated Western thinking from classical antiquity to the end of the seventeenth century, see Thomas Laqueur's *Making Sex: Body and Gender from the Greeks to Freud* (Cambridge, Mass.: Harvard University Press, 1990).

18. Although the discussion below focuses on a *female* literary figure, who subverts the standards in her pursuit for pleasure, the generic *he* is used here as a reflection of the dominant eighteenth-century belief that the normative gender was the masculine one.

19. See, for example, Pollak; Ann Louise Kibbie, "Monstrous Generation: The Birth of Capital in Defoe's *Moll Flanders* and *Roxana*," *PMLA* 110 (1995): 1023-34; Lois A. Chaber, "Matriarchal Mirror: Women and Capital in *Moll Flanders,*" *PMLA* 97 (1982): 212-226; Richetti (1982); and Srividhya Swaminanthan, "Defoe's Alternative Conduct Manual: Survival Strategies and Female Networks in *Moll Flanders*," *Eighteenth-Century Fiction* 15 (2003): 185-206.

20. In *Conjugal Lewdness; or, Matrimonial Whoredom* (1727) Defoe is an ardent supporter of the "companionate marriage," based on the partners' love and mutual respect (Maximillian E. Novak, *Daniel Defoe: Master of Fictions* (Oxford: Oxford University Press, 2001), 678-79). Moll's marital opportunism and the elimination of any emotional

attachments with her spouses epitomise what Defoe considers the most perverse form of "Matrimonial Whoredom," which is bound to lead to disaster. Interestingly, Moll's ending, is far from calamitous.

21. Defoe, 112.

22. Ibid., 118.

23. Swaminanthan, 187, 192, note 18.

24. Ibid., 194, 195.

25. Defoe, 123.

26. Ibid., 327. As it has been suggested by Richetti, the story actually comes to end only when Moll has no more lies to tell. See John Richetti, "*Moll Flanders*: The Dialectic of Power," in *Defoe's Narratives: Situations and Structures* (Oxford: Clarendon Press, 1975), 94-144, p.144.

27. Ibid., 126.

28. Michel Foucault, *The History of Sexuality*, Vol. 1, trans. Robert Hurley (Harmondsworth: Penguin, 1984), 109.

29. Ibid., 109

30. Ibid., 109.

31. Defoe, 137, 138.

32. Ibid., 146.

33. Ibid., 148.

34. Ibid., 419.

35. Ibid., 419.

36. Moll's reaction to her incest is more instinctive, rather than based on reasoning. As Daniel W. Wilson has argued ("Science, Natural Law, and Unwitting Sibling Incest in Eighteenth-Century Literature," *Studies in Eighteenth-Century Culture* 13 (1984): 249-70), the opinion concerning incest was formed via popular legend and tales about deformed offspring, that could not, however, be confirmed by contemporary biology.

37. Imprisonment in Newgate is for Moll both an entrance into Hell (Defoe, 349) and a return to her origins, her birthplace, a symbolic homecoming or re-entry into the womb of her convicted mother. Paradoxically, as Richetti has rightly observed, prison is both a form of social totality that effaces the self, which degenerates into stone, object (Defoe, 354) and a locus of self-regeneration where Moll acquires a coherent subjectivity. "Newgate's confinement brings the experience of the inescapable connection between social circumstances and personality and points implicitly as the resolution of Moll's career to a larger and indeed comprehensive social inevitability" (Richetti, 1999, 63).

38. See Juliet McMaster, "The Equation of Love and Money in *Moll Flanders*," *Studies in the Novel* 2 (1970): 131-44; Carol Houlihan

Flynn, *The Body in Swift and Defoe* (Cambridge: Cambridge University Press, 1990), and Kibbie.

39. Defoe, 62.

40. Ibid., 163.

41. There is, of course, one time in her life that Moll indulges in pleasure that is unrelated to profit. Moll's craving for Jemy, the scene of their parting after the double fraud has been unveiled and their reunion shortly after, as well as her returning his jewels and money to him and her avowals that she's ready to starve with him, are indeed beyond her self-centered logic. One must not forget, however, that the honest clerk waiting for her in London has already been secured, and that her ecstatic month with Jemy has never fooled her into laying all her cards open for him, neither has it prevented their splitting up. As Richetti has pointed out, Moll never loses control of her self as she learns how to "convert spontaneous desire into capable self-possession," and "consistently avoids emotions that cannot be managed, which bring no profit to the self and indeed wear it out" (1975, 103, 138).

42. See Pollak, 12.

43. Ibid., 267.

44. The structure of the novel is, according to Politi, based on the necessity of continual motion, "analogical to Hobbes' mechanics of motion, the rhythms of the plot exhibiting a constant endeavour 'toward' and 'fromward'" (115).

45. Quoted in Bernard Mandeville, *The Fable of the Bees or Private Vices, Publick Benefits, Vols 1, 2*, ed. F.B. Kaye (Oxford: Clarendon Press, 1924, 1966), 1:cix.

46. Mandeville, 1: 20.

47. Mandeville, 1: 19.

48. Despite strong reactions to *The Fable* (by Bishop Berkeley or John Wesley for instance), the book indisputably constituted a major source of inspiration for Adam Smith's *laissez-faire* theory and the utilitarian movement that shaped modern economic thought.

49. Novak, 2001, 610 ff.

50. Defoe, 325.

51. The word "luxury" had three meanings for Defoe and for most eighteenth-century writers, as Novak explains: first, any commodity that was superfluous for maintaining existence; second, a manner of life that was "wasteful of time, energy, and morals," and third, "imported commodities that were neither necessary nor productive" (*Economics and the Fiction of Daniel Defoe*, Berkeley and Los Angeles: University of California Press, 1962, 136). Moll's desire for luxury bears definitely little resemblance to Roxana's corrupted lust for extravagance, reminiscent of the decaying nobility in the courts of Charles II and

George I. Moll's notion of luxury is more closely related to a milder craving for domestic conveniences that sets the market in motion, a form that Defoe had little objection to.

52. Defoe, 397-98, 399.

53. Cited in Kibbie.

54. Mandeville, 1:228.

55. Quoted in Laura Mandell, "Bawds and Merchants: Engendering Capitalist Desires," *ELH* 59 (1992): 107-123, p.116.

56. Defoe's telling confession in the last number of the *Review*: "Writing about Trade was the Whore I really doated upon" (Novak, 2001, 431) suggests that this conflation of the concepts of writing, trading and whoring renders them corrupted and fatal activities, while it simultaneously purges them of their negative hue.

57. As Kibbie interestingly notes, Moll's economic increase, exactly like her biological increase, is incestuous, as the multiplication of her money is the reproduction of kind from kind.

58. In her analysis of Lady Credit, Defoe's favourite Mistress in the *Review*, Kimberly S. Latta argues that despite his profound ambivalence about women in the marriage market, he deviates from traditional, misogynist representations of usury, and refigures Lady Credit as a positive, "'teeming, fruitful Species'," a figure that "corresponds to a new social type, the marriageable woman, as well as to a new economic form, both of which promoted the interests of the increasingly powerful bourgeoisie" ("The Mistress of the Marriage Market: Gender and Economic Ideology in Defoe's *Review,*" *ELH* 69 (2002): 359-83, p.374).

59. For a detailed analysis of the homology between financial credit and literary credibility see Sandra Sherman's, *Finance and Fictionality in the Early Eighteenth-Century* (Cambridge: Cambridge University Press, 1996).

60. "The foundation of the Bank of England [in 1694] represented the modernisation of the financing of the British state," that is, a credit culture closely tied to trade, which had as a result "the rise of London as the world's major credit hub" (Scott B. MacDonald. and Albert L. Gastman, *A History of Credit and Power in the Western World*, London: Transaction, 2001, 133, 134).

61. Throughout Defoe's writings colonial expansion works wonders for the English market: apart from being a source of new wealth, the colonies may solve the problems of overproduction, consumption, and the employment of the poor, advance the value of the land, and improve England's merchant marine and navy (Novak, 1962, 141).

62. Ibid., 154.

63. Defoe, 427.

Select Bibliography

Abelove, Henry. "Some Speculations on the History of Sexual Intercourse during the Long Eighteenth Century in England." *Genders* 6 (1989): 125-30.

Chaber, Lois A. "Matriarchal Mirror: Women and Capital in *Moll Flanders." PMLA* 97 (1982): 212-226.

Defoe, Daniel. *Moll Flanders.* Ed. and Introduction by David Blewett. Harmondsworth: Penguin, 1989.

Flynn, Carol Houlihan. *The Body in Swift and Defoe.* Cambridge: Cambridge University Press, 1990.

Foucault, Michel. *The History of Sexuality*, Vol. 1. Trans. Robert Hurley. Harmondsworth: Penguin, 1984.

Howson, Gerald. "Who Was Moll Flanders?" *The Times Literary Supplement*, 3438 (January 18, 1968): 63-64.

Hunter, Paul J. *Before Novels: The Cultural Contexts of Eighteenth-Century English Fiction.* New York: Norton, 1990.

Kay, Carol. *Political Constructions: Defoe, Richardson and Sterne in Relation to Hobbes, Hume and Burke.* Ithaca and London: Cornell University Press, 1988.

Kibbie, Ann Louise. "Monstrous Generation: The Birth of Capital in Defoe's *Moll Flanders* and *Roxana." PMLA* 110 (1995): 1023-34.

Laqueur, Thomas. *Making Sex: Body and Gender from the Greeks to Freud.* Cambridge, Mass.: Harvard University Press, 1990.

——. *Solitary Sex: A Cultural History of Masturbation.* New York: Zone Books, 2003.

Latta, Kimberly S. "The Mistress of the Marriage Market: Gender and Economic Ideology in Defoe's *Review." ELH* 69 (2002): 359-83.

MacDonald, Scott B. and Albert L. Gastman. *A History of Credit and Power in the Western World.* London: Transaction, 2001.

Mandell, Laura. "Bawds and Merchants: Engendering Capitalist Desires." *ELH* 59 (1992): 107-123.

Mandeville, Bernard. *The Fable of the Bees or Private Vices, Publick Benefits, Vols 1, 2.* Ed. F.B. Kaye. Oxford: Clarendon Press, 1924, 1966.

McKeon, Michael. "Historicizing Patriarchy: The Emergence of Gender Difference in England, 1660-1760." *Eighteenth-Century Studies* 28 (1995): 295-322.

McMaster, Juliet. "The Equation of Love and Money in *Moll Flanders." Studies in the Novel* 2 (1970): 131-44.

Novak, Maximillian E. *Daniel Defoe: Master of Fictions.* Oxford: Oxford University Press, 2001, 2003.

——. *Economics and the Fiction of Daniel Defoe.* Berkeley and Los Angeles: University of California Press, 1962.

Olsen, Thomas Grant. "Reading and Righting *Moll Flanders*." *Studies in English Literature 1500-1900* 41 (2001): 467-81.

Politi, Jina. "Moll's True Name and the Mechanics of Motion." In *The Novel and its Presuppositions,* 114-35. Amsterdam: A.M. Hakkert, 1976.

Pollack, Ellen. "*Moll Flanders*, Incest, and the Structure of Exchange." *The Eighteenth Century* 30 (1989): 3-21.

Porter, Roy. *Enlightenment: Britain and the Creation of the Modern World.* London: Penguin Books, 2001.

Richetti, John. "Defoe: Mapping Social Totality." In *The English Novel in History, 1700-1780,* 52-83. London and New York: Routledge, 1999.

——. "*Moll Flanders*: The Dialectic of Power." In *Defoe's Narratives: Situations and Structures*, 94-144. Oxford: Clarendon Press, 1975.

——. "The Family, Sex and Marriage in Defoe's *Moll Flanders* and *Roxana*." *Studies in the Literary Imagination* 15 (1982): 19-35.

Sherman, Sandra. *Finance and Fictionality in the Early Eighteenth Century.* Cambridge: Cambridge University Press, 1996.

Stone, Lawrence. *The Family, Sex and Marriage in England 1500-1800.* Harmondsworth: Penguin, 1988.

Swaminathan, Srividhya. "Defoe's Alternative Conduct Manual: Survival Strategies and Female Networks in *Moll Flanders*." *Eighteenth-Century Fiction* 15 (2003): 185-206.

Wilson, Daniel W. "Science, Natural Law, and Unwitting Sibling Incest in Eighteenth-Century Literature." *Studies in Eighteenth-Century Culture* 13 (1984): 249-70.

Catastrophic Sexualities in Howard Barker's Theatre of Transgression

Karoline Gritzner

Abstract
    The recent work of contemporary English dramatist and poet Howard Barker offers startling speculations on the theme of erotic sexuality and its interrelationship with death. This paper discusses Barker's "theatre of catastrophe" with reference to theories of eroticism (Bataille), seduction (Baudrillard), and aesthetics (Adorno). In Barker's sexually charged reading of Shakespeare's *Hamlet* in *Gertrude the Cry*; his erotic version of the Grimm brothers' fairytale *Snow White* in *Knowledge and A Girl*; and in his play for three actors and a corpse, *Dead Hands*, erotic desire and the sexual encounter are theatrically articulated as the subversive and destructive effects of consciousness. **Key Words:** theatre, drama, Howard Barker, eroticism, death, sexuality, aesthetics.

> Moments of profound sexual passion cause us – the couple who love – to implore a death, if only from the anxiety that nothing will ever again surpass the *unearthly* quality of this ecstasy. Is it not too perfect to be followed, except by its repetition? The dread of its failing to reappear … the yearning for its reappearance …perhaps the solitary reason for perpetuating ourselves?[1]

    In Howard Barker's plays sexual desire necessarily *complicates* life; it signifies a tragic encounter with the Other and catapults individuals into an awareness of their own limitations and possibilities. Barker calls his distinctive dramatic project a "theatre of catastrophe" in which characters embark upon ecstatic explorations of unlived life, involving the experience of pain and violation but also a recognition of beauty.

    In his most recent non-dramatic text *Death, The One, and The Art of Theatre* – a provocative collection of poetic meditations on the "art of theatre," love and death – Barker contemplates the aesthetic and spiritual quality of tragedy, which considers eroticism and death as its main subjects. Written in a fragmentary, aphoristic style (which is formally as well as thematically reminiscent of Theodor W. Adorno's *Minima Moralia*), *Death, The One, and The Art of Theatre* embraces theatre as a form of art in which the socially and morally impossible becomes possible – theatre is articulated as a space and practice in which the incessant movement of desire produces powerfully seductive verbal and physical images which are harboured like secrets yet revealed without shame.

This book poetically extends a discourse already touched upon in Barker's acclaimed *Arguments for a Theatre*, namely the question of tragic theatre's contested place in a contemporary commodity society characterised by an authoritarian imposition of "light" and a sanitised obsession with health, longevity, and laughter. Tragedy – Barker's Theatre of Death – embraces negativity and the unknown, yet without turning them into "positive," identifiable and verifiable concepts. By cruel necessity death and the beloved ("the one") must remain foreign and intractable to the self. The encounter of the self with the Other in love and in death produces a profound sense of longing and anxiety, which in Barker's theory of tragic theatre is transformed into ecstasy. Barker develops the notion of a tragic, catastrophic theatre in opposition to what he calls the "humanist theatre" which dominates the stage in Britain today – a theatre of issues and education (influenced by Ibsen and Brecht), which is conventionally described as political because it directly confronts the audience with recognisable social problems. Barker's rejection of the concepts of usefulness and moral purpose of theatre has led to an increasing interest in the dynamics of sexuality, eroticism, and death. In Barker's "promiscuous theatre" erotic sexuality, pain, and death are constructed as exclusively personal, solitary experiences, which affirm "the individual's right to chaos, extremity, and self-description."[2] This manifests itself in theatrical explorations of transgressive human behaviour, which eludes mimetic, naturalistic representation.

Although Barker rejects the idea of issue-based, educative theatre that offers the audience recognisable moral arguments, his theatrical project can nevertheless be regarded as a form of cultural critique in the sense of Theodor W. Adorno's notion of non-interventionist (non-engaged) art's critique of society. In numerous writings on art and the culture industry and especially in his late (unfinished) text *Aesthetic Theory*, Adorno argues in favour of aesthetic discourse as a form of human activity in which the non-identical (that which is allowed to exist outside the repressive, administered system) persists without the need to be reconciled.[3] In what he terms the "administered society" (in which human relationships are instrumentalised) the Other, the unknown, the non-identical, and contradiction as such are always forced to be physically and conceptually integrated, whereas in art the Other remains a mystery; meaninglessness can be entertained without the compulsion for positive understanding and resolution. Using negativity as a central aesthetic category, Adorno proposes art as an autonomous and sovereign discourse which has the power to liberate consciousness from the use-oriented logic that dominates the socio-political and economic realms.

The disruptive and subversive quality of the aesthetic in Adorno's theory resembles the quality of erotic sexuality in the dramatic work of

Howard Barker. In Barker's plays, sexuality disturbs the logic of reality ("the sexual is the ungovernable"[4]); erotic desire subverts social meaning, and the individual who finds herself in an ecstatic state of erotic desire can be considered as autonomous and sovereign in relation to her social and political environment. The sexual act is often depicted as a self-absorbed, useless (in the sense of non-productive), transgressive act which fulfils a (negative) function that is similar to the idea of art as negation as put forward by Adorno and articulated by the German philosopher Christoph Menke as representing "a crisis for and a threat to reason."[5]   The sovereign quality of art lies in its potential to disrupt the validity of everyday, non-aesthetic (social and moral) discourse. Art, in other words, has the power to interrupt the logic of the real.

Consequently it can be argued that the aesthetic and the sexual are characterised by a dynamic of resistance to the dominant cultural and social constructions of meaning, identity, and truth. In *Gertrude – the Cry*, Gertrude's and Claudius' love for each other becomes a source of exhilaration and agony. Their illegal sexual bond offends society – especially Gertrude's son Hamlet who in the play is a representative of the new moral order which is authoritarian in its glorification of transparency and its rejection of lying, darkness, and secrecy. After Hamlet's death – he is murdered by Gertrude and Claudius – we hear that he had plans to rebuild Castle Elsinore in glass in order to eliminate secrets and lies and make all private acts immediately visible and accountable. But it is precisely the need for the secret, the longing for darkness and ambiguity combined with a desire to be in a state of not-knowing which adds to the intensity and eroticism of the performance of sexuality in Barker's play.

The notion of ecstasy is of crucial significance to the ways in which sexuality is theatricalised in Barker's work. In addition to the Oxford English Dictionary's definition of ecstasy as "being beside oneself; being thrown into a frenzy or a stupor, with anxiety, astonishment, fear or passion," ecstasy also implies the idea of losing one's centre. In performance of Barker's work this is physicalised in the characters' unbalanced postures and uneven walks. After having killed the old King, Gertrude's posture is slightly distorted – she cannot walk straight anymore. Barker's characters are often dishevelled – their intense emotionality becomes manifest in gestures of physical disarray. The characters experience their erotic encounters with a high degree of self-consciousness, which triggers streams of ecstatic speculation. In *Gertrude – the Cry*, Albert, the Duke of Mecklenburg (who embodies at least three characters from the Shakespearean original: Hamlet's former school friends Rosencrantz and Guildenstern as well as the young Fortinbras whose invasion of Denmark signifies political conciliation at the end of the play) expects nothing less than to be fundamentally disturbed and transformed by his sexual encounter with Gertrude.

> **ALBERT**: I cannot describe the exquisite tension you keep me in I (*He aches*) / I almost think / I do think (*He scoffs*) / I AM AFRAID TO SEE WHAT I SO WANT TO SEE
> **GERTRUDE**: Wait then
> …
> **ALBERT**: I AM IN SUCH A TENDER ECSTASY I WOULD NOT CARE IF I WERE DEAD IF SOME SHOCK STOPPED MY HEART WHO CARES WHO CARES / Say you understand say you know why I stand here and do not run like some mad dog to climb your flesh all mouth and tongue and fists and (*He aches*) / Say you understand (*He shakes his head*)
> **GERTRUDE**: I'll undo the coat
> (*Albert turns from her to avoid the sight. As Gertrude loosens the belt of her coat she gasps*)
> **ALBERT**: I WAIT / I WAIT / I WAIT
> **GERTRUDE**: Idiot
> **ALBERT**: Yes
> **GERTRUDE**: Oh idiot I am your death
> **ALBERT**: BE IT / BE IT (*He turns violently*) / BE MY DEATH GERTRUDE[6]

By desiring Gertrude, Albert welcomes the idea of death into his life – a death that is promised by her sexuality and thus becomes the source of his ecstasy.

In Barker's theatre we witness subjects in process – often the dramatic characters are involved in processes of mental and physical disintegration triggered by erotic and sexual passion. Barker's recent work establishes links with modern French critical theory such as Kristeva's notion of the speaking subject who is not an autonomous, unified self but a subject-in-process who negotiates different, often conflicting levels of signification. Barker's characters are such subjects-in-catastrophic-process: their poetic, sometimes hysterical verbal articulations are informed by (and in reverse have an impact on) bodily drives – the semiotic elements of signification, according to Kristeva. An example of the forceful eruption of the semiotic is Gertrude's mysterious, boundless cry, which cannot be defined or conceptualised: it becomes the central enigma and an obsession for the male characters in the play. The cry is a floating signifier whose meaning forever eludes masculine rationality. It presents an unsolvable yet erotic problem to those who are physically and emotionally involved with the queen and consequently the cry can be read as a symbol of transgressive femininity. The male characters are captivated, mesmerised, and transformed by the cry, and they insist on its repetition. The problem of presence comes into play here: theatre articulates the paradox of presence and the (im)possibility of repetition is an issue in both plays. The cry cannot be repeated in its original form; it always has a different quality: it is first uttered when Claudius and Gertrude kill the old king and couple over the dying body; in this case the cry suggests betrayal. It is again heard every time an order is transgressed, violated, such as in the queen's ecstasy with the duke, and when she gives birth to her child.

In *Knowledge and A Girl* Snow White is also obsessed with repetition and mimicry, and this is captured in dramaturgical terms as well: scenes 1 and 4 begin almost identically: "*A Queen naked in a forest. – Snow White naked in the forest*." Both women have a sexual encounter with the forester, and when it is Snow White's turn, she demands of the forester: "What you do with the Queen my Mother do with me / The same / The same exactly." To which the astonished servant forester replies: "The same is difficult … I'm not the same myself."[7]

The problem of presence is of significance to theatre and sexuality. In his reading of Nietzsche Maurice Blanchot addresses the paradoxical notion of the eternal return of the same. Blanchot argues that there is a fundamental lack of presence – the present as such does not exist (it eludes signification), only the past and the future can be talked about. Yet we have an overwhelming desire for presence, which is perhaps characteristic of the sexual experience – a desire for affirmation, a desire to put a momentary even illusory halt to the alienating flux that defines human experience. But according to Blanchot, the desire for presence is ultimately a desire for death which (like presence) exists beyond or outside the temporal dimension (past-future).[8] The theatrical space offers an encounter with presence and immediacy, which in Barker's work is recognised as a *risk* as it articulates the possibility of a death that is linked to the idea of transgressive sexuality.

The sexual or erotic drive, which in Barker's theatre manifests itself in processes of seduction, is one of the most compelling and indeed potentially most destructive forces at work. The sexual drive brings the characters closest to death; indeed death is the premise upon which sexuality and eroticism assume a theatrical presence. In both plays the promiscuity of the leading female characters means death to other (male) characters who are inexplicably drawn to them.

The role of sexuality in Barker's theatre does not strictly correspond to the Freudian model of the life instinct (libido) as a life-creating and life-maintaining drive. Equally, Freud's thinking about the pleasure principle, which aims at a discharge of tension, is also not affirmed in Barker's theatricalisation of erotic desire. Most relationships in Barker's plays are defined by an immense sexual tension but there is hardly any release of this tension to be found as a result of coupling, or one could say: tension and excitation are not discharged as a result of acts of sexual intimacy, nor is the erotic drive, which compels characters to carry out extreme acts, sublimated or made socially useful in any constructively moralistic manner. Rather than witnessing a discharge of sexual tension in certain explicit acts, in Barker's theatre we are confronted with the growth and complication of characters' lives as a result of their erotic journeys in which they courageously embrace pain and the possibility of (or indeed the hope for) an absence of meaning. In *Death, The One, and The Art of Theatre* Barker draws attention to the "ecstasy of vanishing meaning,"[9] and states that poetic speech – as opposed to the conversation – is "utterance born of an ordeal."[10] The concept of pleasure cannot appropriately be applied to his work because characters do not seek delightful gratification, but they are persistent in their individual discoveries of pain. They are driven into states of agony and in pain they find ecstasy – a heightened, extreme, and sublime form of pleasure. What compels them is the idea of an encounter with the unknown (an "exposure to unknown life"[11]), and it is the unknown that they search for especially in their erotic encounters. As says the King to the Queen in *Knowledge and A Girl* after having speculated about her infidelity: "I never know with you." And the Queen responds: "How good that is / How good you never know with me."[12]

Knowledge in Barker's work only has the *appearance* of possession and control. In other words, the potential of knowledge as a form of, in Adorno's terms, "instrumental rationality" is seemingly acknowledged but persistently challenged. Snow White's attempts to copy her stepmother's sexuality are bound to fail, and her persistence in doing so drives her into a confrontation with her fear ("I'm frightened I am not desirable") and into exile. Knowledge opens up distances between characters and the duality of the known and the unknown translates into a consciousness of the intractable yet absorbing (and erotic) strangeness of the Other. Adorno writes that

> [o]nly by the recognition of distance in our neighbour is strangeness alleviated: accepted into consciousness. The presumption of undiminished nearness present from the first, however, the flat denial of strangeness, does the other supreme wrong, virtually negates him as a particular human being, and therefore the humanity in

him, "counts him in," incorporates him in the inventory
of property.[13]

Theatre problematises the notion of mimetic representation: in
Barker's work erotic desire is signified through certain explicit gestures,
but the cause of desire, its origin, and motivation, are never entirely made
clear. The subject of erotic desire engages in a process of seduction which,
according to Baudrillard, is not production-oriented (unlike the
conventional understanding of sexuality, which has an aim, a goal – the
satisfaction of desire). Seduction, in giving rise to the erotic, is a self-
reflexive process of artifice. In seduction the body becomes aware of its
function as a signifier that is involved in a game, a play of gestures, a
strategy. Seduction is a key element of the theatrical, aesthetic process,
and it shapes our awareness of the self-conscious performance of meaning
in theatre.

Crucial to the seductive nature of erotic sexuality is the principle
of reversibility, which according to Baudrillard is a feminine principle:
woman's power lies in her ability to seduce, and seduction is perceived as
an inversion and reversion of order. Baudrillard opposes the seductive to
the productive principle (of sex) and proposes "[f]emininity as a principle
of uncertainty."[14] One notices the paradoxical position of the female in
Barker's theatre: on the one hand she is the centre of the dramatic universe
(Gertrude's physical presence and the mystery surrounding her cry
dominate the fictional reality), but she embodies a negative, uncertain,
reversible centre; her presence is not static because she transcends the
ordinary terms of definition and rigid conceptualisation pertaining to
empirical (social-realist) discourse.

The central notions of uncertainty and risk in Barker's theatrical
project present another point of contact with literary and critical theory. In
Blanchot's terms, literature in general (and poetry in particular) means
risking language (to write is to risk language), or as Adorno maintains:
modernist art is self-consciously engaged with the endgames of art's
possibility as art – it takes seriously its own possibility of failure. In
Barker's theatre the modernist consciousness of failure is played out on
the level of interpersonal exchange: Barker's dramatic characters are
willing to risk everything – selfhood, power, knowledge, certainty,
meaning – in their passionate journeys towards the irrational, the illegal,
and the catastrophic. In order to emphasise the element of transgressive
passion, a lot of the interpersonal and intimate action involving
heterosexual individuals in Barker's work takes place against a
background of repressive social morality which cloaks itself in the
language of democracy (as in *Gertrude the Cry*) or against a background

of war and dictatorial terror as in *Knowledge and A Girl* where the King is famous for his imaginative inventions of new forms of torture.

The erotic and sexual experience is an experience of wilful yet unexpected self-transformation. The characters long for what is not known and what cannot be known – the cry, for example; or in Snow White's case, the desire to know what it means to be desirable. Barker establishes a link between knowledge and desire, as does Anne Carson in *Eros the Bittersweet* where she states: "That which is known, attained, possessed, cannot be an object of desire."[15] Cascan, the articulate and highly perceptive, "perfect" servant to Gertrude, comments on the queen's adulterous relationship with Claudius:

> All ecstasy makes ecstasy go running to a further place
> that is its penalty we know this how well we know this
> still we would not abolish ecstasy would we we would
> not say this ever-receding quality in ecstasy makes it
> unpalatable on the contrary we run behind it limping
> staggering I saw it there I saw it there – a haunting
> mirage on the ruin of life.[16]

The movement of ecstasy is ultimately a movement towards death, or: the possibility of death becomes a defining quality of sexual/erotic desire. Here Barker's emphasis on the interrelationship of eroticism and death seems to echo Georges Bataille's view that "eroticism opens the way to death,"[17] but there are nevertheless crucial differences between both writers' perceptions of what denotes the erotic. Bataille characterises eroticism (which is an aspect of human sexuality, as opposed to non-erotic animal sexuality) as a force which breaks down the socially perceived discontinuity of being (the "gulf which separates us"[18]) and, like death, engenders a sense of continuity. The dialectic between discontinuity and continuity is essential to reproductive sexuality where two separate, discontinuous, entities (sperm and ovum) unite to form a continuity in death (they lose their previous form) in order to create a new separate being. Batailles' perception of eroticism as a yearning for a lost continuity is Hegelian in its emphasis on a desired sublation of discontinuous, isolated individuality in an experience of unity or reconciliation, which entails a loss of difference – a loss of self. This notion of a "deliberate loss of self in eroticism,"[19] however, is questioned in Barker's work.

Rather than conceiving of theatricalised erotic desire as a means of putting a halt to the perceived discontinuity and alienation of social existence, Barker's theatre is characterised by a sense of permanent discontinuity and rupture resulting from the erotic experience. "The act is false,"[20] says the mother superior in Barker's play *Ursula*, which deals with a group of nuns who entertain an erotic relationship with God but are equally seduced by the idea of human sexual pleasure (which remains a deathly idea). "The act is false" – it promises loss of self but it does not deliver. A conventional idea about sexuality – the idea of the annihilation of consciousness in the sexual act – is overturned and the characters engage in erotic games of seduction in which the reaching of sexual climax is no longer the exclusive aim.

The crisis of self is also articulated in Barker's play *Dead Hands*, performed at the Birmingham Repertory Theatre in 2004, in which the encounter with death prompts an overwhelming passionate desire for "the one." The protagonist Eff arrives to mourn for his father (whose dead body is visible on stage throughout the performance) and is immediately seduced by the dead man's mistress. In the presence of death the erotic assumes a force that is perceived as seductive and threatening at the same time. Erotic pleasure generates a torrent of verbal speculations and heightens Eff's self-consciousness:

> Obviously my brother's here not here not in the room not in the house perhaps I did not suppose him to be lingering on the stair but for all that he might be absent certainly my brother's here no distance could diminish his proximity he sits in his room he sits in a bar he sits for all I know in the buffet car of some great train a glass of champagne in his hand notwithstanding that my brother's here champagne I think not I plucked the word out of the air I was evoking contemplation I was evoking meditation but my brother and champagne it's inconceivable elegance is not the source of his fascination I feel sure you will confirm I am sitting I am not taking your whole cunt in my mouth I am returning to my chair...[21]

As in *Gertrude the Cry* and *Knowledge and A Girl*, here, too, the emphasis is on repetition (the father's mistress adopts a stylised naked position three times) and on the character's compulsive reflections on the repeated act:

> With or without your acquiescence I think it likely Sopron will expose herself to me again and on the third occasion you can be certain I shall not fail to act so what if this renders me pitiful comic or absurd...[22]

The experience of erotic pleasure is presented as deriving from a perception of reality as an *aesthetic* construct which is characterised as process, deferral, and transformation. Adorno's understanding of aesthetic pleasure as a reflection on the "processual event of aesthetic experience" can also serve as an attribute of erotic pleasure in Barker's work.[23]

Barker's theatrical explorations of erotic sexuality and death are imbued by a desire to move beyond the known, beyond the given, beyond the world (reality) as it is known to us. His theatre seeks to be the expression and presentation of "unlived life" in which characters risk their identities and perform illegal acts of transgression often against a background of totalitarian structures, war, and social crisis. Even though Barker rejects the idea of theatre as a moralistic platform for the transmission of knowledge and truth, this does not mean that his theatre has no critical-cognitive value; indeed by refusing to offer the audience simplistic statements about contemporary social problems, by liberating the audience to derive their own contradictory meanings from the theatrical situation, his theatre performs a "negative" function. Barker's work embraces the ideas of uncertainty, "not-knowing," and crisis which are an effect of the ways in which the unspeakable (sex and death) is persistently spoken about on his stage. The dimensions of the erotic and death are liberated from the social discourse of utility, production, and purpose. Erotic sexuality and death are theatrically conceived as the two enigmatic realms of desire that potentially exist (even if only as an idea, a promise or a utopia) beyond the structures of the repressive instrumentalisation of human behaviour, which according to Adorno characterises post-Auschwitz social existence. As Barker states,

> All the sexual transactions in my plays are self-conscious and therefore characterised by desire, a desire which is accumulative, a willed extremity which separates the participants from the cultural milieu in which they live. In all my work I reassert the catastrophic potential of the sexual encounter.[24]

Notes

1. Howard Barker, *Death, the One and the Art of Theatre* (London, New York: Routledge, 2005), 43.

2. Howard Barker, *Arguments For A Theatre*, third edition (Manchester: Manchester University Press, 1997), 123.

3. Theodor W. Adorno, *Aesthetic Theory*, translated by Robert Hullot-Kentor (London: Athlone, 1997).

4. Barker, quoted in Charles Lamb, *The Theatre of Howard Barker* (London: Routledge, 2005), 197.

5. Christoph Menke, *The Sovereignty of Art: Aesthetic Negativity in Adorno and Derrida*, translated by Neil Solomon (Cambridge, Mass.: MIT Press, 1999), xiii.

6. Howard Barker, *Gertrude – The Cry* in: *Gertrude – The Cry and Knowledge and A Girl* (London: Calder Publications, 2002), 58-9.

7. Barker, *Knowledge and A Girl* in: *Gertrude – The Cry* and *Knowledge and A Girl* (London: Calder Publications, 2002), 105.

8. See Maurice Blanchot, *The Step Not Beyond*, translated by Lycette Nelson (New York: State University of New York Press, 1992).

9. Barker, *Death, the One and the Art of Theatre*, 11.

10. Ibid., 9.

11. Ibid., 19.

12. Barker, *Knowledge and A Girl*, 104.

13. Theodor W. Adorno, *Minima Moralia – Reflections From Damaged Life*, translated by E.F.N. Jephcott (London: New Left Books, 1974), 182.

14. Jean Baudrillard, *Seduction*, translated by Brian Singer (London: Macmillan, 1990), 13.

15. Anne Carson, *Eros the Bittersweet* (Princeton, N.J.: Princeton University Press, 1986), 65.

16. Barker, *Gertrude – The Cry*, 10.

17. George Bataille, *Eroticism*, translated by May Dalwood (London: Marion Boyars, 1987), 24.

18. "Between one being and another, there is a gulf, a discontinuity. This gulf exists, for instance, between you, listening to me, and me, speaking to you. We are attempting to communicate, but no communication between us can abolish our fundamental difference. If you die, it is not my death. You and I are *discontinuous* beings." Ibid, 12.

19. Ibid., 31.

20. Howard Barker, *Ursula* in: *Collected Plays, Volume 5* (London: Calder Publications, 2001), 29.

21. Howard Barker, *Dead Hands* (London: Oberon Books, 2004), 27.

22. Ibid., 32.

23. Menke, 14.

24. Lamb, 197-198.

Select Bibliography

Adorno, Theodor W. *Aesthetic Theory*, translated by Robert Hullot-Kentor. London: Athlone, 1997.

——. *Minima Moralia – Reflections From Damaged Life*, translated by E.F.N. Jephcott. London: New Left Books, 1974.

Barker, Howard. *Arguments For A Theatre*, third edition. Manchester: Manchester University Press, 1997.

———. *Collected Plays, Volume 5*. London: Calder Publications, 2001.

———. *Dead Hands*, London: Oberon Books, 2004.

———. *Death, the One and the Art of Theatre*. London, New York: Routledge, 2005.

———. *Gertrude – The Cry* and *Knowledge and A Girl*. London: Calder Publications, 2002.

Bataille, Georges. *Eroticism: Death and Sensuality*. San Francisco: City Lights Books, 1986.

Baudrillard, Jean. *Seduction*, translated by Brian Singer. London: Macmillan, 1990.

Blanchot, Maurice. *The Step Not Beyond*, translated by Lycette Nelson. New York: State University of New York Press, 1992.

Carson, Anne. *Eros the Bittersweet*. Princeton, N.J.: Princeton University Press, 1986.

Lamb, Charles. *The Theatre of Howard Barker*. London: Routledge, 2005.

Menke, Christoph. *The Sovereignty of Art: Aesthetic Negativity in Adorno and Derrida*, translated by Neil Solomon. Cambridge, Mass.: MIT Press, 1999.

Un-sacred Cows and Protean Beings: Suniti Namjoshi's Re-writing of Postcolonial Lesbian Bodies

Shalmalee Palekar

Abstract

My paper examines Suniti Namjoshi's representations of the "raced," lesbian, creative body as a site of both "otherness" and empowerment. By inhabiting the subject position(s) of a diasporic Indian lesbian woman, by operating from multiple liminalities, she engages in a political act, thus opening up spaces in which she inscribes her resistance to stable genres and essentialised traditions. My paper maps out how Namjoshi's writing, with its fluid movement between "authenticity" and dreams, between (corpo)reality and her characters' various manifestations, between split selves and fragmented subjectivities, between playfulness and polemic, crosses boundaries of the gendered body, sexuality, desire, and "race." I posit that among Namjoshi's central concerns are the actual processes of "othering" and marginalisation; that is, the various overt and covert ways in which dominant cultures/discourses create, maintain and perpetuate racist, patriarchal, heterosexist/homophobic ideologies of the ideal/idealised body. Various critics position Namjoshi as an allegorical fabulist, but I will focus, rather, on how Namjoshi's dense, dialogic and multi-layered texts use these protean animal/human bodies to examine questions of community and solidarity, and their implications for minority groups. **Key Words:** postcolonial, lesbian, feminist, Indian, diaspora, literature.

To be a lesbian, a woman of colour, and a migrant is perhaps to be minoritised many times over. Patriarchal discourses have traditionally constructed lesbians as monsters and grotesque aberrations.[1] A lesbian is a disrupter of heterosexist gender dualism. She is threatening because she challenges the hegemony of the "normal" and the "ideal" in relation to the nature of society, family, man-woman relationships and the universality of heterosexuality. An immigrant lesbian of colour is further marginalised, not only in a white, heterosexual, patriarchal paradigm − "where all sexualities, all bodies, and all 'others' are bonded to an ideal/ideological hierarchy of males" − but also by the perpetuation of racist ideologies within Anglo lesbian communities.[2]

Suniti Namjoshi is an Indian lesbian-feminist author, who articulates through her work, the fraught issues that arise from having to inhabit all these subjectivities. To critique her world from that margin is to wrestle with contradictions and paradoxes surrounding issues of identity and self-hood, of self-representation, and agency. The concept of positionality is central to Namjoshi's narratives. Her characters interrogate stereotypes of race, sexuality and gender and the dominant majority's collusion in producing these. By examining the sites at which these discourses intersect and by deconstructing the "meaning" they ascribe, she opens up a "third space" in R. Radhakrishnan's terms – where oppressed and silenced minorities can not only speak, but be heard.[3] These themes and politics are central to Namjoshi's challenging and complex body of work, thus positioning it within postcolonial/feminist debate.

Namjoshi can be positioned as an allegorical fabulist who employs fantasy and irony in her quest for alternative modes of being, and articulates her resistance through transgression rather than aggression, playfully rather than polemically. But going by many reviews, this reading can easily become dismissive, often missing the depth of complexity of her self/re-presentation, and perpetuating the general lack of critical attention paid to her. Among Namjoshi's central concerns are the actual processes of "othering" and marginalisation; that is, the various overt and covert ways in which dominant cultures/discourses create, maintain and perpetuate racist, patriarchal, heterosexist/homophobic ideologies. Radhakrishnan argues that there is a difference between metropolitan hybridity and postcolonial hybridity. He stresses that postcolonial hybridity does not have the "guarantees" of "authenticity" or identity posited by the (Western) secular identity that underlies metropolitan hybridity. Rather, postcolonial hybridity involves a painful "inventory of one's self"[4]; which is to say, the self must be excruciatingly produced to inhabit many discursive positions. This is seen in Namjoshi's work, and is her way of articulating her subject positionality and identity without claims to "authenticity."

Hybridity is never a comfortable "given"; hence there are in her work, deliberate contradictions and provocative position statements on patriarchy, lesbian identity, feminist theory and "Indianness." Through a foregrounding of split subjectivities and selves, she is able to theorise/make visible/legitimise a particular sort of hybrid self, through subversions of institutionalised and systemic erasures. I also see in her work the attempt to articulate and (re)define notions of "community" and "the specificity of parameters of solidarity."[5] Most importantly, Namjoshi's writing demonstrates that finding ways of belonging is indeed different from "fitting in," or "assimilating."

Armed with an enduring suspicion of the human race, and an identification with animals, Namjoshi takes upon herself the task of deconstructing and subverting essentialised traditions and bodies through her fables, tales, poetry and novels. *Feminist Fables*,[6] *The Conversations of Cow*,[7] and *The Blue Donkey Fables*[8] offer alternate realities and different ways of being to those endorsed by Western Humanism. Namjoshi's animals expose the gendered violence and patriarchal morality of traditional fables, thus "her lessons usurp the status quo to endorse feminist thought."[9] Namjoshi's lesbian-feminist politics means that it is difficult to analyse separately the public, the private, the artistic and the theoretical in her writing. She deliberately chooses not to be a "poet of impersonality", [and] "for Namjoshi's art, this policy... has given birth to a genuine poetic voice."[10]

Absurdities abound in Namjoshi's work in all their luxuriant pluralities. The irrational, the fantastic, the symbolical, collide with the pseudo-logical, over-systematised hierarchies of a racist, and heterosexist society. Paradox and contradiction are deliberate discursive strategies, used by the author to provoke readers into making a critical and political response. The result is a trangressive, thought-provoking body of work that resonates with intertextual echoes from different cultural spectrums; a political body of work that aims at locating and foregrounding "difference" on multiple levels, as well as "dykonstructing" hierarchies of power predicated on white, male, heterosexual supremacy.[11]

The 1960s and 1970s feminist and gay liberation movements inspired a distinct body of separatist utopian novels, giving fictional realisation to "woman-identified" all-female societies.[12] These works are important in the sense that they opened up a critical space in which issues of gender and sexuality (especially lesbianism), could be explored in new ways – "a conceptual, representational, erotic space... in which women could address themselves to women."[13] Namjoshi's articulation of separatism in her earlier work, such as *The Conversations of Cow,* means that these works could be read as being a part and product of this lesbian-feminist ideology. Her "dykonstructions" are made even more challenging to read by their focus on how ethnicity and "race" intersect with lesbian-feminism, and by their interrogation of a monolithic Indian identity.

The Conversations of Cow, especially, articulates a complex examination of subjectivity and difference. It opens up a multiplicity of reading positions, and can be read as being problematic in its seeming endorsement of a biologically essentialised separatist politics, and in the way it posits "Indianness" in relation to both Suniti and Bhadravati. But in my opinion, Namjoshi deliberately mobilises certain essentialist discourses in order to foreground the construction of stereotypes and subvert them, and also to constantly provoke readers. The novel is set in the Canada of the 1980s, and has as its protagonists, Suniti,[14] an Indian-lesbian-feminist professor of English, and Bhadravati, a Brahmini lesbian cow, goddess of "a thousand shapes and a thousand wishes."[15]

Namjoshi, with a sharp wit, explores the creativity and subjectivities of an immigrant, lesbian, feminist, separatist through the dialogue between Suniti and Bhadravati; hence creating conceptual spaces that illustrate Suniti's problematic positionality and the socio-cultural forces that impact upon it:

> "Just because I'm a woman and a foreigner, it does not follow I cannot be a university professor." "And a lesbian," B adds, looking mischievous. "But really," she goes on, "English Literature?" "Onlookers," I tell her loftily, "often see more than participants."[16]

Namjoshi attempts to speak for herself, but does so through the use of allegory and fable, and hence elides the fraught issue of "authenticity." But the author still engages in a political act by inhabiting the subject position(s) of a diasporic Indian lesbian woman. Thus Namjoshi's approach to "authenticity" and self-representation can be read in Radhakrishnan's terms:

> an invention with enough room for multiple-rootedness ... [where] there need be no... opposition between authenticity and historical contingency, between authenticity and hybridity, between authenticity and invention.[17]

The novel's disruptiveness, humour and poignancy arise from the disjunctions between Suniti's ways of being and seeing, Bhadravati's Goddess/ lesbian/ cow perceptions,[18] and those of the predominantly white, human/cow world they both must function in.

Namjoshi makes use of both Western and Eastern mythology for her themes, narratives, and characters. For example, in *Feminist Fables,* she has done feminist/ lesbian-feminist rewritings of *Aesop's Fables,* Greek and Roman mythology, fairy-tales, as well as stories from the *Panchatantra.* This is seen clearly in "Case History," which is a reworking of "Little Red Riding Hood."

> After the event Little R. traumatised. Wolf not slain. Forester is wolf... Grandmother dead... Wolf marries mother... Please to see shrink. Shrink will make it clear that wolves on the whole are extremely nice...[19]

In a similar vein we get a rewriting of "Beauty and the Beast," which maps out the damage done by heterosexism and homophobia: "The Beast was a woman. That's why its love for Beauty was so monstrous..." Here Namjoshi subverts the trope of "lesbian as monster" by exposing how phallocentric and heterosexist economies collude to pathologise alternative sexualities. The issue of lesbian invisibility, which resurfaces in *The Conversations of Cow,* is broached in this piece. In the cultural/literary discourses produced within the above-mentioned economies, the Beast is denied access to positive images of self-identification with which to validate same-sex love.

"Man is at the centre. There are no human women."[20] This is a theme that is reiterated in much of Namjoshi's work, including *The Conversations of Cow*. But Namjoshi simultaneously posits the possibility for women to become "woman-identified" and subvert the constructs and constraints of patriarchy. For example, we see that "In the Forest,"[21] the witch in "Hansel and Gretel" is depicted as a source of comfort rather than terror to Gretel; and Sheherazade from "The Thousand and One Nights" refuses the Caliph's offer of marriage and prefers to stay with her sister Dinarzade. Thus for Namjoshi, this notion of the primacy of women's relationships with other women has great subversive potential.[22] She uses it strategically in order to foreground the sexual politics and misogyny in traditional fables and myths, and disrupts their heterosexual imperative and patriarchal closure; thus opening up spaces in which she inscribes her resistance to stable genres and essentialised traditions.

But Namjoshi is also critical of unqualified celebrations of "sisterhood." This concern surfaces in her exploration of racism within Anglo lesbian communities in *The Conversations of Cow,* and in her mapping of the power struggles between women in *The Mothers of Maya Diip.* Her work has been described as "modern parables addressing the contradictions of Lesbian and feminist theory [where] the sexual debates within feminism are distanced by the metamorphosis into animals..."[23] For example, the protagonist of *The Blue Donkey Fables* is a lesbian-feminist Donkey whose "blueness", rather than lesbianism, becomes the site of many debates for the unpacking of biological essentialist theories, as well as "progressive" liberal discourses. (This is a textual strategy Namjoshi uses effectively in *The Conversations of Cow)*.

Namjoshi delights in breaking down boundaries of genre within the narrative paradigm of *The Conversations of Cow*. There is a deliberate fluidity of genres which echoes the fluidity of Suniti and Bhadravati's physical transformations, and suggests that genre/gender-bending is used as a discursive strategy with which to subvert Anglo/phallocentric realities, thus making the text a site which is capable of articulating resistant positions. The use of a talking animal, which functions as a catalyst and drives the action, is a choice evidently in favour of the fable form. But this is a narrative written from a self-consciously Indian lesbian-feminist perspective, with a deliberate foregrounding of its ideology. Therefore, what seems at first to be a light, "transparent" narrative gradually reveals itself as multi-accented, multi-layered. The novel becomes, therefore, a sort of literary archaeological site that invites readers to create and construct meaning – thus subverting the traditional fable's positing of gendered violence and patriarchal morality as "objective" and "universal" truth. Namjoshi explicitly states her desire to open up a dialogue with her readers in the following poem:

> Dear Reader,/ I have the power? I define? And I/ control? But it takes two live bodies, one/ writing and one reading, to generate a sky,/ a habitable planet and a working sun.[24]

The fable is intertwined with science-fiction, romance, Hindu philosophy, absurdist farce, theories of subjectivity and difference, satire and feminist utopia, all of which are both, used and parodied. The structure of Namjoshi's novel demonstrates, in fact, that the political and emotional concerns of a non-Anglo, lesbian, feminist do not necessarily fit into a linear, realist narrative. Content (corporeality, search for identity, articulating marginalised selves), as well as form (mixing novel, fantasy, theory, science fiction-utopia, poetry and fable) point to an engagement with the development of a new lesbian-feminist art form.[25] Suniti's narrative is elliptical, and though it ends on a happy note it does not have closure imposed upon it, because the "end" of the narrative is the beginning of Suniti's writing the narrative. In the intricate dance of woman and cow, neither Suniti nor Cow ever give or accept neat, tidy, easy answers. Throughout the novel, Suniti searches for spaces and discursive gaps, into which she can speak her voices so that she will be heard. As Spivak points out:

> For me, the question "Who will speak?" is less crucial than "Who will listen?" "I will speak for myself as a Third World person" is an important position for political mobilisation today. But the real demand is that, when I speak from that position, I should be listened to seriously,   not   with   that   kind   of   benevolent imperialism...[26]

Namjoshi — through Suniti, and Cow in her many manifestations — breaks many silences and strategically disrupts notions of the "proper," through her transgression of genre boundaries, and her protean bodies and stylistic experiments. In fact, Namjoshi plays interestingly with the literary convention of a heavenly Muse:

> I'm down on my knees, waiting for the goddess to manifest herself. When I open my eyes, The Cow of a Thousand Wishes is standing before me on green turf. Daffodils and crocuses grow at her feet, though, incongruously enough, the cow herself is a Brahmini cow.[27]

Thus the Goddess/Muse is a cow, and a Brahmin one at that. By simply juxtaposing these incongruities, Namjoshi creates a hybrid, disruptive symbol. It brings together the literal and the fantastic, the bizarre and the banal, the divine and the bovine. In colloquial English usage, the adjective "cow" functions in a derogatory sense to mean a large, slow-witted woman. In Vedic Hinduism, on the other hand, the cow is constructed as a Holy Mother whose every secretion is sacred.[28] Cow fits into neither the former nor the latter category,[29] thus patriarchal language is subverted with the Hindu mythoscape. Again, contrary to literary conventions, the agent of inspiration and/or wish-fulfillment arrives *before* we know the nature of Suniti's quest. Cow is also a lesbian, as Suniti finds out soon after:

> "I ought to tell you," Cow informs me, "that this is a Self-Sustaining Community of Lesbian Cows." I scrutinise Cow. So, Cow and I have something in common.[30]

Also importantly, Cow is never a silent Muse, but an articulate, strongly opinionated one. Their relationship has deliberate echoes of the ancient Indian guru-shishya (teacher-student) tradition. But both the teacher and student are not only female, they are "out" lesbians. Furthermore, the student is actually allowed the space to question, disbelieve, even talk back, which could be seen as subversive in itself, even in many contemporary educational contexts. Therefore Namjoshi uses the character of Cow to subvert both, Western literary, and Hindu-Brahminical traditions.

There is a constant questioning, challenging, re-defining of boundaries, socio-cultural conditioning and role-playing right through the novel, especially when Bhadravati decides to "become" a white, heterosexual man because she is tired of being economically disempowered and "exotic." It is interesting to note that people's reactions to Suniti and Bhadravati change dramatically as soon as they are perceived as being a heterosexual couple, Sue and Bud – even though tensions arise from the "interracial" relationship:

> As we're leaving the maitre d'hotel says, "Bring her again. She's beautiful." Bud looks smug. "There, Suniti. Aren't you pleased?" "No. If you went into a parking lot with a foreign car, it's exactly what the attendant might say to you."[31]

Through the protean Cow, Namjoshi makes a succinct comment on the creation of minorities by the dominant majority:[32]

> It is only because married people and the bourgeois family are given such authority within a sexist/heterosexist culture, that Lesbians become nebulous unpersons.[33]

Some lines in the novel suggest that sometimes Suniti does feel like a "nebulous unperson". Typically, Namjoshi carries this sense of alienation and disorientation from the self to its surreal extreme – Suniti wakes up one morning to find herself in bed with her. They think, feel and act in almost precisely the same ways, look identical, but have two separate bodies. Yet this manifestation, S2, is not just a replica or copy, but an actual second Suniti. S2 is a necessary step in Suniti's search for a legitimate identity – a process of discovering/constructing/reclaiming different aspects about herself and being able to articulate them towards achieving an inner coherence. It is significant, therefore, that Suniti starts to experience a genuine empathy for S2. The creation of, and necessity for S2 could be seen as tying in with Radhakrishnan's analysis of postcolonial identity as excruciatingly produced through multiple traces, which I have discussed earlier.

Similarly, when Suniti encounters racism at a hotel, the issues raised by Namjoshi are more complex than Suniti's reaction suggests. The author explores the material and ideological specificities that constitute Suniti as "powerless" in this context; Suniti is constructed as "racial other" and "non-man" by the waitress, which makes the waitress – rather than Bud – the perpetrator of oppression. This tactic disrupts simplistic connections between gender and power (man/perpetrator, woman/victim), and debunks the liberal feminist assumption of a sisterhood based purely on gender, that transcends ethnicities, cultures, histories and classes. "Sisterhood cannot be assumed on the basis of gender; it must be forged in historical and political practice and analysis."[34]

I suggest that Namjoshi deliberately and strategically sets up binary oppositions but the author's depiction of racism in Anglo lesbian communities shows that she is aware of the various contexts, asymmetries and histories that can disrupt these dichotomies. This awareness comes across clearly in later works such as *The Mothers of Maya Diip*. This novel is a study of oppression and unequal relations of power within a mythical matriarchy. Maya Diip is an island ruled by the Ranisaheb, whose title, as the Blue Donkey points out, means "Queen. It does not mean the Feminist Poetry Collective."[35] Namjoshi clearly implies that essentialised gender binaries have to be unpacked and dismantled in order to achieve any sort of progress – the mere inversion of binaries is not enough. This matriarchy, with its worship of motherhood, abuses of power, class hierarchies, intolerance of difference, and complete devaluing of one gender/sex is no different from a repressive patriarchy.

This examination is more challenging and subtle in *The Conversations of Cow*. Bhadravati claims that men are colonisers from Mars and that to be a Martian, and gain access to "Martian circles", all that is needed is some make-up and appropriate padding – thus implying that men only impersonate "received" and stereotypical notions of masculinity, which are easily duplicated with the right "equipment." An implicit comment on the "performed" nature of gender itself, once again emphasising the potential for subverting the fixity of phallocentric representation.

The humanising of/identification with animals also raises complex issues of interpretation. What does it mean in terms of the strategies Namjoshi deploys in her writing? A passage from Namjoshi's non-fiction shows that her Hindu roots play a strong part in shaping her consciousness and voice, particularly in relation to her use of and identification with talking animals.[36] Romila Thapar contends that in Hindu teachings:

> Considerable emphasis is placed on the universal quality of all human beings, on the values of tolerance and compassion, and on the need for harmony [between humans and nature] through recognition of the rights of each – all of which would lead to spiritual peace.[37]

Namjoshi uses this tenet that both humans and animals have souls and are therefore part of the whole fabric of creation, which explains to an extent, why she humanises animals. But she then uses the technique/strategy of anthropomorphism to subvert these constructs. Through her use of human animals, she is able to both, effectively problematise the uncritical acceptance of the teachings of Hinduism, and critically examine the debates of lesbian-feminist theory.

Namjoshi's work also raises the question of "imagined realities" in relation to inhabited realities.[38] This is seen especially in the invention of a self-sustaining collective of lesbian cows. This invention be read as a self-critique of the longing for a pure space of marginalism beyond the cultural-political, a space that is transcendent of ideological interpellations and regimes of power.

But the cow-collective simultaneously posits another possibility, and that is — an exploration of ways of belonging, through an examination of the notion of community. Radhakrishnan contends that minority communities must share "worldviews, theories, values and strategies" in order not to be disempowered and co-opted.[39] In the context of the end of *The Conversations of Cow*, the invention of lesbian cows can be read as Namjoshi's attempt to depict a solidarity between minorities which is achieved slowly and is fraught, but is ultimately empowering. It is a concept of community that has the space for "multiple-rootedness," which breaks down the epistemological opposition between "authenticity" and "invention", but which does not, in the process, posit an "authentic" hybridity.

On one level, Namjoshi constantly fulfils stereotypical Western expectations in relation to "Indianness," with regard to Suniti, and Suniti's attitude to white men, women and white cows — Suniti is a small, brown, Hindu-Indian woman who believes that Bhadravati the Brahmin cow is a Goddess. But apart from being an outspoken lesbian-feminist, Suniti also has an ironic awareness of Cow's "colonial" fondness for scotch and water, and that this makes Cow a scotch and water guzzling Brahmin Goddess with a contrived American accent.

Many of the cow-human relationships illustrates what Chandra Talpade Mohanty contends is the potential of "imagined community"; in the sense that it is an alliance across divisive boundaries, which emphasises the political, rather than essentialist notions of "biology" or "culture" as a basis for alliance.[40] The use of allegory and fables, and specially the use of "human" animals, is a form/style/tactic that has been appropriated by "post-colonial/postmodern" writers like Salman Rushdie. This tactic enables them to highlight and drive home the various points they make about difference on a multiplicity of levels. It is true that Cow does appear "magically" out of the blue. It is also true that Cow's appearance both, disrupts the banality of Suniti's everyday life, and yet, reinforces it through the very "humanness" of Cow. But there is more than just literary defamiliarisation going on here; Namjoshi explores what it is to write out of multiple liminalities, and yet instead of betraying anxieties of "unbelonging," her work embodies plural possibilities − and does this without losing its sharp and witty edge. All the characters in the text talk volubly, laugh, cry, fall in love, fall out of love, ponder the meaning of life; interactions between characters are "normal," except some of them are cows, and change at will into women, men or Goddesses.

> "But, of course, B, you are always you whoever you are − if you see what I mean." What on earth do I mean?... I decide to do nothing. I shall treat B exactly as though she were B, which she is, who she was, well as she would have been.[41]

It is possible to approach Namjoshi's works in a sequential manner and read them as increasingly moving towards non-hegemonic forms. For example, in her second-last book *Building Babel*, Namjoshi has been exploring how the Internet can be used as a medium for a dense text and poetry. The book includes an electronic chapter which readers can add to, opening Babel to everyone.

Namjoshi's examination of Indian lesbian-feminist subjectivities and selves means that new spaces, new images, new languages, new creativity, new bodies can emerge. These non-hegemonic forms combined with lesbian sexuality allow for new resonances and symbols, as well as provide for new relationships between one's selves, between women and between minorities. Thus Namjoshi's narratives move away from isolation and move towards formulating a concept of community; they effectively thematise and validate marginalised or resistant feminist/ lesbian/ migrant/ postcolonial selves and identities. In effect, Namjoshi makes possible, and affirms, new ways of belonging.

Notes

1. Patricia White, "Female Spectator, Lesbian Specter," in *Sexuality and Space,* ed. Beatriz Colomina (New York: Princeton Architectural Press, 1992), 132.

2. Teresa de Lauretis, "Sexual Indifference and Lesbian Representation," in *The Lesbian and Gay Studies Reader,* ed. Henry Abelove et al. (New York and London: Routledge, 1993), 144.

3. R. Radhakrishnan, "Postcoloniality and the Boundaries of Identity," *Callaloo* 16.4 (1993): 755.

4. Radhakrishnan, 753.

5. Ibid., 760.

6. Suniti Namjoshi, *Feminist Fables,* (Melbourne: Spinifex Press, 1993).

7. Namjoshi, *The Conversations of Cow,* (London: The Women's Press Ltd., 1985).

8. Namjoshi, *The Blue Donkey Fables* and *The Mothers of Maya Diip,* (New Delhi: Penguin Books India, 1991).

9. Diane McGifford, "Suniti Namjoshi (1941-)," in *Writers of the Indian Diaspora: A Bio-Bibliographical Critical Sourcebook*, ed. Emmanuel Nelson (Westport, CT and London: Greenwood Press, 1993), 293.

10. Ibid., 292.

11. A term coined by Meeta Chatterjee in her PhD-in-progress, English Department, University of Wollongong. Used with her permission.

12. Diane Griffin Crowder, "Separatism and Feminist Utopian Fiction," in *Sexual Practice, Textual Theory: Lesbian Cultural Criticism,* eds. Susan Wolfe and Julia Penelope (Cambridge, MA and Oxford, UK: Blackwell Publishers, 1993), 237.

13. de Lauretis, 141.

14. I will refer to the author as Namjoshi, and the character as Suniti so as to avoid confusion.

15. Namjoshi, *Conversations*, 122.

16. Ibid, 34.

17. Radhakrishnan, 755.

18. Patricia Duncker, *Sisters and Strangers: An Introduction to Contemporary Feminist Fiction,* (Oxford, UK and Cambridge, MA: Blackwell Publishers, 1992), 161.

19. Namjoshi, *Feminist Fables,* 3.

20. Ibid., "Exegesis," 53.

21. Ibid., 95.

22. In fact Namjoshi subtitles this piece "For Adrienne Rich - if she would like it," which suggests that she has consciously based it on Rich's concept of a "lesbian continuum."

23. Duncker, 59.

24. Namjoshi, *The Blue Donkey Fables,* 51.

25. McGifford, 293.

26. Gayatri Chakravarty Spivak, "Questions of Multiculturalism", in *The Post-Colonial Critic: Interviews, Strategies, Dialogues,* ed. Sarah Harasym (New York and London: Routledge, 1990), 60.

27. Namjoshi, *Conversations,* 13.

28. W. J. Wilkins, *Hindu Mythology: Vedic and Puranic* (Bombay: Rupa & Co, 1986), 339.

29. Though Cow does operate on one level as "Kamadhenu," the "Cow of Plenty," yielder of all that is wished. This aspect is underscored at the end of the novel, in Suniti's invocation to Cow.

30. Namjoshi, *Conversations,* 17-18.

31. Ibid, 105.

32. Also see J. Pugliese, "Language and Minorities," in *Minorities*, edited by Shirley Fitzgerald and Garry Wotherspoon, 192-215 (Sydney: State Library of NSW Press, 1995), 193. In his analysis of ethnic minorities, Pugliese says: "What is this seemingly homogeneous other (majority) against which minorities emerge? The majority's very identity is staked out in the manoeuvres by which it defines its others," that is; any history of minorities also functions as a tacit history of aspects of a perceived majority.

33. Duncker, 61.

34. Chandra Talpade Mohanty, "Under Western Eyes," in *Third World Women and the Politics of Feminism,* ed. Chandra Talpade Mohanty et al. (Bloomington and Indianapolis: Indiana University Press, 1991), 56-58.

35. Namjoshi, *The Mothers of Maya Diip,* 114.

36. McGifford, 293.

37. Romila Thapar, *Ancient Indian Social History: Some Interpretations* (Bombay: Orient Longman, 1978), 27.

38. Radhakrishnan, 769.

39. Ibid., 767.

40. Mohanty, 4-5.

41. Namjoshi, *Conversations,* 51-53.

Select Bibliography

Bhabha, Homi K. "The Other Question... Homi Bhabha Reconsiders the Stereotype and Colonial Discourse." *Screen* 24.6 (Nov-Dec, 1983): 18-36.

Butler, Judith. *Gender Trouble: Feminism and the Subversion of Identity.* New York and London: Routledge, 1990.

Chatterjee, Meeta. "Humour in Indian Literature Written in English."

Incomplete PhD Dissertation, University of Wollongong.

Carlston, Erin. "*Zami* and the Politics of Plural Identity." In *Sexual Practice, Textual Theory: Lesbian Cultural Criticism*, edited by Susan Wolfe and Julia Penelope, 226-236. Cambridge, MA and Oxford, UK: Blackwell, 1993.

Cranny-Francis, Anne. *Engendered Fictions: Analysing Gender in the Production and Reception of Texts*. Kensington: New South Wales University Press, 1992.

Crowder, Dianne Griffin. "Separatism and Feminist Utopian Fiction." In *Sexual Practice, Textual Theory*, edited by Susan Wolfe and Julia Penelope, 237-250. Cambridge, MA and Oxford, UK: Blackwell Publishers, 1993.

Duncker, Patricia. *Sisters and Strangers: An Introduction to Contemporary Feminist Fiction*. Oxford, UK and Cambridge, MA: Blackwell, 1992.

Faderman, Lillian. *Surpassing the Love of Men: Romantic Friendship and Love between Women from the Renaissance to the Present*. New York: William Morrow, 1981.

Guha, Ranajit, ed. *Subaltern Studies I: Writings on South Asian History and Society*. Bombay: Oxford University Press, 1982.

Gunew, Sneja and Kateryna O. Longley. *Striking Cords: Multicultural Literary Interpretations*. Sydney: Allen & Unwin, 1991.

Hoagland, Sarah Lucia and Julia Penelope, eds. *For Lesbians Only: A Separatist Anthology*. London: Onlywomen Press, 1988.

Landry, Donna and Gerald Maclean, eds. *The Spivak Reader: Selected Works of Gayatri Chakravorty Spivak*. New York and London: Routledge, 1996.

Lauretis, Teresa de. "Sexual Indifference and Lesbian Representation." In *The Lesbian and Gay Studies Reader*, edited by Henry Abelove et al., 141-152. New York and London: Routledge, 1993.

McEwen, Christian, ed. *Naming the Waves: Contemporary Lesbian Poetry*. London: Virago Press, 1988.

McGifford, Diane. "Suniti Namjoshi (1941-)." In *Writers of the Indian Diaspora: A Bio-Bibliographical Critical Sourcebook*, edited by Emmanuel Nelson, 291-297. Westport, CT and London: Greenwood Press, 1993.

Mohanty, Chandra Talpade. "Under Western Eyes: Feminist Scholarship and Colonial Discourses." In *Third World Women and The Politics Of Feminism*, edited by Chandra Talpade Mohanty, Ann Russo and Lourdes Torres, 51-80. Bloomington and Indianapolis: Indiana University Press, 1991.

Namjoshi, Suniti. *Feminist Fables*. London: Sheba Feminist Publishers,

1981.

——. *The Conversations of Cow.* London: The Women's Press Ltd., 1985.

——. *The Blue Donkey Fables* and *The Mothers of Maya Diip.* New Delhi: Penguin India, 1991.

Penelope, Julia and Susan Wolfe, eds. *The Coming Out Stories.* Watertown, MA: Persephone Press, 1980.

Pugliese, Joseph. "Language and Minorities." In *Minorities,* edited by Shirley Fitzgerald and Garry Wotherspoon, 192-215. Sydney: State Library of NSW Press, 1995.

Radhakrishnan, R. "Postcoloniality and the Boundaries of Identity." *Callaloo* 16.4 (1993): 750-771.

Rich, Adrienne. "Compulsory Heterosexuality and Lesbian Existence." *Signs* 5.4 (1980): 631-660.

Spivak, Gayatri Chakravarty. "Strategy, Identity, Writing." In *The Post-Colonial Critic: Interviews, Strategies, Dialogues,* edited by Sarah Harasym, 35-49. New York and London, Routledge, 1990.

——. "Questions of Multiculturalism." In *The Post-Colonial Critic: Interviews, Strategies, Dialogues,* edited by Sarah Harasym, 59-66. New York and London, Routledge, 1990.

Thapar, Romila. *Ancient Indian Social History: Some Interpretations.* Bombay: Orient Longman, 1978.

White, Patricia. "Female Spectator, Lesbian Specter." In *Sexuality and Space,* edited by Beatriz Colomina, 131-160. New York: Princeton Architectural Press, 1992.

Wilkins, W. J. *Hindu Mythology: Vedic and Puranic.* Bombay: Rupa & Co., 1986.

Desire-less-ness

Fiona Peters

Abstract

Desire, specifically but not exclusively sexual, is usually taken as a "given" in discussions and theoretical debates concerning sexuality. The purpose of this paper is to begin to question this, and to ask whether or not a concept of desire-less-ness might be useful as a means of understanding some contemporary manifestations of anxiety and cultural lethargy. The paper employs a psychoanalytic methodology, specifically drawing on the work of Jacques Lacan, Julia Kristeva, and Slavoj Zizek. Firstly I explain the specific concept of desire that underpins my argument, before elaborating a historical and theoretical conception of desire-less-ness. Finally, I turn to a literary representation of a desire-less individual, Patricia Highsmith's Tom Ripley, to illustrate my argument. **Key Words:** desire, desire-less-ness, anxiety, symbolic order, psychosis, subject.

1. Introduction

What might it mean *not* to desire? Is desire, especially sexual desire, an innate "given," or is it, on the contrary, constructed? Is it possible to function as a non-desiring human being? And would that be the same, or closely aligned to, the situation of the asexual person? And in what ways do we *all* nowadays lead lives that are so satiated by our expectations and assumptions of desire that we fail to recognise both its inevitability and concurrently, its impossibility?

Julia Kristeva argues that "there are lives not sustained by *desire*, as desire is always for objects. Such lives are based on *exclusion*."[1] So, according to Kristeva, the life not based on desire is a life of exclusion. I will be exploring the nature of that exclusion, specifically but not exclusively, through a literary example, and considering what might take its place.

2. Desire

According to contemporary psychoanalytic theory, desire may become displaced by a crippling and constitutive anxiety, one that clings to its function of keeping the subject at a distance from the object, especially a possible love-object:

> ...anxiety occurs not when the object-cause of desire is lacking; it is not the lack of the object that gives rise to anxiety but, on the contrary, the danger of our getting too close to the object and thus losing the lack itself.

> Anxiety is brought about by the disappearance of desire.[2]

Thus anxiety (expressed as lack of desire) functions as a mechanism to keep the object (the love object, the sexual relationship, and so on) at a distance.

Read psychoanalytically, the non-desiring individual cannot be said to be lacking something constitutive and pre-given. Instead of fantasy existing as confirmation of a pre-existent latency of desire, it in effect creates it: "it is only through fantasy that the subject is constituted as desiring. *Through fantasy we learn how to desire.*"[3] Thus those who do not desire are fundamentally threatening to the rest of the desiring universe. Excluded from full appropriation into the symbolic universe, to be non-desiring challenges the very status of our conception of the human subject.

3.   Desire-less-ness

So...what do I mean when I begin to approach the question of desire-less-ness (and this is clearly not to be confused with the Buddhist meaning of the term)? Firstly, to be non-desiring in the sense in which I approach it doesn't necessarily mean to be non-sexual. Neither am I concerned here with decisions to become celibate for a certain period of time. It might rather be that the objects that we think we desire, by their over-proximity and their multiplicity, are capable of reducing us to a desireless state. Aligned to that, what conception of desire can be articulated prior to thinking about desire-less-ness?

Desire cannot be positively identified, being only capable of a negative theorisation. According to Lacan, desire is always barred, it always misses its object, it is never involved in a relationship of reciprocity. In his formulation it must be distinguished from the *drive* that in turn always, in psychoanalytic conceptions, contains within it an element of aggressivity. Paul Verhaeghe argues:

> The drive means that one lets oneself go, driven by something else, something coming from an uncontrollable and timeless other place. The field of the drive lies outside consciousness, in a strange but necessary mix of aggression and Eros.[4]

So the drive is, literally, something that drives the subject to places where he/she may not consciously wish to go. The drive is *not* an instinct, but *is* instinctual; as Laplanche and Pontalis state, it is a dynamic process consisting in a *pressure*...which directs the organism towards an aim. According to Freud, a drive has its *source* in a bodily stimulus; its *aim* is to eliminate the state of tension obtaining at the instinctual source; and it is in the *object*, or thanks to it, that the drive may achieve its aim.[5]

Freud shifted his conception of the drive particularly at the time of the development of his ideas concerning the *beyond* of the pleasure principle, yet he always held that the drive is sexual in nature. This plays a huge role in his emphasis on the centrality of sexuality – something that he always argued for despite the division that this insistence caused within the psychoanalytic community.

For Lacan, the Freudian drive fits into his configuration of need, demand, and desire. As for other animals, the human being is subject to a series of biological instincts like hunger, which are capable of being satisfied. What differentiates the human animal, according to Lacan, is that it not only manifests needs, but makes *demands*. The demand for love is the most central but, at the same time, the most impossible to meet. For Lacan, this differentiation from other animals occurs because of the ways in which, for the human being, language intervenes to act as a mediation between the drive and its fulfilment – in other words and according to Lacan, the human child becomes situated, and in many respects trapped, within the linguistic, or more broadly symbolic, framework.

Within language, once a need is signified, it becomes a demand – to speak to another is to demand a response. For Lacan there is a continuous gap between a simple biological need and human demand – and, according to him, it is in this gap that desire is to be found. In other words, we might *need* food to satisfy our biological hunger, but the demand that we make is for more than any simple meal could possibly satisfy – satiation is always just beyond our grasp. The demand for food then, is never just made simply for the satisfaction of our immediate hunger, but is rather a manifestation (a very important one) of the demand for love.

In psychoanalytic theory, this desire that occurs within the gap between need and demand is unable to attain satisfaction, insofar as desire implies a goal or an end point. It is goal-less and the many apparent goals that endlessly arise before us are never enough – desire is merely displaced from object to object. It is fantasy that plays a key role here, for example in the process of falling in love. According to Lacan, there can be no sexual *relation*ship – precisely because in a sexual relationship, the one desires *not* the other but *their* desire.

We can read in Lacan's work the extent to which the loss inherent in the assumption of sexuality theorised as *difference* leans towards a construction of the "One," both holding out the promise of totalisation and concurrently withdrawing it. In *Seminar XX* he argues:

> Love is impotent, though mutual, because it is not aware that it is but the desire to be One, which leads to the impossibility of establishing the relationship between "them-two" (*la relation d'eux*). The relationship between them-two what? Them-two sexes.[6]

Suzanne Barnard points out that the desire not *for*, but *to be* One that the sexually differentiated subject experiences (usually categorised as the phallic signifier),

> stands ultimately for the impossibility of signifying sex. As such, it can be understood to represent both a traumatic failure of meaning and the impossibility of ever fundamentally anchoring or positivising the subject.[7]

Thus, "ever achieving one's gender or even accomplishing one's sexuality"[8] is barred from the subject as a loss that is *inherent* rather than a more or less pathological aberration. The sexual subject, as defined by a sexual difference that is predicated on loss and lack (the gap into which desire falls), constantly slips through the net of the binaries that attempt to define it:

> Hence, sexual difference can be understood to stand for that which forever eludes the grasp of normative symbolization. The obsessive individual and cultural reiterations of the "surface" of sexuality – the seeming reality of the sexual relationship, as it is divided into binaries, such as male and female, masculine and feminine, hetero-and homosexuality, and so on – only cover up this fundamental dehiscence of the sexual subject.[9]

This notion of dehiscence, of a concurrent splitting and spilling of the inherently ignorant and flawed human subject, marks the Lacanian treatment of gender and desire. While individual sexual relationships are of course possible within this theorisation, Lacan always stresses the *impossibility* of the sexual *relationship* as such. This failure cannot be surmounted; indeed, any attempt to do so flees from the traumatic consequences of the imposition of the Real into the structures of sexuation and falls back upon, according to Suzanne Barnard, "the accepted logic of sex and gender, particularly as those terms have structured the essentialist-constructionist debates among American feminists and gender theorists."[10]

Not only do I desire the other person but I also, more importantly, desire the desire of the other person – I seek his/her desire for me and want/demand this to be recognised. Within a dual relationship, this recognition is *never* sufficient, but it is in the sexual relationship that the tragi-comedy of desire, according to psychoanalysis, is most clearly played out. There is, specifically, no "authentic" underlying layer of desire.

Within contemporary psychoanalytic discourse, desire is a key point of departure. It is most explicit in the vagaries of the sexual relationship, however desire drives and determines every human and social interaction. Whether or not it be for social success (*I* want it because *you* want it), desire exceeds every experience or object on the infinite transition to its next goal and the goal after that.

However, it is clear that there is today a cultural injunction to enjoy, to achieve sexual satisfaction and gratification, to perform, to have fun, in other words to attain one's desire. In Lacan's formulation of desire, this simply increases the pressure on the subject and, it can be argued, in effect leads to an increasingly anxious culture. Zizek offers an example:

> Let us recall the figure of the father who advises his son on sexual exploits: if the father warns him against it, formally prohibits him from dating girls etc; he, of course, between the lines only propels the son to do it, i.e. to find satisfaction in violating the paternal prohibition; if, on the contrary, the father in an obscene way directly pushes him to "behave like a man"and seduce girls, the actual effect of this will probably be the opposite (the son's withdrawal, shame of the obscene father, impotence even.[11]

Being *told* to enjoy – to desire, I am arguing, may thus lead to an excess of anxiety, bringing with it its concurrent affect, lack of desire, a withdrawal from the desiring process. In this model, anxiety is deployed as a painful yet nonetheless protective strategy against the vicious and, to use Zizek's language, obscene injunction to enjoy, at all costs. It could be argued that, once stultified by the weight of this anxiety, meaningful actions become more difficult, even impossible to instigate.

To place this briefly within a cultural and historical framework, Lacan famously argues against the dominant mode of post-war ego psychoanalysis in the United States. He believes that ego-psychology was both a symptom and a perpetuator of infantalism:

> The academic restoration of this "autonomous ego" justified my view that a misunderstanding was involved in an attempt to strengthen the ego in a type of analysis that took as its criterion of success a successful adaptation to society – a phenomenon of mental abdication that was bound up with the ageing of the psychoanalytic group in the diaspora of the War and the reduction of a distinguished practice to the "American way of life."[12]

This attempt to strengthen the ego and at the same time to utilise psychoanalysis to aid and abet conformity to a culture that promises payback for desire whilst constantly manufacturing more is contradictory according to Lacan. A consequence of this, it can be argued, is the upsurge in passivity arising from a nascent anxiety within a cultural mood that has been described as "the complacency of despair."[13] Julia Kristeva has argued that attempts to alleviate or deny this anxiety by the elevation of ego-strengthening in relation to "having it all," especially where sexual "liberation" is concerned, or the "injunction to enjoy," instigates a particular psychic pain. She argues that literary works may be read and utilised to try to begin to understand specific historical-cultural impasses, times when the excess of psychic pain is revealed as trauma unrelieved by narcissistic pleasure. Along with Lacan, she finds it impossible to ignore the impact of the Second World War on the psychic life of the individual in the cultural formulations that followed: "That pressure found its intimate and inevitable repercussion in psychic pain. An inescapable urgency, the pain nonetheless has remained…invisible, unrepresentable."[14] Kristeva argues that the violence of the twentieth century instigated "the violently intense deflagration of psychic identity,"[15] which, it can be argued, may lead to an overdetermination of desire.

Paul Verhaeghe states:

> This is the new command of the super-ego – enjoy now, enjoy fully and as long and as much as possible. The universal contemporary leitmotif is "have it now."[16]

Have it now, anywhere, our desires unchecked. But not, as I have shown, according to Kristeva and other analysts working with a "new" type of patient manifesting what Lacan describes as the increase in the pressure for pleasure that conversely leads to a lack of the very thing we think we can attain, pleasure itself. This results in a massive and undefined anxiety.

For Lacan, the arena of the Real underlies that of the Symbolic Order that, while implicated in the construction and mediation of desire, is both unstable and fragile. The Real (precisely not reality) is present as a chasm of inertia, empty time free from the pleasure principle or the command to enjoy. It can be argued that the inert is, in its passivity, resistant to mindless proliferation and concurrently to the endless running motor of sexual desire. In some respects, it can be utilised as cultural critique, one that transposes the seeming negativity of passivity and inertia into a radical disavowal of the rigid structuring of the symbolic within today's cultural milieu.

Lacan argues that anxiety must be attached to an object yet we never know precisely what or where those objects are situated. Thus its utilisation as a shield, keeping the dangers of desire at bay. For Zizek, Eduard Munch's *Scream* presents the modernist exemplar of anxiety:

> The standard designation by which *Scream* conveys anxiety is therefore appropriate – provided that we conceive of the notion of anxiety in its strict Lacanian sense – as the effect which registers the subject's panic reaction to the <u>overproximity</u> of the object cause of desire.[17]

Within the discourse of the post-modern, however, according to Zizek we clutch at our individual sinthomes to stave off the horrors of confronting our particular object-cause of desire. The concept of the sinthome is developed from the Freudian notion of symptom, but having lost the cause and effect relation that as Zizek relates above, can still be discerned in *Scream*. The sinthome, having lost the cause and effect correlation, becomes not a representation of a trauma, a symbolic means of allowing trauma to be read (and thus analysed) but, rather, a means of non-representation. According to Zizek, this then elevates a perverse enjoyment that evades the easy clarity of the injunction to enjoy. Sarah Kay explains:

> The symptom becomes the <u>sinthome</u>, the manifestation of the subject's enjoyment which he cannot give up but should embrace as "what is in him more than himself"...its symbolic dimension declines and the

subject's   imaginary   relation   with   enjoyment
correspondingly increases in importance.[18]
In this sense sinthomes are the non-symbolised knots that hold our
psyches together and always escape the simple yet overwhelming
injunction to enjoy – instead we enjoy our symptoms. The sinthome works
within psychoanalytic discourse to counter the loss inherent in the
assumption of sexual difference: the pressure to reach towards the One
that I have described – can either be mediated by the sinthome or can
otherwise slide into passivity.

The linked concepts of passivity and inter-passivity are,
according to Zizek strategies more and more widely deployed as strategies
for coping with the injunction to enjoy. An example he uses is that of the
practice of noting than an interesting programme is coming on television,
but at that time we want to go out, or do something (or nothing) else, so
we set the VCR. We record it, take it out of the machine, label it and put it
on a shelf, never to watch it. We have thus allowed the machine to watch
it for us, but conversely have not "missed out" on any aspect of our desire.
This inter-passivity is thus a way of appeasing the injunction to enjoy and
its concurrent anxiety without the need to actively pursue our desire.

Desirelessness takes this much further. The depressive, for
example, is so flooded with anxiety that she cannot perceive of any object-
related goals. The multiplicity of objects and the expectations thrust onto
the individual may become so overwhelming that the symbolic universe
becomes something to flee from. According to Zizek, notions of "the act"
and "action" are opposed – the act for him shakes the symbolic order,
activity by contrast fortifies its symbolic codes. The notion of the *act* is
therefore theorised as anti-symbolic, radical and disruptive in the sense
that action or activity cannot be.[19] As Sarah Kay suggests: "The Zizekian
act is a paroxysm that shakes the symbolic order; activity, by contrast,
consoles its users and fortifies its codes."[20] In this sense the definitive act
is that of suicide, or conversely a withdrawal from the symbolic order
through psychosis – both options offer an escapism that dissociates the
subject from the symbolic and the concurrent burden of desire and guilt:
"What releases us from this enslavement, Zizek contends, is the ethical act
which suspends the Oedipal law by reopening the abyss of psychosis
within it."[21] However, while the symbolic or oedipal law can be
suspended in this fashion, the subject thus affected remains either
stultified within a depressive position or conversely, may be classified as a
sociopath, unable to relate to others in any meaningful fashion. It is within
the space of literature that we can encounter figures who may be able to
live and function without desire.

4. Tom Ripley

Author Patricia Highsmith, from her first novel *Strangers on a Train* (1950) to her last, *Small g: a Summer Idyll* (1995), was always concerned with the levels of anxiety that the pressure to desire and concurrently to engage fully with the world, exerted on her protagonists. Something resembling an ontological blankness lies at the heart of her writing, a nothing underpins her tantalising plots and characterisations. Her work is classed as crime fiction, and it could be argued that it is exactly the looseness of the mystery genre that gives space for the expression of such a void: that the search for the criminal, their guilt or culpability, justice and retribution allow these texts to highlight the insubstantial and relative nature of truth and morality. While the criminal may be captured and punished, this is often merely a legalistic and *structural* victory for the Law or the good. It is in the character of Tom Ripley, her own favourite "hero," the multiple killer who nonetheless detests murder and whose exploits range over five novels, that Highsmith produces, in contrast to her other angst-ridden characters, a figure who can, happily, live and function without desire.

For Zizek, Ripley is an exemplar of what he terms normal psychosis:

> He is the ultimate psychotic, the best exemplification of what Lacan had in mind when he claimed that normality is the special form of psychosis – of not being traumatically caught up in the symbolic web, of retaining "freedom" from the symbolic order.[22]

Tom Ripley is Highsmith's amoral and desireless hero. His lack of engagement with other people on anything but a surface level is underpinned throughout the novels by an almost overwhelming anxiety, reflected in a concurrent level of discomfort for the reader. He exists precisely as a void, unfathomable and non-sexual. (Even though he marries, his sex life is instrumental and routine.) It can be argued that his distance from the subjective universe relates to his lack of integration into the symbolic order in the Lacanian sense:

> One way to read Ripley is as an angelic figure, living in a universe which as yet knows nothing of the Law or its transgression (sin), and thus nothing of the guilt generated by our obedience to the Law. This is why Ripley feels no remorse after his murders; he is not yet fully integrated into the Symbolic universe.[25]

Thus Ripley evades the strictures of the super-ego, remaining primarily within the visual, Imaginary realm. Throughout the novels, he utilises the structures of the symbolic without recourse to its defining, limiting and prohibitive functions. In other words, Ripley can *act* the reasonable, rational man, and in fact *be* all that this entails, yet be devoid of content in the form of guilt, emotion and desire. Thus he exists as a functioning individual who refuses (indeed cannot) enter into the flawed dialectic of sexual desire (and is very content without it). The Tom Ripley of Highsmith's novels is threatening precisely for this reason; although he kills when he feels he has no other option, it is his lack of subjective engagement rather than any murderous impulse that renders him so disturbing.

The construction of a "hero" who lacks conventional feelings of guilt, desire, and conscience is the central and defining feature of these novels, and may partially explain some readers concurrent fascination and resistance. Anthony Minghella, in his 2000 film adaptation of the first Ripley novel, *The Talented Mr. Ripley*, attempts to humanise Tom, but in doing so negates the power, the challenge, and destabilising effects of the character. According to Zizek, Minghella is defeated by Ripley's unfathomability: "Minghella's *Ripley* makes clear what's wrong with trying to be more radical than the original by bringing out its implicit but repressed content. By looking to fill in the void, Minghella actually retreats from it."[26] In the film, Minghella gives Ripley a repressed homosexuality, inventing an entirely new character for the purpose of drawing this out. At the same time he imbues Ripley with feelings of remorse for his murders. While Minghella believed that he was working against Hollywood norms by giving Tom a gay identity, he in fact shies away from the more subversive and dangerous representation of…precisely nothing.

When portrayed within literature, desire-less-ness (especially lack of sexual desire) is most clearly perceived when combined with a lack of conscience and humanity. Tom Ripley is the most challenging and dangerous literary portrayal of all, not because he kills but because he embodies a void, a lack of engagement, managing to live well and comfortably while holding the world, of others, of desire and of intersubjectivity, successfully at bay. This, perhaps, also helps explain the "difficulty" many readers have with Highsmith's work: not the substance of her texts but their peculiar insubstantiality, desire-less-ness as art.

Notes

1. Julia Kristeva, *Powers of Horror: An Essay on Abjection*, trans. Leon S.Roudiez (New York: Columbia University Press, 1982), 6, original emphasis.

2. Slavoj Zizek, *Looking Awry: An Introduction to Jacques Lacan Through Popular Culture* (Cambridge, MA: The MIT Press, 1991), 8.

3. Ibid., 6, original emphasis.

4. Paul Verhaeghe, *Love in a Time of Loneliness* (London: Rebus Press, 1999), 143.

5. J. Laplanche and J. B. Pontalis, *The Language of Psychoanalysis*, trans. Donald Nicholson-Smith (London: The Hogarth Press, 1985), 215, original emphasis.

6. Jacques Lacan, "On jouissance," in *Encore, the Seminar of Jacques Lacan, Book XX, On Feminine Sexuality, the Limits of Love and Knowledge, 1972-1973*, trans. Bruce Fink (New York: W.W. Norton and Company, 1999), 4.

7. See Suzanne Barnard, "Introduction," in Suzanne Barnard and Bruck Fink, eds., *Reading Seminar XX: Lacan's Major Work on Love, Knowledge and Feminine Sexuality* (Binghamton: State University of New York Press, 2002), 10.

8. Ibid., 11.

9. Ibid.

10. Ibid., 7.

11. Slavoj Zizek, "The Interpassive Subject," *The Symptom Online Journal* 3 (Autumn 2002), www.lacan.com, 6.

12. Jacques Lacan, *Ecrits*, trans. Alan Sheridan (London: Tavistock Publications, 1977), 37.

13. Paul Bowyer, *By the Bomb's Early Light: American Thought and Culture at the Dawning of the Atomic Age* (Chapel Hill: University of North Carolina Press, 1996), 350.

14. Kristeva, 22.

15. Ibid., 138.

16. Verhaeghe, 132.

17. Slavoj Zizek, *Enjoy Your Symptom! Jacques Lacan in Hollywood and Out* (New York: Routledge, 2001), 115, underline in original.

18. Sarah Kay, *Zizek: A Critical Introduction* (Cambridge: Polity, 2003), 80, underline in original.

19. In his essay "Why is Woman a Symptom of Man?" Zizek asks: "And what is the *act* if not the moment when the subject who is its bearer *suspends* the network of symbolic fictions which serve as a support to his daily life and confronts again the radical; negativity upon which they are founded." See Zizek, *Enjoy Your Symptom!*, 53, original emphasis.

20. Kay, 86.

21. Ibid., 111.

22. Slavoj Zizek, *The Fright of Real Tears: Krzystof Kieslowski Between Theory and Post-Theory* (London: British Film Institute, 2001),145.

25. Slavoj Zizek, "Not a Desire to Have Him but to be Like Him," Review of Andrew Wilson, *Beautiful Shadow: A Life of Patricia Highsmith, London Review of Books* 25.16 (21 August 2003), www.lrb.co.uk, 2.

26. Ibid., 4.

Select Bibliography

Barnard, Suzanne and Bruce Fink, eds. *Reading Seminar XX: Lacan's Major Work on Love, Knowledge and Feminine Sexuality.* Binghamton: State University of New York Press, 2002.

Bowyer, Paul. *By the Bomb's Early Light: American Thought and Culture at the Dawn of the Atomic Age.* Chapel Hill: University of North Carolina Press, 1996.

Kay, Sarah. *Zizek: A Critical Introduction.* Cambridge: Polity, 2003.

Kristeva, Julia. *Powers of Horror: An Essay on Abjection,* translated by Leon S.Roudiez. New York: Columbia University Press, 1982.

Lacan, Jacques. *Ecrits,* translated by Alan Sheridan. London: Tavistock Publications, 1977.

——. *Encore, the Seminar of Jacques Lacan, Book XX, On Feminine Sexuality, the Limits of Love and Knowledge,* translated by Bruce Fink. New York: W.W. Norton and Company, 1999.

Laplanche, J. and J. B. Pontalis. *The Language of Psychoanalysis,* translated by Donald Nicholson-Smith. London: The Hogarth Press, 1985.

Verhaeghe, Paul. *Love in a Time of Loneliness.* London: Rebus Press, 1999.

Zizek, Slavoj. *Looking Awry: An Introduction to Jacques Lacan through Popular Culture.* Cambridge, MA: The MIT Press, 1991.

——. *Enjoy Your Symptom! Jacques Lacan in Hollywood and Out.* New York: Routledge, 2001.

——. *The Fright of Real Tears: Krzystof Kieslowski Between Theory and Post-Theory.* London: British Film Institute, 2001.

——. "The Interpassive Subject." *The Symptom Online Journal* 3. (Autumn 2002). www.lacan.com.

——. "Not a Desire to Have Him but to be Like Him." Review of Andrew Wilson, *Beautiful Shadow: A Life of Patricia Highsmith. London Review of Books* 25.16 (21 August 2003). www.lrb.co.uk.

PART III

Bodies: Representations of Gender Identities

Underneath the Clothes – Transvestites without Vests: A Consideration in Art

Barbara Wagner

Abstract

This essay considers the problem of gender transgression by using examples of the art of the 1970s through 1990s. Thus, the point of interest is not cross-dressing but rather the performance of a corporeal identity that is wrongly understood as a contrary one. The chosen examples refer to the problem of assuming a gender identity reduced to the outward appearance. I would like to maintain the necessity of clearly defined boundaries for a "complete" gender transgression – as this is suggested by the hegemonic binary gender categories. Yet, such boundaries do not exist, as the artworks demonstrate. **Key Words:** cross-dressing, hegemonic binary gender model, gender identity, transgression.

1.   Introduction

Every day we meet people and classify them consciously or unconsciously into categories.[1] As the first of all categories we choose the determination of gender,[2] although the gendered body is hidden underneath clothes.[3]

Nevertheless, we assume that the assignment we have made is correct, even if we cannot examine the body and search for the existence of suitable genitals. We expect the congruence of appearance and presence or absence of the signifying genital, which is, according to Lacan, the phallus. So we make our decision for one of the two given possibilities of determination: male or female.

In this essay I would like to question what happens to the process of determination as soon as a gendered body is *undressed*. This situation seems to clarify the gender assignment because we are in the position to search for the presence or absence of the phallus directly. But what occurs to the classification if the body image transgresses the definite division of sexes within the hegemonic binary gender model? Is, then, the phallus still the signifier of the gender assignment? What kind of transgression is presented?

Contemporary art offers examples of gender performances that question the assumed congruence of outward appearance and "unmistakable" gender assignment bound up with the presentation of the body. As these examples will demonstrate, it makes no difference when and where they emerge from as cultural background.[4] The problem remains the same. In transvesting the given gendered body image, artists illustrate two problems of assignment within the hegemonic binarism: the determination of gender by the signifier and the lack of an appropriate designation of the presented body image.

2.   Vito Acconci – Conversion Without Changes

The first example I would like to look at is Vito Acconci's three-part film *Conversions* (1970-71), where he tries to achieve the most radical transformation of his personal identity by choosing another sex. Therefore, in the first part of the movie, he burns off his chest hair with the flame of a candle as a kind of auto-aggression against his male body of which he tries to get himself. He also pulls and forms his breast in order to attempt a female appearance. In the second sequence of the film, Acconci "removes" – as he has said[5] – his penis between his legs and walks, runs, and jumps – imitating everyday life actions, even though they are restricted, caused by the hidden penis in the third part of his performance. As another degree of comparison he denies the presence of his penis by putting the "removed" penis into the mouth of his partner, Katy Dillon. She moves behind him on her knees, trying to keep his penis in her mouth.

He demonstrates within these moving pictures the limited possibilities of performing transsexuality being presented by the body itself and how unconvincing this performance is. The breasts do not keep their artificially formed feminine appearance, nor can Acconci move with the hidden penis in an approximately "normal" way. Not even the assistance of his partner can obscure the fact that the body image presented is a constructed seemingly "natural" relation between gender identity and sexuality. Even though Acconci tries to "remove" his maleness by jamming the penis between his legs, he also forms his breasts – as the female substitute for the penis.[6]

This clumsy conversion of the body's appearance reminds one of the everyday problems of male-to-female-transsexuals living in the pre-operative stage of their conversion with a male body, with the existence of the signifier as "the absolute insignia of maleness."[7] Its presence "remembers" in every move they make that they have to live with the "false" body, and this limits their movements considerably.

Even on the level of reception, the hidden phallus remains "visible," caused by the unnatural movements of the performer. By "removing" or denying the penis in two of the three sequences of the film, the signifier remains the decisive attribute of the gender identity. The body of the artist *is* and *stays* male in his appearance and identity, since the artist is focusing on first and second gender assignments, while transforming his bodily gendered identity. The performed gender identity cannot fulfil the aimed at female body image. So the "conversion" has to fail as long as the penis is to be assumed.

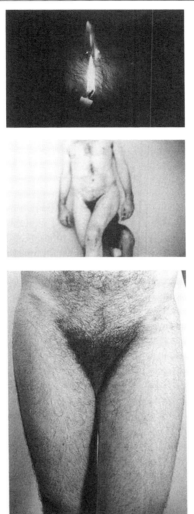

Figure 1: Acconci, Vito, *Conversions* (1971). Production Stills. ©Vito Acconci, 1971. Courtesy of Gladstone Gallery, New York.

Even during the third phase of transgression, when Katy Dillon tries to hide the penis in her mouth, the absence of the signifier is not given. On the contrary, this attempt to deny the existence of the male gender identifier is emphasising the "maleness" of the artist dominating as performer his assistant by forcing her to follow on her knees.

The performer is getting more and more sexualised within the three parts as a contradiction to the intended "conversion." The more Vito Acconci tries to attempt a female outward appearance, the more he is emphasising his male gender role. Being reminded of the threatened loss of the penis by the restricted movements of the body, the performer concentrates on his signifying gender assignment. He, as an artist, calls this process a "conversion" and never speaks of a transgression – a step beyond gender identity. His body remains the same. Nevertheless, the conversion of the bodily gender identity seems to be impossible without the assistance of Vito Acconci's female partner.

This kind of performance does not lead to an "opposite" body image presenting a female gender identity. What is shown is an artificial construction of a gender assignment, concentrating on the *surface*, on the *appearance* of the body.

3.   Lynda Benglis – Pin Up the Phallus

This phenomenon is comparable to the photographic performance Lynda Benglis created as an advertisement in the November issue of the magazine *Artforum* in 1974 – initially to be printed as a centrefold, imitating the presentation of pinup girls in magazines like *Playboy*. There she also cannot deny the identity of her gendered body. Her outward appearance, the bronzed and oiled and therefore fetishised body, is to be identified as obviously "female" – due to the absence of the penis. And this signifier she appropriates to herself by presenting a huge dildo. But Lynda Benglis furthermore imitates in her transvestive performance the affected macho-like male posture: she spreads her legs and fingers; she raises the left shoulder and opens her mouth.

As the photography is taken from a perspective slightly from below, Lynda Benglis as performer is looking down at the viewer, maintaining her self-consciousness and power, gained by the appropriated phallus. By doing so, she manages to direct the view of the onlooker to the phallus, who now is the centred item in the reception, as he is finally the one who categorises the gender-identity. Actually, Lynda Benglis reduces the distinctive mark of gender assignment in her photographic performance to a dummy, made of plastic. She usurps a for females not conceded power by using the dildo as substitute for the signifier in order to "complete" her body image, which cannot show the presence of the signifier by itself. This assumed power she emphasises in a simulated self-conscious posture.[8]

Due to this presentation – phallus and posture – the performed image of the gendered body should be categorised as a male one. But the way she performs this "other" gender identity is too obvious in order to obscure the fact of the basically given gender identity. Even the often attributed "androgynous" appearance cannot be confirmed. By using this provocative posture Lynda Benglis demonstrates the artificial and constructed way of identifying genders by focusing on the signifier. So, in this subversive act, it is evident how easily the sign can be replaced. This also provokes castration anxieties. Furthermore, she insinuates the contemporary discussion of power and powerlessness within a binaristic gender framework: By using an oversized and double-headed dildo she points out the two directions of power and powerlessness. One end of the dildo seemingly comes out of her body in an erect phase – the stage imminent before penetration and therefore the time of subjugating the woman. This visualises at the same time the situation of powerlessness from the perspective of the penetrated woman.

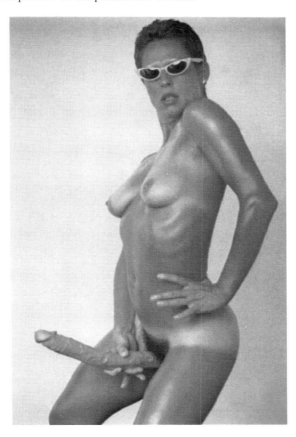

Figure 2: Benglis, Lynda, Advertisement, *Artforum* (November 1974). © Lynda Benglis, 2005. Courtesy of Cheim & Read, New York.

The other end of the dildo, ending at Lynda Benglis' vagina, leads the outward signifier of male power into her body. Yet, it is not only the erected penis pressing her into this decidedly female gender role. The predominance of the male gaze reflected within this photographic performance – published in a magazine – also makes her being turned over wholly on the power represented by "being" the phallus in terms of Lacanian theory. Following this direction, the distribution of power is now contradictory. She is the powerless one to be penetrated and to be punished for her acting.

Lynda Benglis reflects contemporary gendered, sexist problems that she noticed in media during the Nixon administration.[9] She performs the specific way in which this problem is gendered and therefore a specific topic for the Women's Liberation Movement during the early 1970s: concerning the image of woman in mass media, the sexual liberation movement, and the new gender role to be practiced. The unbecoming appropriation of the phallus as the sign of power cannot cancel out the female identity but also emphasises the inferior position as a woman, still linked with the pre-dominance of Sigmund Freud's theories of the penis as the signifier of patriarchal power. These are the reasons why the attribution "androgynous" as an expression of sexual equality functions so paradoxically.[10]

4.   Yasumasa Morimura – Focused Desire

Such an ascription applies even more so to the photographic performance *Fugato* of Yasumasa Morimura, as soon as he makes up his body, wears a wig and imitates with his masqueraded body the role of a certain woman in his photographic performance from 1988. The evidently feminine face contrasts with the male figure of the body. Morimura imitates Eduard Manet's 1863 painted portrait of *Olympia* in the position of the body and the way the portrayed woman is looking at the onlooker. He predetermines the frame of reception: his left hand covers the region of his body where the sex of the undressed body is usually identified. He is holding a corner of the coverlet in his right hand, framing the signified area of the body, to be continued by the outstretched right leg. Furthermore, the proportions of the spaces in the picture, being separated by the masquerading hand, follow approximately the idea of the Golden Cut. Another very important tool is the frame of the paravent in the background behind the artist. The red-golden lustrous border ends as a straight vertical exactly above the region of the body, where the signifier is to be estimated. This could be read as an erect penis as well.

Figure 3: Morimura, Yasumasa, *Portrait (Futago)* (1988). Colour photograph with brushed on varnish, 82 2/4 x 118 in. (92.108.A-D). Carnegie Museum of Art, Pittsburgh; A. W. Mellon Acquisition Endowment Fund.

Paraphrasing Manet's *Olympia*, Morimura ostensibly takes a decided female gender role as a servant of sexual desire. But the way the desired body is presented deviates from the traditional scheme of the balance of power between subject and object, model and onlooker. It is not the naked model who is subjugated under the view of the desiring onlooker. Her view out of the image – provided that Olympia *is* female – resists the subjugation. Her self-consciousness represents her power over sexual desires, which cannot be fulfilled. She is the one, leaving the corset of gender roles. "She is the masculine of 'masculinised'; she is 'boyish,' aggressive, or androgynous."[11] It is not the hand as a mask, questioning the sex of the body. Morimura emphasises in one aspect the bodily assignments. But he also takes the impression of the view into consideration: The subject becomes object and furthermore realises his new role as being observed by his own desires, refused by the desired body, since Olympia ignores the offered flowers from her suitor, presented by her servant – another role that Morimura undertakes within this performance.

The subliminal association of the phallus as an initially neutral, distinctive mark and the penis as an organ excludes the female gender identity from a positive self-definition, since that identity is marked by the absence of the sign. What the artist presents in his performance remains the male gaze on an "incomplete" female body image. By doing so, imitating a decidedly feminine model in combination with emphasising the existence of the hidden phallus, the ascription as "androgynous – effeminised" gender-identity has to be questioned.

Morimura's construction of an ostensibly female body image, trying to represent a female gender identity, is and stays a male attempt from the outside. His performance neither offers a female identity that is convincing (in terms of perception) nor offers a male identity, represented by the power of the performer and the performed identity. His gender construction, furthermore, presents in no way an androgynous ideal, since within the performance the balance of power between the two given gender identities does not exist.

So, his performance visualises a deviation from the "pure" difference as a binary construction of gender assignment, because there is no appropriate designation for the transgressive body image, offered as the object of the gaze. Yasumasa Morimura presents his body image without any gendered relation and forces the viewer to consider his culturally pre-determined perspective of perception in categorising body images into one of the two "given" gender identities. Even though the artist visualises not only a transgression of gender but also of culture, the question of percepting a gendered body image is still the same. There seems to be a "pure" difference, distinguishing female from male identity and using the penis – identifying the penis with the phallus – as signifier in Japanese culture as well as in European and North American reception. This goes along with Jacques Lacan's division of "having a signifier" or "being the signifier," separating male and female categories.

It still remains a transvesting, a masquerading in the sense of superficiality, even though Manet and Morimura demonstrate a kind of mirror, enabling the viewer to discover his own desire by looking at the undressed body of a prostitute.

5.   Matthew Barney – Three are One Sex
In contrast, Matthew Barney presents in *CREMASTER 4* (1994) – a movie series in five parts, where the subject is the descending of the testicles in different phases – a multiple copy of the perfectly made and embodied imagination of androgyny represented by three models. These fairies do not seem to be humans at all with bodies bearing sex characteristics and navels. They are rather myths, representing the "perfect" androgyny. Matthew Barney masks the bodies of the actors, that is, masks several body parts, where a specific gender identity could be determined. This "neutralisation" of the appearance continues in the shape

of the bodies: He chose models whose bodies were formed by bodybuilding in a literal sense, so they lose their sexual identity on first view.

On the level of narrative these three fairies fulfil a mediating and an assisting role. The fairies take both female *and* male gender roles. They mediate between two storylines within the movie and they assist male actors in order to enable them to obtain their gender identity. The fairies themselves are changing their roles in every sequence in which they take part.

Figure 4: Barney, Matthew, *CREMASTER 4: FAERIE FIELD* (1994). Production still. ©Matthew Barney, 1994. Photo: Michael James O'Brien. Courtesy of Gladstone Gallery, New York.

Within this seemingly absolute balance of gender determination the protagonists represent the centre of the five parts of the CREMASTER-cycle. The eccentric arrangement of the "neutrality" within the number of five movies, where a symmetrical split is possible, is comparable to the use of space Morimura presented for his photographic performance, using the Golden Cut.

Therefore the three fairies represent in their bodily appearance the symmetrically arranged construction of balance: Even though the bodies are partly masked, not only the presence of the signifier settles the gender-identity, but also the appearance of the bodies itself. Matthew Barney takes three different types of models to represent three kinds of gender identity.

Type 1 is rather female, which is indicated by two knots on the top of the wig – the testicles are ascended. Also, the physiognomy is seemingly more female. Type 2 appears more androgynous and has therefore four knots as a sign of balance. The face of the protagonist is "sexless." Type 3 seems to be rather male, shown by the two knots on the bottom of the wig, like descended testicles. Here the appearance of the actor ostensibly is harsh and male.

Since Matthew Barney denies the view of the signifier by masking, he leads the search for criteria to an inward sign, but doesn't give any help for reception, where to look for it. He still is bound up with the anatomical idea,[12] and so with succeeding in representing the "neutralisation" of the bodies by eliminating the signs of gender assignment, restricted to the binarism. He causes confusion for the reception of these body images and provokes the creation of new definitions in order to categorise the gender identity of the fairies. Some of the classifications are as follows: "sexless," "androgynous," "ambisexual," "ambigendered," "perverse," "completely androgynous." Indeed, the three actresses cannot obscure their gender identity: the make-up and the accessories indicate the female identity, don't they? Actually, within this movie there is one sequence offering the "correct" ascription of the fairies' gender identity: All three enjoy a picnic all alone. They don't have to fulfil any assigned gender role. Dressed in baroque-like dresses the three "ladies" are sitting in the green, having fun, playing ball – or is that playing with balls?! But how can we be sure that these ladies *really* are ladies? Never look under a lady's skirt! The voyeurs won't find what they are looking for. Everything is well hidden underneath a mask. And this mask is nothing other than our everyday appearance – the clothes. Even underneath the clothes there is no truth, since our behaviour and our gender performance characterise the gender-assignment as well. The fairies rather represent the importance of our roles in everyday life than only two possible gender identities. The identity is more than the presence or absence of the phallus as signifier.

6.   Conclusion

All four examples always choose the gendered body as a medium for two gender assignments that have to be differentiated: the original body of the performer *and* the other body image that is to be achieved. In order to determine the particular performed gender identity we take a look at the undressed body. Here, the presence of the phallus as a signifier seems to enable us to categorise the body definitely to one of the two defined gender-assignments given by the hegemonial binarism. So we assume a "pure" difference between the varied gendered bodies: The presence of the signifier and the absence as oppositional binarism lead to a value of the determinating sign which threatens to lose the balance between the two given gender assignments. The subliminal association of the phallus as signifier and the penis as an organ exclude the female gender identity from a positive self-definition and therefore over-emphasises the "patriarchal symbolic order."[13]

At the same time, this binarism is representing a frame for a difference that we cannot perceive because the signifier is hidden underneath the clothes. But we perceive images of gendered bodies in everyday life that tell us if there *is* the signifier or if the image as "no-image" *is* itself the signifier[14] – by following Jacques Lacan's division of "having a signifier" or "being the signifier" in order to distinguish the two sexes.

Thus, the given examples should have made clear that it is still the phallus that is defining the gender of the body, even when "another" sex is presented. The deviation from the "pure" difference as a binary construction of gender assignment is questioning not only the value of the signifier as a determinating sign.

It also visualises the problem of giving the presented image an appropriate designation with regard to gender identity: The evasive use of the prefix "trans" cannot solve this problem as long as the original body is still gendered, predetermined, and an unchangeable medium – not even surgery may completely change a body's origin!

Proceeding on the assumption that using the prefix "trans" means a transgression, this also means there is something like an unmistakable boundary in the context of gender identity.[15] To transgress these boundaries then means: leaving the territory, leaving the original gender identity completely. But none of these premises are fulfilled: neither in the artworks where we still see the original body image, even though it is masked and the signifiers were hidden respectively presented, as in the case of Lynda Benglis. Nor does the performance of transsexuality lead to the result that should be achieved.[16]

The various possibilities of "being in-between," of being in a "nowhere-land" in art *and* life breach the hegemonial binarism of gender assignment. Furthermore the possibilities question the valorising status of the phallus as a signifier of the gender assignment practice that is still predominant in our society, since his presence is emphasised even though well hidden.

Notes

1. Maren Lorenz, *Leibhaftige Vergangenheit. Einführung in die Körpergeschichte* (Tübingen: Edition diskord, 2000), 25.

2. Suzanne J. Kessler and Wendy McKenna, *Gender: An Ethnomethodological Approach* (New York: John Wiley and Sons, 1978), 2.

3. Carol Hagemann-White, "Wir werden nicht zweigeschlechtlich geboren," in *Dis/Kontinuitäten: Feministische Theorie*, ed. Hark Sabine (Opladen: Leske & Budrich, 2001), 31.

4. Vito Acconci is an American artist, like Lynda Benglis and Matthew Barney. Yasumasa Morimura lives and works in Tokyo, Japan.

5. Quoted in Amelia Jones, "Dis/playing the Phallus: Male Artists Perform their Masculinities," in *Art History* 17.4 (December 1994), 565.

6. Felix Boehm, "Über den Weiblichkeitskomplex des Mannes," in *Schriften zur Psychoanalyse*, ed. Deutsche Psychoanalytische Gesellschaft (München: Oehlschlaeger 1978), 8.

7. Robert Stoller, *Sex and Gender*, Vol. 1 (New York: Science House, 1968), 186.

8. Leslie C. Jones, "Transgressive Femininity: Art and Gender in the Sixties and Seventies," in *Abject Art. Repulsion and Desire in American Art, Selections from the Permanent Collection, Whitney Museum of American Art, New York* (New York: Whitney Museum of American Art, 1993), 53.

9. Sandra Ballamore, "Lynda Benglis' Humanism," *Artweek* 7.21 (May 1976), 6. It was "to mock the idea of having to take sexual sides – to be either male or female… Also I was mocking the media. It was a very Nixonian time; the media was very much in question."

10. For reactions to the performance, see Leslie C. Jones, 52.

11. Timothy J. Clark, *The Painting of Modern Life. Paris in the Art of Manet and his Followers* (Princeton: Princeton University Press, 1986), 132.

12. Matthew Barney describes this circumstance as the relationship between an athlete and his body. See the interview Amine Haase,"Vom ausstieg und vom Abfall. Oder: Wie das Innere nach außen gekehrt werden kann," *Kunstforum International* 162 (November-December 2002), 327.

13. Elizabeth Grosz, *Jacques Lacan. A Feminist Introduction* (London, New York: Routledge, 1990), 116.

14. Claudia Reiche, "Cyberfeminismus, was soll das sein? " in *Gender Revisted*, eds. Katharina Baisch et al. (Stuttgart, Weimar: Metzler 2002), 182f.

15. Gesa Lindemann, Geschlecht und Gestalt. "Der Körper als konventionelles Zeichen der Geschlechterdifferenz, " in *Auge und Affekt. Wahrnehmung und Interaktion,* ed. Koch Gertrud (Frankfurt a. M.: Fischer-Taschenbuch-Verlag., 1995), 87.

16. Susanne Schröter, *FeMale. Über Grenzverläufe zwischen den Geschlechtern* (Frankfurt a. M.: Fischer-Taschenbuch-Verlag, 2002), 213.

Select Bibliography

Ballamore, Sandra. "Lynda Benglis' Humanism." *Artweek* 7.21 (May 1976): 5-6.

Boehm, Felix. "Über den Weiblichkeitskomplex des Mannes." In *Schriften zur Psychoanalyse,* edited by Deutsche Psychoanalytische Gesellschaft, 80-99. München: Oehlschlaeger, 1978.

Clark, Timothy J. *The Painting of Modern Life. Paris in the Art of Manet and his Followers.* Princeton: Princeton University Press, 1986.

Garber, Marjorie. *Vested Interests: Cross-Dressing and Cultural Anxiety.* New York: Penguin Books, 1992.

Grosz, Elizabeth. *Jacques Lacan. A Feminist Introduction.* London, New York: Routledge, 1990.

Haase, Amine. "Vom ausstieg und vom Abfall. Oder: Wie das Innere nach außen gekehrt werden kann." *Kunstforum International,* 162 (November-December 2002): 326-329.

Hagemann-White, Carol. "Wir werden nicht zweigeschlechtlich geboren." In *Dis/Kontinuitäten: Feministische Theorie,* edited by Hark Sabine, 24-34. Opladen: Leske & Budrich, 2001.

Hirschauer, Stefan. *Die soziale Konstruktion der Transsexualität.Über die Medizin und den Geschlechterwechsel.* Frankfurt a. M.: Suhrkamp, 1993).

Jones, Amelia. "Dis/playing the Phallus: Male Artists Perform their Masculinities." *Art History* 17. 4 (December 1994): 546-584.

Jones, Leslie C. "Transgressive Feminininty: Art and Gender in the Sixties and Seventies." In *Abject Art. Repulsion and Desire in American Art. Selections from the Permanent Collection, Whitney Museum of American Art,* 33-58. New York: Whitney Museum of American Art, 1993.

Kessler, Suzanne J. and Wendy McKenna, *Gender: An Ethnomethodological Approach.* New York: John Wiley and Sons, 1978.

Lindemann, Gesa. "Geschlecht und Gestalt. Der Körper als konventionelles Zeichen der Geschlechterdifferenz." In *Auge und*

Affekt. Wahrnehmung und Interaktion, edited by Gertrud Koch, 75-92. Frankfurt a. M.: Fischer-Taschenbuch-Verlag, 1995.

Lorenz, Maren. *Leibhaftige Vergangenheit. Einführung in die Körpergeschichte*. Tübingen: Edition diskord, 2000.

Reiche, Claudia. "Cyberfeminismus, was soll das sein?" In *Gender Revisted*, edited by Katharina Baisch et al., 173-187. Stuttgart, Weimar: Metzler, 2002.

Schröter, Susanne. *FeMale. Über Grenzverläufe zwischen den Geschlechtern*. Frankfurt a. M.: Fischer-Taschenbuch-Verlag, 2002.

Stoller, Robert. *Sex and Gender*, Vol. 1. New York: Science House, 1968.

Of Swords and Rings:
Genital Representation as Defining Sexual Identity and Sexual Liberation in Some Old French *Fabliaux* and *Lais*

Tovi Bibring

Abstract
This paper explores, in a restricted inventory of lais and fabliaux, what some specific representations of lower body parts teach us about the way medieval people conceptualised their sexuality. In a first step we shall examine chosen metaphors referring to genitalia and how they are related to gender expectations. We shall then see how genitals are taught and learned within the context of first sexual experiences. Finally, we shall ask what place they have in constructing sexual identity and in contributing to a new sensibility of sexual liberation. **Key Words:** phallic symbols, feminine orifices, gender, sexual identity, potency, sex.

1.   Introduction

The crude language of the Old French fabliaux and the elaborated metaphors of the Old French narrative lais are two different forms with one common aspiration: to find sexual identity and sexual liberation through the description of the wonders of the intimate body. When in the fabliaux vaginas are not referred to by the word *con* (cunt), they are described, in explicit graphical language, as a kind of hole or entrance. The oft-mentioned *vit* (prick) can then be compared to someone or something intruding into this hole.[1] In the lais, implicit metaphorical language designates the same organs sometimes by the same metaphors (rings, fountains, doors, swords, horses) but in a more refined way, in line with courtly dictates.

During the past twenty years major studies have treated the genital question of the fabliaux.[2] Philippe Ménard, Charles Muscatine, and R. Howard Bloch focus on linguistic levels and procedures in the persistent description of genitalia.[3] Sarah Melhado White's *Sexual Language and Human Conflict in Old French Fabliaux* draws parallels between economic shortage and sexual frustration and considers gender issues such as the misogynistic representation of the vagina as a dirty, inferior genital. John Baldwin's *The Language of Sex* proclaims that the evocation of sexual parts is intended to defy the courtly, and the theological sexual discourses. In *Gender and Genre in Medieval French Literature*, Simon Gaunt offers a *constructionist* reading of genitalia (gender can be manipulated) instead of an *essentialist* one (biological differences define gender).

Genitals per se are referred to less often in studies of Old French romances and narrative lais.[4] Those stories, as Baldwin affirms, conceal the body under the clothes.[5] Rare and exceptional are the cases when genitals are explicitly named. Erotic narration of nudity merely consists of female breasts, skin, tights, neck; it is taboo when dealing with the male body. It is through symbolical discourse that we can detect genitals' representation in the courtly vernacular genres.

My aim in the present paper is to read the narration of genitalia both in lais and fabliaux, and to trace their roles in the understanding of the self as a sexual entity. The sexual organs sometimes receive the stereotypes attributed to gender expectations. Men who possess testicles attached to their penises are authoritarian and dominating. Aroused moist vaginas correspond to the moist humour of women who have no spine and are emotional, tearful, and indiscrete. Submissive towards men, they can be ordered to speak; they are traversed and penetrated by the rude overbearing penises, and their sexual appetite is insatiable. In some other cases genitals are shaped by the forms of characters' sexual fantasies. I shall examine closely the meaning of such perceptions of sexuality.

2.   Swords, Rings, and Some Other Physical Miracles

Reserved to men, valorised by their hardness, length, and sharpness, pulled out of a sheath hanging from the haunches and returned thereto, *Swords*, (or for that matter arrows, lances, or knives) become a banal, cross-cultural phallic symbol. Any weapon is manipulated by the *Hand* which in itself registers as phallic, as a result of its illustrative physics and of the use of the same verbs such as "to take," "to extend," or "to beat" (in the fabliaux the sexual act is often described as the penis beating the vagina), which it shares with the "third hand." Swords and hands are also associated with manly authority since they are used to produce symbolical gestures during official, religious, and social ceremonies led and directed by men. The weaponry lesson in the *Lai de Tyolet* consists of questions asked by Tyolet about armory and answered by the guiding knight.[6] Overwhelmed by the hard and sharp sword and the long lance, Tyolet starts his adult life. Instead of whistling, he is ready to kill with a sword; therefore he is ready to become a man by taking the hand of the princess of Logers.

But taking a woman's hand, that is, marrying her and being sexually united with her is different from taking a woman "by the hand" when "hand" subsumes the man's virile exploits. A woman taken "by the hand" is led to become the man's carnal possession. When she is taken by the right (positive) hand, it means that she consents and even desires. Being taken by the left signifies that she is being forced. When Graalent in the lai of the same name is about to rape the fairy, he takes her "par la main senestre." Desiré, the hero of a lai of his own, requests and grants the fairy's love and takes her "par la mein destre." In the *Lai de Tydorel*, the narrator mentions that the queen was taken by the left hand, whereas the queen herself insists it was done by the right hand. In both versions there is no doubt that the lover's gesture of grabbing by the hand, prefigures the sexual act, that is to say, the penis's act.

In the fabliaux some erections are described as a raising of the hand, but what is of most interest for us is the change of gender perception, when the female characters use their hands. In Jean Bodel's *Le Sohait des vez,* a woman concludes a deal by pulling her hand towards a merchant in her dream of a prick market. She buys "a prick with a prick," or at least a metaphor for one. On this occasion her hand slaps and awakens her husband who forgot his matrimonial duty earlier that evening. Not only does she replace his penis with the one she acquires, she is also *beating him* with *her* hand. And this goes even further. When the intrigued husband hears about his wife's dream he puts his penis in her hand, to see if it might be worth anything. This is a complete reversal of sexual roles: it is no longer a woman who submits her body to a man but the man who submits his organ to the woman's authority.

Another fabliau woman who leads her husband by the hand towards her sexuality is the one from *La Sorisete des Estopes*. An ignorant virgin peasant believes that a vagina is a mouse. When he explains to his wife that the mouse ran away, she reassures him that it came back home. She then takes him by the hand and teaches him how to caress the mouse in order not to scare it in the future. As women who are taken by the hand discover the robust nature of penises, this peasant discovers the muddiness of the vagina. In this piece the hand takes on its phallic significance by showing the woman's superiority, in actions and in mind, over her husband.

Though unaware of Freud's notion of the *vagina dentata*, the peasant and the fableor represent a misogynistic concept of femininity (the vagina as a teethed, harmful animal). Nevertheless it is hard for me to see in this fabliau merely a "conventional message: women are devils," as White concludes.[7] The text obviously is not pro-feminine: the woman fornicates with the priest; her mother conspires with her; the female sexual appetite is never satisfied (the wife has sex both with her husband and the priest on the same day). Still, each spouse made an effort to approach the other. The peasant was ready to go and get his wife's vagina. On his way he even tried to learn about it. The wife did accept the intimacy with him. She did take it upon herself to reassure him, even though she could have easily continued her manipulation.

Horses in the courtly pantheon are loyal animals, signs – identifying signifiers – of knightly social status and position.[8] Just like sexuality, they can be domesticated or undomesticated, and when domesticated they can be tied up or out on the loose. Indeed, when Marie de France's Lanval or the anonymous Graalent set their horses free to eat, they meet the seductive fairy. Whether Lanval is invited to her bed, Graalent rapes her, but the pattern here is clear. Whenever the horse is freed, uncontrolled, momentarily forgotten, another horse propels his body into action. In many cases the girl will be discovered washing in the river. The male looses his horse, and the female gets wet. In the fabliau *La Damoisele qui ne pooit oïr parler de foutre*, David identifies his "so stiff and hard, that it can pierce a wall" penis with a pony. When he complains about its thirst, the girl invites it to drink from her fountain. "My horse is hungry, can you feed it?" clearly means "my penis is hard, is your vagina moist?" [9]

Li lais de l'espine tells the story of a forbidden love between the king's only son and his stepmother's daughter. Discovered in each other's arms and bodies, they are separated. When the young boy embarks on a dangerous adventure, his beloved awakes from a dream in a forest under a prickly bush. She recognises him as the man that approaches her and watches him fight a mysterious knight. When he triumphs, he is awarded with a magical horse that never has to eat provided that he is tied. After overcoming two other knights, the boy takes his stepsister and marries her. The emblem of the horse is an attempt by the narrator to permit those two lovers to marry. The horse staying tied and fasting means that no sexual activity is permitted. Food, we will see throughout our study, is compensation for sex. The only way those two lovers can be together is if their love can be fraternal, political maybe, but not sexual. However, platonic marriages cannot last forever, especially when the spouses are in love. The queen releases the horse. That is the final note of the lai. The discontinued sexual love is now possible, the horse is untied. [10]

Appealing to and essentially reserved for men, inhabited by marvelous female creatures, the *Forest* metaphorises the female body. It is a common place for adventures to happen in courtly literature and consists of two spaces. [11] The outer zone – near the castle – is where aristocrats, accompanied by their circle of favourites and servants, go hunting, one of their preferred leisure activities. The inner zone is kept for a young knight unaccompanied, where supernatural adventures occur, mostly in the form of meeting a fairy and hunting a magical white animal. [12] The second zone is to be read, from our perspective, as a passage leading to female sexuality. As one penetrates deeper into the forest, one gets closer to the sexual opportunity. In the lays *Desiré*, *Graalent*, *Guingamor*, and *Lanval*, the physical relationships are entered into within the forest's depths. The marvelous fairies are incarnations of male sexual fantasies. Described as young, inexperienced maidens, the *puceles* execute all that which a man desires, providing him with wealth, bravery, and sexual partnership.

The anonymous writer of the *Lay del Trot*, inspired by André le Chapelain's allegorical story about the four-doors-assimilated-into-vaginas palace, trims it into an episode that takes place in a forest. Lorois embarks there in the first place because he wants to hear the singing of the nightingale, an allusion to a sexual quest. He comes upon two parades of women. The first consists of those who are peacefully carried by their rich horses and accompanied by the men they love the most. They are followed by unaccompanied women riding in a trot. The first are the women who during their lives served Amor; the latter are the ones who did not. They are doomed to an eternity of "trot" – not one moment of rest. Once again riding is associated with copulating, and horses with penises. In that spirit, the moral is provided by a proverb explaining, "he who shuts his stables will lose his horse, which will depress him." Like André's *De Amor*, this text reflects that society is constructed on the assumption that the orifice in the women's body was created to be filled.[13] Women who keep their bodies closed to men should be warned. On judgment day they will be sentenced like heretics and criminals. Women who prefer to be unvisited, to define their individuality apart from men, misread their destination: if they won't serve men, they will go to hell; that means they have no place in male shaped society.

Rings symbolise the bond of fidelity and loyalty when given by a lord to his vassal or by a man to his bride. But, when the ring is given by a woman to her lover, it alludes to the giving of her vagina to him. The troubadour Guilleum de Poitier says that he received "her loving and her ring." The inscription on the ring of Sister of Pleasure from the courtly tale *Frayre de Joy e Sor de Plaser* indicates: "I am the ring of Sister of Pleasure, the one who has me, will have her."[14] The only way Guingamor from the lai by the same name can see his lady friend is if he does not lose the ring she gave him. With the ring in his possession, he can see her, laugh with her, and lie with her.

In the fabliau *L'Anel qui faisoit les vets grans et roides*, attributed to Haiseau, the enchanted ring is removed from the finger of the beholder. The man who takes off his ring can no longer have his prick big and stiff, until the clergyman who finds it and is subjected to mockery returns it to him. This fabliau concentrates on the physical aspects of manhood and does not concern any particular female character. The man who lost the ring cannot perform, either with his wife or with other partners. The ring stands in for the vagina. Vaginas in the heterosexual "real" life make this kind of effect on men; enchanted rings are only the signifiers. Whether the man is married (having the cleric around makes us believe this is not impossible) or not, in a symbolic way the loss of the ring indicates an

adulterous liaison. In typical tales we read about specific wives who
fornicate with their local priests. The morality is the same: when one
leaves his ring(woman) unguarded, someone else sees and seizes it
immediately. If he is discovered, he is chased away (or, when he is a
fabliau priest, he is castrated, beaten, or killed), and the owner regains
possession of the ring.

The discussion about being reduced to only genitals is not
reserved strictly for women. Dismembered men, or men with soft
members, are also useless to women. Simon Gaunt points out correctly
that in fabliaux where men are thought to be without solid genitals or any
genitals at all, they are "portrayed as replaceable, expendable, or
unnecessary."[15] Worthless otherwise, they exist merely to provide services
using their "tool." This question is also the subject of several courtly tales
and judgments. Should a woman whose lover's virility was mutilated stay
with him or leave him? Marie de France consecrates the lai *Chaitivel* to
that question. Other male lovers in the lais' tradition embody female
sexual desires. Similarly to the fairies, they appear as marvelous creatures
and present themselves to sexually frustrated wives as does Marie de
France's Muldumarec in *Yonec*, or the knight in *Tydorel*, which we will
examine subsequently.

Whether men look at women as metonymies for their vagina or,
vice versa, women see men as penises, the substitution is not in itself
degrading. Metonymy here shows that, at all times, people understand
themselves as sexual entities and aspire to legitimate sex as part of their
existence. In that game, a woman without a vagina and a man without a
penis are indeed useless. We can argue whether it is decent, moral, or
appropriate to look for nothing but sex, but in such discourse it is
admissible to search for a mate that can provide you with it. Tales whose
subject is the sexual desire of men and of women, and which are not about
raping or manipulating but about mutual consent, have to understand men
and women as bearers of genitals.

3.   Private(?) Lessons in Sexual Identity

The first step to obtaining a sexual identity is the study of the
other's mature and different sexual organ. It is an initiation for sexual
experience. Both the virgin married man in Gautier Le Leu's *Le Sot
chevalier* and the about-to-lose-her-virginity girl in *L'esquiriel* learn about
the other sex organs in order to be able to function sexually. The first one,
a virgin married man who has never seen a vagina before, gets an
anatomical lesson from his mother-in-law. The mother-in-law embodies
here the role of the helping fabulous fairy from the marvelous courtly
tales. Instead of being a young, mysterious, and spiritual advisor, she is
old, exposed, and has down-to-earth advice. Her lesson is very simple and

based on observation. She exposes her body and asks the knight what he sees. The latter describes the feminine miracles as two holes, the higher one: "is longer than it is wide/ – and what about the one alongside?/ – Madame, shorter, that is my sense/ – beware of introducing your prick there. Hence,/it was not made for that act/ to put in one's prick is a big misconduct."[16] There is an ambiguity concerning the knight's heterosexual identity. He has never seen or touched a female body; he has to be warned of the anus; and while repeating out loud the instruction to only "fuck the longer one," he is overheard by his guests. *Hole* in French comes in the masculine form; the guests understand that their host wants to "fuck" the tallest of them. Because of all that, he is the Silly Knight, but is he so silly to actually desire men? The fableor gradually inserts the same-sex elements, but he does not cross over the taboos of the medieval discourse about man's love. All obscurity is lifted, the knight satisfies his wife's longer hole, and by means of a comical twist the guests escape.

His heterosexual "infantile discovery and socialisation[17]" consists of the recognition that one, sexuality is anatomical and technical, and two, it isn't discrete or intimate. Nevertheless, in his ignorant way he turns the natural sexual activity into a *learned* material, he adopts a sexual identity.

E. Jane Burns comments, "it is significant that the unknowing knight's instruction comes from a woman speaking to ensure another woman's pleasure."[18] Unlike this mother or the one in the *Sorisete*, the alliance between mothers and daughters, isn't always the case. Some mothers try to prevent their daughters from any illicit sexual activity – such mothers as the queen from *Espine* and the one from the fabliau *L'esquiriel*

The young girl's sexual education in *L'esquiriel* consists of noticing the specific manly organ only to take the required distance from it, as the mother teaches: "Above all things, pay attention /That thing you must not ever mention/That men carry hanging."[19] But the instruction comes too late. The girl is already preoccupied by this marvelous pendulum, and she insists on receiving the following forbidden information: "Mother, she says, tell me now /What is its name and how/Shut up daughter, to say I dare not/Is that the thing my sire HAS got ?/That in between his legs is pendent."[20] After tiring her mother this way, she finally learns the name of that *thing*, and she indulges herself by repeating the word *prick* over and over again:

> Prick, she says, praise the lord, prick! Prick I'll say
> throughout the entire day today. /Prick, alas! Prick says
> my father/Prick says my sister, prick says my brother
> /And prick says our nanny /And prick at every nook, and
> prick at every cranny /Prick say everybody as much as

> they desire, /Even yourself, for sure, my mother /you say
> prick. And me, silly unfortunate, /would I do otherwise
> and prick won't articulate?[21]

By acting in spite of her mother's wishes, the teenage rebellious girl
defines herself as a sexual entity naturally aware of and intrigued by the
differences between the sexes. If women, and especially young unmarried
girls, are not supposed to say such words, it does not mean that they are
not sexually aroused. If we follow the mother's logic that forbidding the
word forbids the act, by being brave enough to pronounce the forbidden
word, the girl is soon to be ready to pass to the act.

The next step of her sexual investigation is to fulfill her curiosity
as the potential behind the word. It is just in this moment that Robin, who
overhears the conversation, enters the play. He holds his erect penis
beneath his trousers and presents it as a squirrel. Norris J. Lacy finds no
logic in the fact that Robin has to invent a euphemism for his penis. But
Robin invents the euphemism for an *erect* penis. Even if the maiden
noticed that all men carry something between their legs, even if she saw
the connection between this "fish" and his desire to swim in the female
pond, as she says, it is plausible to think that she hasn't yet seen it or felt it
erect.[22] When she sees Robin she deduces that what he "grabs by the
hand" is a verbally disguised penis. She demonstrated earlier her
familiarity with the organ's position or, as Lacy puts it, "adequate
knowledge of human anatomy."[23] But it may be the first time she sees it in
a sexual way. So every man has a *vit*, but one man that grows a squirrel
can introduce her to the desired, yet unnamed, experience. Instinctively the
girl has already perceived the two stages of sexuality. A *thing*, or as she
now knows to say, a *vit* is what separates women from men. What brings
them together is a metaphorical image. Robin builds his strategy exactly
on that gap. He fancies the girl's virginity; therefore he registers himself
on a sexual level, and therefore the call of the metaphor. He would like to
leave the girl in the anatomical-linguistic stage, where no euphemism is
required since sexuality or desire are not evoked. Just as men have a *vit*
women have a *con*. There is no harm in pronouncing such words. The
confusion between the sexual and the anatomical body will, in Robin's
mind, permit the penetration. His squirrel will get the nuts, but the girl will
not be alarmed; her *con* will not be awarded with lustful designation. This
is of course very misogynistic, but Robin is the male's voice of the fabliau.
He defines sex as a something only men desire, and that decent girls,
unless fooled, shouldn't put out. He also considers the female as objects of
only male satisfaction. He looks for plausible sexual experiences that can
be provided by a girl's orifice. He ignores her desires, pleasures, and
satisfaction. Even symbolically, the *con* stays in an inferior linguistic

level. Only, things might be quite different. This girl is neither an object nor a fool.

As Lacy claims, the girl "understands that the reference is a metaphor and chooses to play along. To take her as victim or dupe is a misreading."[24] She plays along because what "stands" now in front of her eyes is an opportunity to actually engage in the act. Were she to argue with Robin, prove his ruse, she would harm her initial intention. When Robin is inside of her, she enjoys it so much, she tires him out, asks for more, and is disappointed when the squirrel is no longer hungry. It is Robin who should have learned his lesson when he heard the girl exhausting her mother; it is he who becomes an object to satisfy her desires.

The sexual lesson is part of initiation in chivalric life in *Tyolet*. Tyolet lives with his mother in the forest. He owns this extraordinary gift, the ability to hunt for their living by whistling and thus attracting the game. Thanks to this gift Tyolet stays innocent because he never has to fight, or to put himself in danger. The day he is old enough to leave this protective environment, he meets an animal that does not obey his whistle. Following it, Tyolet is present when it metamorphoses into a knight. Since he has never seen a man before (the only human being he knows is his mother), he is stupefied and cannot stop staring at the marvelous body. Like the silly knight and the squirrel-fond girl, Tyolet's first step is observing; unlike them Tyolet learns first about his own sex's body.[25] The metamorphosed knight teaches Tyolet the two important lessons about manhood. The first one reflects a humanistic criticism of society, where knights are nothing but "chevaliere beste" (knight-beast), which kill other beasts like them. The second lesson is about "weaponry." Tyolet asks, and the knight answers. The narration corresponds primarily to the arms and their use in battle, but the sword's blade is described as sharp and hard. Tyolet continues his investigation and asks about "that long thing that the knight carries." For the first time the knight hesitates before answering this particular question, and only after making sure that Tyolet is ready to know the answer ("would you like to know? – yes, by all means") does he respond with doubled sense verse: "A lance that I bear on/in me."[26]

4.   The Fantasy of Sexual Liberation

Young knights find adventures in the forest, a place where they can set sexuality free. Female sexual liberation entails the quest for sexual happiness, for fulfilling sexual relations, and the possibility of separating a good sexual life from emotional love. That is the main wish of the queen from *Tydorel*. The ten years of sterility that she had with her beloved husband end when she meets the mysterious knight and conceives Tydorel. Even though she loves the man she is married to, she is not happy with their sexual life. Euphemistically she can not have a child. Once she meets a "good" lover, she immediately conceives. In the courtly discourse that cannot talk freely about orgasms, they are disguised behind the debate of an heir. Saying that, I don't intimate that in a different layer of reading the question of mothering a son as a part of accomplishing a social role and maintaining a position in the king's court isn't possible. But a pluralistic reading is one of medieval literature's characteristics. It seems pertinent for me, then, to suggest that an unequivocal reading such as Monique Ipotési's, arguing that "here there is only a question of procreation" and that the only one who desires is the male fairy, misses an important element of the lai.[27]

When Tydorel's mother awakens alone from her dream, and sees the knight, he promises her a unique opportunity for happiness, for *Joie*, a term used to designate the physical aspect of love. Thirty lines of sexual insinuations anticipate this very close *joie*. Starting when some of the queen's ladies-in-waiting eat fruit before falling asleep, temptation and conception are nearby. It continues with the knight's exploits: he finds and climbs his horse, finds his swords and his armor and wears them, puts the queen on the horse's neck, enters the forest depths, arrives at the river, which he penetrates, swims across to the other side, with the water covering his front, and then comes back. We can now recognise the virile space and body that are presented by the horse and the sword and the virile activity of coming and going, of passing from one edge to another. The female space and body are represented by the forest and the river, and by the passivity of the female character (but this passivity is only analogical to the sexual act, not to sexual desire or seduction). When he finishes swimming he tells the stupefied lady that has been watching him: "par ceste voie vien e vois."("This is the route through which I come and go.") This could easily be a fabliau verse, because not only of its use of the assonance of v (as in *vit*), but also its description of intercourse.[28] And intercourse there is just after the knight speaks his prophesy out loud.

Le Sohait des vez deals with a similar problem. The sexually frustrated wife does not accept sexual deprivation. She understands the wrong that her husband for whom she had been virtuously waiting for three months, and who fell asleep before making love to her, has done.[29] We are told in the prologue that she loves him very much. Apparently she does not plan on cheating on him, but she looks for a way to be satisfied within the borders permitted to her. Those borders, at that stage, are her unconsciousness, her dream, her fantasy. In real life, since she is a virtuous woman (*preudefame*) she cannot explicitly demand sex; she would be disdained by her husband as a glutton. Lying next to him, she has her dream of a prick market. She examines all the sizes, colors, and shapes of the object that could replace her malfunctioning husband. She finally picks up the largest. Hungry for love, she imagines the quantity of

her desired dinner rather than the quality thereof. The quality would have
been her beloved husband. Since over dinner she served him the best part
of the meat, she hoped to be served with the best part of him. But the
quantity is the immediate satisfaction of her desire, which now, when it is
unrecognised by the man, passes from love to hunger. When she finds the
largest penis, she proceeds to step two: transporting the imagined/
dreamed world into reality, respecting the double rules of decency. She
cannot masturbate with the chosen penis, since masturbation is as bad as
the other crime, of frontally soliciting her husband to pay his matrimonial
debts. Both of them must be awakened. At that point the genius of Bodel
interferes. As we have seen, the wife raises her hand to shake on the deal
only to slap her husband and to wake him. Since they share a rare
intimacy, she is asked to recount and recounts her dream, which excites
him. Threatened by his poor instrument that "isn't even worth a cent," he
is ready to prove that even if his wife will have to live with such a
disappointing virility, it can at least fulfill her needs. He replaces her
sexual fantasy and becomes her sexual partner.

This inaugurates the eternal debate about whether size matters or
not. A big penis is an aphrodisiac. A man with a large member
immediately becomes a sexual object for a woman and the subject of her
fantasies. The size of the penis is directly connected to her sexual appetite,
but it is also a source of jealousy for men. White sees in the proliferation
of the organ "an unreal omnipotent penis, enviable by male and female
alike," responsible for materialistic riches of different kinds. It is for her "a
metaphor of well being that is not merely sexual."[30] But the sexual aspect
is remarkably pertinent in *Le Sohait* and also in the fabliau *Le Fevre de
Creil*, in which the blacksmith's wife cannot wait another moment for her
husband to leave town after she hears his own description of his
apprentice's virility:

> Lady, says he, I have never seen such a great
> member/Nor that I know of nor do I remember…/to be
> stiff in hot foot/and just as well to be so boot/.../One fist
> of width and two fists long/Never were there holes that
> are so oblong/That inside of them it could pound /Also it
> is perfectly round.

On the very first occasion the woman finds, she visits the well-equipped
young man desiring to fulfill her sexual desire. By trying it with someone
who is God's gift to women, she demonstrates her liberation; she decides
to act. What she wants from him is his body and not any other richness. He
is her husband's apprentice, hierarchically lower than her, and
consequently less wealthy. Knowing that it is just a dismembered object of

desire, the wife of the merchant of Douai chooses a large penis. Both husbands realise that they are not physically blessed, and this hurtful truth propels them to take the necessary measures to preserve control over their wives. The merchant makes peace and love with his wife, while the tricked blacksmith catches and warns his.

The *Lai d'Ignaure* deals with other jealous husbands. But the notion of size is translated here into the notion of potency. It is not the physical size of Ignaure's penis that is discussed but his physical ability to be the simultaneous lover of twelve mistresses. Discovered by a traitor that reveals this to the husbands, Ignaure is killed: his penis and his heart are torn out of his body, cooked and served to the ladies as their last supper, because they go on hunger strike thereafter.

Ignaure is a perverse version of the legend of the *Eaten Heart* in which an adulterous liaison ends when the lover is killed and his lady is served his heart. Renaut de Beaujeu, to whom the text is attributed, merged another medieval tradition into this lai: castration as the punishment for forbidden love. Both in the courtly genre and in the fabliaux, an adulterous lover is threatened with this chastisement. Based on the principle of an eye for an eye, there is no sweeter revenge for a betrayed husband, than to castrate his enemy. When the twelve husbands capture Ignaure they decide to punish both the vigorous lover and the ladies: "On the forth night, from the knight/We shall cut off the organ of delight/Which they thought was very nice/And we shall make each lady eat a slice."[31] The light tone almost hides the cruelty that it describes and continues to be almost amusing when the lai turns out to be a lament for the loss of an attractive and well-functioning penis. Ignaure's body is described, for instance, as consisting of "the nicest and best formed members." There isn't a specified one member, but a global physical atmosphere. Another lady talks about his "gentle body," and a third one regrets his eyes and flanks, two sexual metaphors. Of course, a man can have clear beautiful eyes and solid sides, but I suspect that the mention specifically of those two parts reminded the medieval audience of male sexuality. The urethra is described as an eye in *Le Sohait*. Flanks are a common euphemism for sex in the romance tradition. The impotent lovers are those who were injured in their sides and are no longer able to perform.

5.   Conclusion

The narrator of *Le lay del Lecheor* allows a woman to state the painful or maybe enjoyable truth: men distinguish themselves only because they love cunts – that is reason enough to compose a lai in the cunt's honor! This can be read as a misogynistic statement, but since the lai does enumerate all the noble activities required to get to the female orifice, which is not that easy to achieve, the lai is an amusing light example of the ambivalence of genital representation. On the one hand, representing female sexuality as an entrance is demeaning for the woman, as she is understood as an imperfection, as torn, or as subject to intrusion. The penis presented as a weapon, conquers the woman, as a warrior conquers a land. She is then dominated by him, subject to his authority. On the other hand, some passages into the feminine are traversed with fright. Vaginas, or their depictions as forests, rivers, fountains, are rendered valuable by their depth, darkness, and dangers. Most fabliaux reduce the whole of the female essence to the hole of the female entrance, and the meeting of the vagina or the well engorged penis implies nothing but an opportunity for sexual togetherness, desired both by men and women. In the narrative lai men penetrate feminine zones as part of their initiation (and destiny) towards adult social life.

Whatever genre we choose to read, it remains that they are both vehicles for expressing sexual fantasies, lust, and needs by describing the intimate body at intimate moments. Learned, imagined, and desired genitals reflect social position and motivation of the individual as part of his quest for sexual liberation and sexual identity. Although the authors of lais and fabliaux are (with the exception of Marie de France) men, and although the sexual identity is still restricted to heterosexuality and the sexual liberation to fantasy, a new sensibility regarding the notions of females' rights to satisfying sex, expressed and experienced sexual identity, and aspiration for sexual liberation is injected in filigree.

Notes

1. For lists of designations of male and female genitalia see Charles Muscatine, *The Old French Fabliaux* (New Haven: Yale University Press, 1986), 186-189.

2. For an exhaustive analytical bibliography of studies of the fabliaux see Brian Levy, *The Comic Text, Patterns and Images in the Old French Fabliaux* (Amsterdam: Rodopi, 2000).

3. Muscatine, 1986, Philippe Ménard, *Les fabliaux: Contes à rire du Moyen Age* (Paris: PUF, 1983) ; R. Howard Bloch, *The Scandal of the Fabliaux* (Chicago: The University of Chicago Press, 1986).

4. See Glyn Burgess, *The Old French Narrative Lay: an Analytical Bibliography* (Cambridge: D.S. Brewer, 1995).

5. John W. Baldwin, *The Language of Sex: Five Voices from Northern France around 1200*, (Chicago: University of Chicago Press, 1994), 100.

6. Unless otherwise mentioned, the pieces I am working with here are anonymous. Citations and references are to the following: for the

fabliaux, Willem Noomen, ed., *Nouveau Recueil Complet des Fabliaux, vol. I-VIII* (Assen: Van Gorcum, 1983-1994); for the narrative lais, Alexandre Micha, ed., *Lais féeriques des XIIe et XIIIe siècles* (Paris: Flammarion, 1992); for Marie de France's lais, Laurence Harf-Lancner, ed., *Lais de Marie de France* (Paris : Lettres Gothiques, 1990)

7. Sarah Melhado White, "Sexual Conflict in Old French Fabliaux," *Comparative Studies in Society and History* 24 (1982): 185-210, 206.

8. Bernard Ribémont, "Renaut et le cheval," *Reinardus* 7 (1994) : 127-142. Here, as elsewhere at times, my translations are adaptations. English translations are usually in prose, and, accordingly, they lose something of the magic of the original. My adaptations preserve the rhyme in order to give an example of the formal charm of the tales.

9. "Figures of equitation are inevitable; one may 'ride indoors' (en loge) or 'mount without reins or saddle.' Too much sex in *La Veuve* is to squeeze the mare" (Muscatine, 110).

10. Other members of the animal kingdom allude to genitalia. For example, the snake by its form and the brusque way it ejaculates its poison is used to describe the traitor in *Tyolet*, and refers to his manhood. Gauvain tries to prevent the wrong consumption of sexuality by preventing the wrong marriage or that no one will take with another one's *hand*, the dreadful snake out of the *bushes.* For the vagina as gluttonous animals and especially as a pig see Gary D. Mole, "Du bacon et de la femme. Pour une relecture de *Barat et Haimet* de Jean Bodel," *Néophilolgus*, 86.1 (2002): 17-31.

11. The forest is opposed to the civilized courtly world. It is a place into which one can escape before reintegrating into society: men in different stages of madness (Merlin, Yvain), lovers (Tristan and Iseult), and disappointed knights (Lanval). See Jacques Le Goff, *L'imaginaire médiéval* (Paris: Gallimars, 1991) and Francis Gingras, *Erotisme et merveille dans le récit français des XIIe et XIIIe siècles* (Paris : Champion, 2002), 250-258.

12. About the eroticism of the white animals see Gingras, 211-221.

13. See Bruno Roy, *Une Culture de l'équivoque* (Paris : champion 1992), 82.

14. "Anelle suy de Sor de Plaser, / Qui m'aura leys pora aver," v. 233-234, *Frayre de Joy e Sor de Plaser*, in *Nouvelles courtoises Occitanes et Françaises*, eds. Suzanne Méjean-Thiolier and Marie Françoise Notz-Grob (Paris: Lettres Gothiques, 1997).

15. Simon Gaunt, *Gender and Genres in Medieval French Literature* (Cambridge: Cambridge University Press, 1995), 267.

16. All translations of texts and criticism are mine : "Il est plus lons qu'il ne soit les/ -Et confais est cil par dalés ?/ -Dame, plus cors, ce m'est avis./-Gardés en cel n'adoist vos vis, / Car il n'est mie a cel ués fais:/ Qui vit y met, c'est grand mesfait," v. 71-76. *Le Sot chevalier*, in Noomen, 5(1990), 329.

17. Bloch, 120.

18. E. Jane Burns, "Knowing Women: Female Orifices in Old French Farce and Fabliau," *Exemplaria* 4 (1992): 81-104, 99.

19. "Sor totes choses garde bien/Que tu ne nomer cele rien/Que cil home portent pendant," v. 25-27. *L'esquiriel*, in Noomen 6(1991), 44.

20. "Mere, dist ele, dites moi/Comment il a a non et qoi/Tais toi, fille, je ne l'os dire./ Est la riens que a mon sire / Entre les jambes li pent, dame ? " v. 27.4-27.8. In ibid., 45.

21. "Vit, dist ele, Dieus merci, vit!/ Vit diré ge, cui qu'il anuit./ Vit, chaitive ! Vit dir mon pere, /Vit dit ma suer, Vit dist mon frere, / Et Vit dist nostre chanberiere ;/ Et vit avant et vit arriere, / Vit dist chascuns a son voloir ! Vos meïesme, mere, por voir/ Dites vit. Et je, fole lasse,/ .Qu'é forfet que vit ne nomasse? " v. 43-52. In ibid., 45-46.

22. Medieval lack of privacy could have led to earlier visions of sex.

23. Lacy, Norris J. *Reading Fabliaux*, (New York: Garland Publishing, 1993), 82.

24. Ibid.

25. This passage is also somewhat ambiguous with regards to a repressed homosexual identity.

26. " -Veus le savoir?-Oïl, par foi/ Une lance que port o moi," v.181-182 *Lai de Tyolet*. In Micha, 192.

27. Monique Ipotési, "L'interdit sexuel dans le lai de 'Tydorel,'" *Lecture* 7-8 (1981) : 91-11.

28. About the assonance and puns of *vit* see Muscatine, 112- 113.

29. There is a gap between what is said in the prologue ("the merchant absent for *three* months," v.11) and the complaints of his wife ("I didn't sleep with him for *two* months," v.58). Is it an innocent mistake of the fableor or the copyist, or, alternatively, is it a parody of the wife's "perfect" fidelity?

30. White, 198.

31. "Au quart jor (prendons) le vassal/ Tout le daerrain member aval/ don't li delis lor soloit plaire, /Si en fache on un mangier faire, " v. 541-544. Renaut de Beaujeu *Le lai D'Ignaure ou le Lai du prisonnier*, edited by Rita Lejeune (Bruxelles: Palais des Académies, 1983).

Select Bibliography

Aubailly, Jean-Claude. *La fée et le chevalier : Essai de mythanalyse de quelques lais féeriques des XII e et XIII e Siècles*. Paris: Champion, 1986.

Bec, Pierre. *Burlesque et Obscénité chez les troubadours, le contre texte au Moyen Age*. Paris: Stock, 1984.

Bloch, R. Howard. *The Scandal of the Fabliaux*. Chicago: The University of Chicago Press, 1986.

Burgess, Glyn. *The Old French Narrative Lay: An Analytical Bibliography*. Cambridge: D.S. Brewer, 1995.

Burns, E. Jane. "Knowing Women: Female Orifices in Old French Farce and Fabliau." *Exemplaria* 4 (1992): 81-104.

Cooke, Thomas D. "Pornography, The Comic Spirit and The Fabliau." *The Humor of the Fabliaux: A Collection of Critical Essays*, edited by Thomas D. Cooke and Benjamin L. Honeycutt, 137-162. New York: Columbia University Press, 1974.

Dubost, Francis. *L'Autre, l'Ailleurs, l'Autrefois. Aspects fantastiques de la littérature médiévale*. Paris: Champion, 1991.

Gaunt, Simon. *Gender and Genres in Medieval French Literature*. Cambridge: Cambridge University Press, 1995.

Gingras, Francis. *Erotisme et merveille dans le récit français des XIIe et XIIIe siècles*. Paris: Champion, 2002.

Ipotési, Monique. "L'interdit sexuel dans le lai de *Tydorel*". Lecture 7-8 (1981): 91-110.

Lacy, Norris J. *Reading Fabliaux*. New York: Garland Publishing, 1993.

Levy, Brian J. *The Comic Text: Patterns and Images in the Old French Fabliaux*. Amsterdam: Rodopi, 2000.

Melhado-White, Sarah. "Sexual Language and Human Conflict in Old French Fabliaux." *Comparative Studies in Society and History* 24 (1982) : 185-210.

Méjean-Thiolier, Suzanne and Marie Françoise Notz-Grob, eds. *Nouvelles courtoises Occitanes et Françaises*. Paris: Lettres Gothiques, 1997.

Ménard, Philippe. Les Fabliaux : Contes à rire du Moyen Age. Paris : PUF, 1983.

Mole, Gary D. "Du Bacon et de la femme: Pour une relecture de Barat et Haimet de Jean Bodel." *Néophilolgus* 86.1 (2002): 17-31.

Muscatine, Charles. *The Old French Fabliaux*. New Haven: Yale University Press, 1986.

Pearcy, Roy J. "Modes of Signification and the Humor of Obscene Diction in the Fabliaux." *The Humor of the Fabliaux: A Collection of Critical Essays*, edited by Thomas D. Cooke and Benjamin L.

Honeycutt, 163-196. New York: Columbia University Press, 1974.

Roy, Bruno. *Une culture de l'équivoque*. Paris: Champion, 1992.

Only with You – Maybe – *If* You Make Me Happy:
A Genealogy of Serial Monogamy as Governance and Self-Governance

Serena Petrella

Abstract

In my research, I explore governance practices in the Western world. I study how individuals are governed and govern themselves through the deployment of bio-political power in neo-liberal, "free" market regimes. Specifically, I analyse the administration of citizens' lives through the regulation of sexual conduct. I observe how different types of sexual identifications and practices are consistent with the political agendas of neo-liberal regimes and of late-phase capitalist economies, as well as characteristic of their inherent contradictions. I investigate how such sexual matrices of behaviour and subjectivation have become entrenched through processes of normalisation, which support and reproduce systemic bio-political power.[1] The object of my inquiries is the norm of monogamy. In this project I intend to illustrate a framework to study how the norm of monogamy has emerged and become a powerful symbolic fabrication in the social. I first discuss previous work done on the topic and offer my critiques of it, then I propose an analytical methodology to better explain and analyse the emergence of serial monogamy. Secondly, I argue that serial monogamy is presently acted out in a "political ethics" of existence that articulates itself along ontological, de-ontological and teleological lines. Through this "ethics of the self," individuals attempt to reach the "truth" about their humanity and achieve its highest potential by measuring the success of their emotional and sexual relationships. **Key Words:** monogamy, normalisation, genealogy, sexuality, sex, the gendering process, the heterosexual matrix, sexual identity, abject identity, sexual ethics.

1. Introduction

In the Western world, the great majority of people share a substantial portion of their lives with one partner. Adherence to the norm of monogamy begins in youth: upon entrance into the sphere of the sexual, we pair up. Many individuals now engage in long-term life partnerships that may or may not be marriage. Sequential partners are acceptable and individuals can, throughout their lives, have a varied array of sexual experiences. Generally, though, we tend to pair up in multiple yet exclusive relationships.

Sexual expectations surrounding pairings presently seem to be articulated along a narrative of satisfaction. Genders follow "scripts" of specific lifestyles that inform decisions on both life goals and expectations. Sexual fulfilment and pleasure are to be given and received back, as they are now symbolically constructed as key requirements for a satisfactory mature union. In the present social, sexual intercourse and love are connected to the concept of the "relationship." This means that the monogamous norm is embraced at the onset of pairing up, in the teen years. In the context of sexual engagements, the institution of marriage has lost its primacy and is being substituted by the relationship, which is a new form of monogamous engagement where sex finds its justifications as tool in the quest for love, self-actualisation and satisfaction, not necessarily reproduction. The trend of serial monogamy for the sake of satisfaction is common to both heterosexualities and homosexualities. According to Giddens, the idea of "relationship" is as paramount in gay, lesbian, and queer sub-cultures as in the hegemonic counterpart. An increasing proportion of gay men and the majority of lesbian women, are at any one time in a live-in relation with a partner, and seem to have preceded the majority of the heterosexual populace in developing relationships.[2]

Deviance from the norm of serial monogamy does occur. Specific lifestyles may diverge from the monogamous norm, at least temporarily. A "single-by-choice" individual may juggle different sexual encounters, or short- to long-term relationships, without settling into an exclusively monogamous pairing. Polyamorous lifestyles, where partners suspend sexual monogamy and at times emotional monogamy are possible but rare. Divergence from the norm of monogamy may be acceptable during a certain period in a person's life but, if prolonged past a certain age, it becomes suspect, potentially interpreted as a sign of either emotional immaturity or dysfunction. Enterprising, fulfilled, and successful adults are expected to embody a specific "sexual citizenship," characterised by the "possession" in love and care of a partner, and monogamous sexual conduct. It is possible to blunder, to choose a companion unwisely. Thus, extra-relational/marital affairs are tolerated, as long as they function as an interim, as intermediary steps in the quest for a new exclusive pairing. Thus we live under a hegemonic regime of serial monogamy, where fidelity to a single partner is the norm.

What has brought me to study the norm of monogamy is the apparent misalignment of, on one side, a politics of emancipation (our sexuality has been "liberated") and, on the other, a politics of conservative containment (sexual "permissiveness" is a sign of social and moral decline). Adherence to the first trend would entail greater sexual freedom: if we are technically "free" to be polyamorous, why do the majority of people engage in monogamous conduct? On the other hand, we cannot explain our sexual habits to be "contained" according to conservative doctrine. Higher numbers of teenagers now engage in sex, at younger ages than before; queer and homo sexualities, recently considered "deviant," are tolerated; these trends, alongside the celebration of recreational and pleasure-driven sexuality, appear to be indicative of non-adherence to conservative agendas.

This paper investigates how serial monogamy is a symbolic normative construct through which individuals measure their "ontological selves" and strive for emotional and sexual fulfillment, in ethical projects of self-actualisation. This symbolic monogamy has slowly morphed into a sexual morality that prescribes an ethics of "love quests" through serial but exclusive pairing. Yet, as a norm it not only acts as a containment field, but it creates a nexus for resistance. Notions of sexual identity and normal behaviour, even when designed to marginalise the "abnormal" and chastise or reform the "deviant," set up schemas for subjectification; thus, inadvertently, they create matrices for "abject" recognition. They therefore act as mirroring ontological nexuses that open up an "ethical" negotiation for subject positions *in relation* to the norm.[3]

2.   Critique of Previous Work and a Discussion of Genealogy as Method

The research approaches that in my opinion have dealt with the relational arrangement of monogamy more exhaustively and pertinently are the sociological studies of the 1960s and 1970s and the evolutionary approaches in anthropological and socio-biological research.

In the 1960s and 1970s, social research closely mirrored the open-mindedness and wish for change that could be observed in larger social and cultural realms. Increasing rates of divorce and the cropping up of non-traditional and extramarital sexual contracts were considered proof that an old conservative regime of sexual economy was on its way out.[4] In this light those institutionalised customs and habits that supported monogamy in Western societies were interpreted as suspect, but more importantly, as unnecessary. It was during this period that research on old and new forms of relational arrangements flourished. New familial structures that went beyond the exclusive dyadic pair were enthusiastically investigated. Examples of this type of research focused on mate swapping, swinging and group marriages as new, groundbreaking sexual and familial arrangements.[5]

In the minds of evolutionary theorists, human sexuality presently exhibits traits that are the result of genetic or behavioural selection for species survival. Heterosexual attraction is widely thought to be a physiologically inscribed genetic prophecy or an adaptive strategy for the survival of the species. Monogamy, although recognised not to have been, historically and culturally, the sole sexual conjoining among humans, is understood to be the most successful reproductive strategy, and this "fact" is offered as justification for its global popularity. According to anthropological and socio-biological research, monogamy's origins and persistence find its basis in the reproductive needs of the human species.

Interestingly, these approaches have produced conflicting explanations for the "rise" of monogamy in humankind. The first model is based on differentiation in gender behaviour, and posits the male as strategically promiscuous, the female as discreetly monogamous. The committed pair eventually evolves out of these opposing mating strategies, as it is the more successful model for raising offspring.[6] The second approach offers a very different picture of the sexual past of our ancestors and describes non-monogamous conduct as characteristic of both genders. It explains monogamy and adultery as a "couplet," or as the two sides of the same reproductive strategy. Both genders' tendency to be promiscuous is geared to increase reproductive success and add variety to the "gene-pool."[7]

There are a number of foundational problems with the first approach to the study of monogamy. Firstly, it has a strong humanist slant that non-problematically ascribes to ideals of human rationality, agency, historical progress and civility. These assumptions have been questioned and made suspect in structuralist and post-structuralist research. Moreover, stratification issues of class are simplistically overlooked in such works, as the majority of families and subjects studied belong to the middle class. Similarly, issues of gender, race and ethnicity are ignored and there is no commitment to studying the patriarchal, neo-colonial and culturally hegemonising forces at play in the social. No attention is dedicated to self-regulation in individuals and to how specific codes of conduct are embedded, along gender, class and race-specific trajectories, in the constitution of "subjects" of a "civil society."

The evolutionary approaches to the study of monogamy also present a number of problematic characteristics. Most importantly, they share the assumption that all human rituals concerning courtship and mating, marriage and divorce can be understood as scripts by which men and women seduce each other in order to replicate themselves. All monogamous conduct is conflated into one foundational and basic drive: reproduction. It is evident that these approaches fail to even consider the discursive dimension of sexuality, and the hegemonic gendering structures of the heterosexual matrix, nor are they aware of their collusion in their creation and reproduction.

The evolutionary approach takes heterosexual attraction for granted, and sets out to theorise from a very problematic point, that of the "natural," heterosexually reproducing, dyadic pair. All human sexual behaviour, including present non-reproductive plasticity, is reduced to the intrinsic "need" of species survival. Although these approaches can still be considered useful in thinking back in time, to speculate upon our primordial beginnings, they are not very helpful in explaining recent attitudes and sexual behaviour in the social. They also define and attach sexual characteristics and propensities to a (heterosexual) sex, and then non-problematically "paste" the same characteristics to the gay and lesbian genders.

More broadly, a number of general problems are shared by both approaches. First, both formulations take a trans-historical approach, where material and cultural differences across time and space are effaced for the strategic purpose of producing condensed grand-theories of human development. Second, they make an over-simplified connection between human behaviour and the material/economic realm, and are therefore unable to effectively tackle issues of stratification and patriarchy. Third, their refusal to consider the discursive formation of sexual traits and gender scripts of behaviour, which vary drastically from culture to culture and from specific historical periods to others, effectively disable them from approaching monogamy as a regulatory mechanism of conduct and self-conduct that is historically specific and culturally contingent.

I will now propose a new methodological approach for the study of monogamy in the present social. As an "effective historicist" and (de)constructivist,[8] I interpret sexuality to be historically contingent and culturally specific. Present day monogamy, in my opinion, is a normative assemblage that emerged out of the bio-political machinations of the police state of the eighteenth century.[9] As such, it is a bundle of competing authoritative discourses on human sexuality. Aspects of it may have been "deployed" at a time when they made "oeconomic" sense (that is, marriage incentives to resolve high percentages of illegitimate births), yet these deployments have taken on a life of their own. Operationalised by different authorities (medical, educational, philanthropist), forgotten, re-discovered, manipulated, changed, the present variegated morphology of the norm of monogamy has emerged out of the deployment of the technology of sexuality. Its study should be cognisant of its discursive depth, and adopt a methodology for study designed to "dissect" it "layer by layer." Most importantly, this methodology should dedicate attention to its "normative" nature, and be able to map out its homogenising *and* heterogenising tendencies.[10]

Michel Foucault's research focuses on the constitution of subjectivities, and his work offers an orientation to theorising and analysing practices, their constitution and their effects on subjects. This approach is intrinsically anti-humanistic and is useful in avoiding different problematic issues in social theory, among them the debates over objectivism versus subjectivism, individuality versus totality, and structure versus agency. I shall refer to this approach as the genealogical method. I have chosen to adopt it because it is particularly effective in de-centring metaphysical conceptions of agency, in avoiding totalising accounts of social life and in emphasising the contingent and historical aspects of everyday life. Theorists working in the Foucauldian tradition have devoted themselves to each one of these lines of inquiry. These studies of governance focus on the conglomeration of strategies, tactics, calculations, and reflections that police the "conduct of conduct" of human beings.[11]

The genealogical method is particularly useful in analysing the rise of bio-politics in the Western world, and can interpret the governance of individuals as the deployment of two practices: the anato-politics of the human body and the bio-politics of populations. The first is primarily economic; it is comprised of practices that aim to maximise an individual's usefulness. The second is primarily concerned with biology, and is characterised by all practices concerned with health, life expectancy and longevity of a population; it specifically intervenes into reproduction.[12] These governance practices operate at the abstract level as speculative discourses, and take the form of concrete arrangements, or technologies of power, which have colonised our social, political, and economic lives. Within this, the deployment of sexuality is one of the most influential. Sex as a category is important, politically, as it functions as the axis along which the two poles of bio-power have gained access to individuals' lives. The regulation of sexual conduct is the entrance point for power to both the life of the body and the life of the species. Governance of sexual practices is thus tied to the economic maximisation of the individual's body, and the overall fostering of the populace.[13]

At this point I shall illustrate the ways in which I will approach the systematic study of the hegemonic norm of serial monogamy. The following grid for analysis is derived from Foucault's discussion of regimes of "Truth" as result of the intersection of power and knowledge.[14] He identifies four types of technologies of power/knowledge: technologies of production, technologies of power, technologies of sign systems and technologies of the self.

Technologies of production are applied to produce, transform, or manipulate things. These technologies are related to monogamy through all practices that inform material relations, thus in an "economic" sense, as those regulatory interventions geared towards the reproduction of life. Research in this area will devote itself to a historical study of familial structures, and investigate the shifts in their formation from early capitalist to present late-phase economies, to establish in what way they foster or undermine monogamous arrangements. Technologies of power determine the conduct of individuals and submit them to certain ends or domination, in processes that effectively "objectivise" the subject. My analytic efforts in this area focus on authoritative structures and investigate how they organise their efforts in deploying monogamous conduct in the individuals they govern. Technologies of sign systems discursively employ signs, meanings and symbols of signification for regulatory purposes. My discussion of the technologies of sign systems on monogamy concentrates on the symbolic signs that inform this specific sexual practice. Technologies of self-governance allow individuals to affect by their own means, or with the help of others, a certain number of operations on their own bodies and souls, thoughts, conduct and way of being, so as to transform themselves in order to attain a certain state of happiness, purity, wisdom, perfection, or immortality.[15] My studies discuss at length how individuals come to espouse and embody discursively constructed sexualities, in practices of self-affirmation and discovery. These "embodiments" take place according to three different self-inscribing dimensions: an ontological dimension, a de-ontological dimension, and a teleological dimension.

3.   Serial Aspects of Monogamy in the Present Social

Serial monogamy as normative construct rests on a broader technology of sexuality. In the present social human intelligibility is made available to individuals through two founding operations. The first is the gendering process that occurs at birth (nowadays even in uterus), and the second is the heterosexual matrix, which normatively orders individuals according to erotic direction. Through the heterosexual matrix, argues Judith Butler, pleasures and sensation stemming from sexual activity, as well as biological traits and drives, are ordered under a fictitious coherence through the invocation of a sexed identity. Within this logic of sexual identity, sex itself is posited as a biological cause for pleasure; sex determines pleasure's direction, its destiny, and meaning. The production of sex as a category of identity allows for its discursive regulation to take place. If no individual can be taken as human, or recognised as human, unless coherently marked by sex, then the category of sex establishes a principle of intelligibility for humanity.[16]

This conceptualisation of sexuality makes evident the political "nature" of the primacy and naturalness of the heterosexual drive. To conceive heterosexual coupling as "naturally" deriving from a biologically dictated human sexuality, allows two operations: first, the institution of the hetero norm; second, intervention in case of deviation. But there is more. The heteromatrix does not stop at erotic direction; normatively, it dictates "volume" as well. It is normal only to have one partner at a time. In the sociological work done so far on intimacy and relationships, this particular issue has not been problematised in a satisfactory manner. In my opinion, sociological research still has to address how heterosexual normativity and couplehood are related to each other. Studies on intimacy take the monogamous aspect of relationships for granted.

I argue that this lacuna can be resolved by investigating how present ideals of emotional and erotic fulfillment are fashioned *out of the pair*, in historical evolutions of signs and sign systems that effectively fuse self-actualisation to the ability to successfully commune with another. There is a nexus here: technologies of sexuality produce a "normal" heterosexual subject that *is* monogamous; consequently, all "pursuits of happiness" within relationships will tend to re-contextualise and reproduce this monogamy. It is important to clearly tease out that the "normal" subject of sexuality is a *monogamous* subject. Authorities of power/knowledge discursively stipulate appetite according to gender, which is then pathologised if unbound or misdirected. Next, the subject infolds these schemas *ethically*, because he/she desires to be "normal," or else, she/he rejects or, at least, partially rejects them, again *ethically*, because engaged in politics of subjective resistance. Within normative monogamy then, a number of covert machinations are embedded, which provide individuals with matrices for life trajectories that are passively and actively taken up. I shall describe each machination and offer examples of potential "ethico-sexual" engagement.

If the first machination operates at the ontological level, the norm of hegemonic heterosexual monogamy would provide individuals with a schema of sexual "self-recognition," or a matrix of basic human intelligibility, articulated in the gendering process of identification into complementary sexes. The surface of the body is made to coincide with a sexual configuration: the subject is educated into the appropriation of a sex. Later an abject ontology might emerge. In a "normalised" individual, monogamous heterosexual conduct is enacted as an expression of a "natural" sexual development. In another individual, one who resists the "hetero" side of normativity, homosexual monogamy is enacted. Yet another individual, resisting the "economic" side of normativity, engages in polyamoury.

The second machination relates to the position of a subject in relation to the precept one intends to follow. Tied to the next step of ascetic elaboration, it provides individuals with "options" of behaviour that are stipulated and made available in the socio-cultural realm. For the heterosexual single male, a promiscuous model for sexual engagement might be available, while for a heterosexual female, a more monogamous lifestyle might be invoked. Yet, later on both might be expected to "settle down" to a more mature, thus "monogamous," lifestyle. The same life trajectories could apply to homosexual individuals.

The third machination in normative serial monogamy would provide a teleology for human fulfilment, a "mythological life-script." It is a symbolically construed "life goal" that individuals come to yearn for in the hopes of experiencing "love" with another, reaching "emotionally mature sexual ecstasy," and achieving an "ultimate human potential." Its hegemonic character suggests a prophecy for erotic direction that can only be mastered by enacting the economy of heterosexual erotic desire, or the pursuit of a heterogeneous object-choice. Again, in a perfectly normalised individual, hetero-monogamy is enacted with the aspiration it provides an avenue to the "ultimate" experience in sexual and emotional fulfilment. The same teleology may be at play in another individual who, however, engages in homosexual monogamous conduct. A counter-teleology is projected by yet another person who engages in bisexual non-monogamous conduct with the political ambition of living a more "authentic" life.

The fourth machination of hegemonic normative monogamy operates de-ontologically, by providing individuals with a plan for "moral action" in their sexual lives. The "ethics" of heterosexual monogamy suggests that this dyadic arrangement is the only acceptable form of sexual and emotional connection. Its intrinsic moral imperative positively encourages individuals to subject themselves to the in-folding of the hetero-monogamous norm. In a "hetero" normalised individual and also in a "homo" normalised individual, monogamy is discreetly enacted because avoidance of promiscuity allows them to feel "moral," "at peace," and "honorable" with regards to a love pledge or contractual arrangement made to a partner. Another individual leads a sexually promiscuous life yet is "faithful" to a code of emotional monogamy, stipulated with his/her long-term partner. In yet another individual, sexual promiscuity and emotional polyamoury are enacted as "politics of resistance" to a social world that has been actively rejected.

As we have seen, basic ontological self-recognition is founded on the acceptance of the embodied ordinance as male or female. Thus, to a specific morphological concavity corresponds the female gender and all the cultural behaviours attached to it, while to a morphological convexity corresponds the male gender, and the cultural masculine agglomeration of behaviours related to it.

Secondary ontological self-recognition is founded of erotic direction: the normalised individual is attracted to heterosexual object choices. Yet this is fractured further, into a secondary gendering process, which Butler terms abject recognition: this consists of a partial acceptance of embodied ordinance (still as female/male) yet a resistance to heterosexual object choice normativity. Thus more possibilities are opened up for the erotic functioning of subjects: an embodied male subject can be attracted to another male subject; similarly a female can be erotically driven towards another female. Also, a subject can be attracted to things (fetishism), find sexual stimulation through specific acts that have nothing to do with gender (SM), or not need sexual object choices at all (auto-eroticism in specific subcultures such as body building or asexuality). These subjects can come to feel "at peace" and manage to live against the normalising culture around them, or to be happy in spite of it – resistance to the norm becomes the ontological foundation of self-recognition.

These ontological stipulations are problematised further. Ontological grounding then is not simply a matter of self-recognition of sexual identity schemas and of the operationalisation of erotic direction schemas. It also rests on an invocation that one *other* (*your* other) recognise you, every day, in a process that marks and reiterates ones' symbolic existence. Moreover, it rests on the "acting out" of a discursively constructed and culturally specific notion of unity (*being* the couple). The subject of normalised monogamy then does not consider itself fully "complete" without the relational grounding that the other gives it as its partner.

The schemas of sexed self-recognition and the erotic behaviours attached to them, including the more indirect ones (serial monogamy), create the mask and script according to which we come to recognise ourselves (in ontological ethics) and interface with the socio-cultural symbolic order (in strong or abject accordance to the norm). This process of subject formation is a constant suturing over of the subject-that-should-be (culturally given) and the subject-that-is (phantasmatic ethical approximation of the cultural model). In this process, we temporarily "find" or "locate" ourselves, and this "topological fixing" is crucial. We need the mirage of stable subjectivity to function, and we create it by juggling and enacting different versions of subjectivity models normatively "fed" to us. The subject temporarily escapes this ontological alienation by embodying the norm.

The subjectivity models imposed on subjects are never stable within the symbolic realm of culture. They are themselves in flux, caught up in the belligerently discursive clashes of competitive authorities (the notion of intimate pairing is a good example of this). Some norms have reached a level of universal status that makes them appear a-temporal and natural (male and female sex). Others have not (monogamy).

4.   Conclusion

In conclusion, I have presented a plan for study for the norm of monogamy that can account for its socio-historical emergence and analyse its present heterogeneous forms. I argue that ethical re-formulations and manipulations of the norm of monogamy arise from the intrinsic characteristics of a larger habitus at play in the social, that of "self-actualising identity," so dearly celebrated in Neo-Liberal democracies. Its essentially critiquing tendency effectively clashes with traditional versions of the hetero-monogamous norm, and pushes towards renegotiations that erode its borders and undermine its erotic strategies. These processes should not be mistakenly interpreted to be emancipatory trajectories, but should rather be understood as processes of "infolding" of subjective articulation.

Notes

1. Michel Foucault, *The History of Sexuality, Vol. I: An Introduction* (New York: Pantheon, 1978), 139-40.

2. Anthony Giddens, *The Transformation of Intimacy. Sexuality, Love and Eroticism in Modern Societies* (Cambridge: Polity Press, 1992), 15.

3. Michel Foucault makes this point when discussing homosexual ontologies as related to the medical definition of the sexual abnormal. The gay movement utilised the medical definition of homosexuality as a tool for resistance against the oppression of homosexuality. Michel Foucault, "Sex, Power, and the Politics of Identity," in *Michel Foucault: Ethics, Subjectivity, and Truth*, edited by Paul Rabinow (New York: The New Press, 1994), 168.

4. James R. Smith, and Lynn G. Smith, *Beyond Monogamy. Recent Studies in Sexual Alternatives in Marriage* (Baltimore: The Johns Hopkins University Press, 1974), 36.

5. Gilbert D. Bartell, "Group Sex Among Mid-Americans," in *Beyond Monogamy. Recent Studies in Sexual Alternatives in Marriage*, edited by James R. Smith and Lynn G. Smith (Baltimore: The Johns Hopkins University Press, 1974), 185-201. Larry L. Constantine and Joan M. Constantine, "Sexual Aspects of Multilateral Relations," in *Beyond Monogamy: Recent Studies in Sexual Alternatives in Marriage*, edited by James R. Smith and Lynn G. Smith (Baltimore: The Johns Hopkins University Press, 1974), 268-289.

6. Helen E. Fisher, *Anatomy of Love: The Natural History of Monogamy, Adultery, and Divorce* (New York: W. W. Norton & Company, 1992), 66.

7. Sarah B. Hrdy, *The Woman That Never Evolved* (Cambridge: Harvard University Press, 1981).

8. Mitchell Dean, *Critical and Effective Histories* (London: Routledge, 1994), 18.

9. The proliferation of political technologies that invested the body, health, modes of subsistence, and lodging from the eighteenth century onward, found their unifying pole in what was called *policing*, defined here as all methods for the qualitative development of a population and the strength of a nation. The science of policing consisted in regulating all that related to the condition of a society, in seeing that all

state practices contributed to the welfare of the members that composed it. Its aims were to employ all state efforts in serving to fortify and increase the state's own power and, by ensuring public welfare, strengthen its populace. Jacques Donzelot, *The Policing of Families* (New York: Pantheon Books, 1979), 7.

10. Normative assemblages, such as monogamy, appear to stem from naturally occurring characteristics in humans, but are actually discursive invocations that produce the object in question in a way that has two effects: the first is it makes it suitable for regulation; the second, it creates a marker for human intelligibility. In their analysis of normative bio-politics, Nikolas Rose and Mariana Valverde argue that the norm appears to emerge "out of the very nature of that which is governed," ("Governed By Law," *Social and Legal Studies* 7.4 (1998): 573), by which they mean that "normativity" is invoked and legitimated by its "normality" (that is, a normal child, a normal family). Governance through norms then complicates the distinction between the licit and the illicit as it introduces an "impersonal" judgement of each individual in relation to the collectivity of which they form a part. In this manner the normative order, as it governs "for the sake of" society, gains legitimacy simply through its normative quality. In a circular relation of capillary power, normative governance and the social laws produced within it actually institute the realm of the social itself. Rose and Valverde, 573.

11. Michel Foucault "Technologies of the Self," in *Technologies of the Self: A Seminar with Michel Foucault*, edited by Luther H. Martin, Huck Gutman, and Patrick H. Hutton (Amherst: University of Massachusetts Press, 1988), 16-49.

12. Foucault, 1978, 139-40.

13. Foucault, 1978, 145-46.

14. Michel Foucault, "Omnes et Singulatim: Towards a Criticism of Political Reason," in *The Tanner Lectures on Human Values. Vol.2*, edited by Sterling M. McMurrin (Salt Lake City: Utah University Press, 1981), 81.

15. Michel Foucault, 1988, 81.

16. Judith Butler, "Sexual Inversions," in *Foucault and The Critique of institutions*, edited by J. Caputo and M. Yount (University Park: Pennsylvania State University Press, 1993), 89.

Select Bibliography

Bartell, Gilbert D. "Group Sex Among Mid-Americans." In *Beyond Monogamy. Recent Studies in Sexual Alternatives in Marriage*, edited by James R. Smith and Lynn G. Smith, 185-201. Baltimore: The Johns Hopkins University Press, 1974.

Butler, Judith. "Sexual Inversions." In *Foucault and The Critique of Institutions*, edited by J. Caputo and M. Yount, 81-98. University Park: Pennsylvania State University Press, 1993.

Caputo, J. and M. Yount. *Foucault and The Critique of Institutions*. University Park: Pennsylvania State University Press, 1993.

Constantine, Larry L. and Joan M. Constantine. "Sexual Aspects of Multilateral Relations." In *Beyond Monogamy. Recent Studies in Sexual Alternatives in Marriage*, edited by James R. Smith and Lynn G. Smith, 268-289. Baltimore: The Johns Hopkins University Press, 1974.

Dean, Mitchell. *Critical and Effective Histories*. London: Routledge, 1994.

Donzelot, Jacques. *The Policing of Families*. New York: Pantheon Books, 1979.

Fisher, Helen E. *Anatomy of Love: The Natural History of Monogamy, Adultery, and Divorce*. New York: W. W. Norton & Company, 1992.

Foucault, Michel. *The History of Sexuality Vol. I: An Introduction*. New York: Pantheon, 1978 [1976].

——. "Omnes et Singulatim: Towards a Criticism of Political Reason." In *The Tanner Lectures on Human Values.Vol.2,* edited by S. McMurrin, 225-245. Salt Lake City: Utah University Press, 1981.

——. "Technologies of the Self." In *Technologies of the Self: A Seminar with Michel Foucault*, edited by Luther H. Martin, Huck Gutman, and Patrick H. Hutton, 16-49. Amherst: University of Massachusetts Press, 1988.

——. "Sex, Power, and the Politics of Identity," In *Michel Foucault. Ethics, Subjectivity and Truth*, edited by Paul Rabinow, 163-174. New York: The New Press, 1994.

Giddens, Anthony. *The Transformation of Intimacy. Sexuality, Love and Eroticism in Modern Societies*. Cambridge: Polity Press, 1992.

Hall, Stuart and Paul du Guy. *Questions of Cultural Identity*. London: SAGE, 1996.

Hrdy, Sarah B. *The Woman That Never Evolved*. Cambridge: Harvard University Press, 1981.

Martin, Luther H., Huck Gutman, and Patrick H. Hutton. *Technologies of the Self: A Seminar with Michel Foucault*. Amherst: University of Massachusetts Press, 1988.

McMurrin, Sterling M. *The Tanner Lectures on Human Values.Vol.2*. Salt Lake City: Utah University Press, 1981.

Rabinow, Paul *Michel Foucault. Ethics, Subjectivity and Truth*. New York: The New Press, 1994.

Rose, Nikolas. "Identity, Genealogy, History." In *Questions of Cultural Identity*, edited by S. Hall and P. du Gay, 128-150. London: SAGE, 1996.

Rose, Nikolas and Mariana Valverde. "Governed By Law." *Social and Legal Studies* 7.4 (1998): 569-579.

Smith, James R. and Lynn G. Smith. *Beyond Monogamy. Recent Studies in Sexual Alternatives in Marriage*. Baltimore: The Johns Hopkins University Press, 1974.

Stanton, Domna C. *Discourses of Sexuality: From Aristotle to AIDS*. Ann Arbor: Michigan University Press, 1992.

PART IV

Legality, Bureaucracy, Religion, and Sexuality

A Project for Sexual Rights: Sexuality, Power, and Human Rights

Alejandro Cervantes-Carson and Tracy Citeroni

Abstract

Using the debate between Foucault and Habermas as theoretical background, we aim to advance a political and normative project for the international establishment of sexual rights as human rights. Given the current and dominant social organisation of sex and gender, we believe that there are pressing demands for designing and establishing normative standards that allow for the protection of sexual difference and the affirmation of sexual diversity. While fully acknowledging the disciplining risks of any normative project, we articulate the cultural, social, and political conditions necessary for two distinct sets of rights. First, we discuss the possibility of negative sexual rights capable of protecting the sexual integrity of historically marginalised individuals and groups that are targets of heterosexist violence. Second, we call for the development of positive sexual rights capable of simultaneously affirming both sexual diversity and sexual lives filled with pleasure. The justification and acceptance of negative sexual rights, we argue, only require a politics and ethics of tolerance. By contrast, positive sexual rights demand a different political and ethical paradigm, one of recognition. Ultimately, the political project of sexual rights seeks to debunk male hegemony over the practice and discourse of sexuality, and to decentre heterosexuality altogether. **Key Words:** domination; ethics and politics of tolerance; ethics and politics of recognition; hegemonic masculinity; heterosexism; human rights; power relations; sexual identity; sexual rights; social movements.

1. Introduction

The first two articles of the Universal Declaration of Human Rights are set to establish the unrestricted universality and comprehensive reach of this international normative document. "All human beings are born free and equal in dignity and rights" is the opening statement of article 1. In turn, article 2 makes sure that "everyone is entitled" to "all the rights and freedoms" that are determined in the Declaration, and clearly precludes any recourse to social discrimination or exclusionary practices on the basis of "race, colour, sex, language, religion, political, or other opinion, national or social origin, property, birth, or other status."

The reference to "sex" in the Declaration is not a general reference to sexuality or sexual diversity but rather to sex and gender differences, and more specifically to the practices of sexism and gender discrimination. The term "sex" signals the existence of a system of social inequality and mistreatment whose exclusionary practices are set outside the normative boundaries of human rights and are pronounced as illegal, illegitimate, and as counter universal forces to the spirit and the objectives of the Declaration. Therefore, the purpose of including the term "sex" is to assure and defend "the equal rights of men and women" (as stated in the fifth paragraph of the preamble), and to protect these basic rights against the destructive forces of sex discrimination and gender inequality.

However, sexuality is painfully absent from any normative considerations in the Universal Declaration of Human Rights. Furthermore, since 1948 and after half a century of international normative work, there has been a complete lack of development of rights for sexuality, as well as any significant instruments to protect against heterosexism and homophobic practices of discrimination and violence.[1]

Using the debate and the re-casting of the debate between Foucault and Habermas on power as a theoretical background,[2] this paper advances a political and normative project for the international establishment of sexual rights as human rights.

Given the current and dominant social organisation of sex and gender, we believe that there are pressing demands for designing and establishing normative standards that allow for the protection of sexual difference, as well as for the affirmation of sexual diversity.

While fully acknowledging the disciplining risks of any normative project of this nature, we articulate the cultural, social, and political conditions necessary for two distinct sets of rights: on the one hand, the need for negative sexual rights capable of protecting the sexual integrity of historically marginalised individuals and groups that have become targets of heterosexist violence; on the other, the push for positive sexual rights capable of simultaneously affirming both sexual diversity and sexual lives filled with pleasure.

We argue that the justification and acceptance of negative sexual rights only require a politics and ethics of tolerance. By contrast, positive sexual rights demand a different political and ethical paradigm, one of recognition. Yet, the political project of positive sexual rights seeks ultimately to debunk male hegemony over the practice and discourse of sexuality, and to decentre heterosexuality all together.

Despite the limits of sexual identity-based social movements, we believe that their social and cultural impact has been crucial, and allows us to claim that the project of negative sexual rights is today feasible. Furthermore, we also claim that the political project of positive sexual rights is currently possible because of the undomesticated emancipatory potentials of these movements, and because of a profound thought transformation that has occurred in social theory and philosophy that enables us to think and live sexuality as a non-essential, decentred, fluid, and relational condition and identity. Finally, we argue that this opens the possibility of severing the link that sex, sexuality, and sexual identity has to power.

2.   The Need for Negative Sexual Rights

Given the current conditions of power relations, gender inequality, and heterosexism under which societies live today, we believe that the need for a construction of sexual rights as a set of normative mechanisms for protecting the sexual integrity of individuals and groups requires very little moral justification. In fact, the presence of patterns of violence and social behaviour that place under constant jeopardy sexual choices and the integrity of groups of people is reason enough not only to argue in favor of negative rights, but to demand norms and laws capable of avoiding and punishing crimes, as well as recognising, granting legitimacy, and protecting a diverse definition of sexuality and a diversity of sexual choices and activities.

The first problem, however, is that any political project that aims to promote, construct, and consolidate norms that protect sexual integrity and allow for diverse sexual choices to take place will require critical forms of social recognition. On the one hand, of course, they necessitate the basic social recognition that violence should not occur, but perhaps most importantly that violence against sexual diversity is illegitimate and that there should be no place for it within social relations. On the other, they call for a social acceptance that sexuality has a very wide array of expressions, choices, and orientations beyond what has been defined as socially normative.

A critical recognition of sexual diversity, however, requires more than protective mechanisms against violence and the social "acceptance" of sexual difference manifested. For sexual diversity to emerge as a legitimate multiplication of forms of sexual self, normative sexual self requires decentring. A "normal" sexual self that is defined within one group of manifestations (hegemonically masculine heterosexuality) will perceive and interpret every other sexual self as deviant, to the extent that it is seen to take place (only) outside the boundaries of that defined normality. This definition of sexual normalness has, at best, very little space for sexual difference. Placed at the center of the cultural labeling process, of discourse formation, and of the production of knowledge, the "normal" sexual self describes and evaluates sexual expressions, behaviours, and preferences as variations of its thematic existence or as deviations from it. Again, within this frame of normalness sexual difference, at best, has a tolerated space. Sexual difference is allowed to coexist with normal sexuality if it is deemed not to be threatening, remains under the gaze and control of sexual normativity, or has been domesticated in such a way that it can be seen to be part of the horizon of normality in the future. This tolerated or domesticated space is far from a space that engenders social recognition of sexual diversity.

The symbolic and physical violence that is directed towards non-normative non-heterosexual expressions, individuals, and groups can be managed and administered by a politics of tolerance, without affecting the centrality of heterosexuality (and its hegemonically masculine and heterosexist discourses) for the construction of sexual identity. Tolerance creates a social space on the fringes of heterosexuality, or outside the periphery of its boundaries, where undefined sexual difference is allowed to exist, and where sexual deviance can be marginalised, contained, and kept in the shadows.

In fact, one might even argue that tolerance becomes a way of filtering and normalising sexual difference, and most importantly of protecting the political centrality and the discursive centeredness of "normal" sexual self. On the one hand, it allows for a renovation of the historical and contextual criteria for defining normalness by selectively incorporating, in ripe and appropriate moments, bits and pieces of sexual difference. On the other, it creates a social and cultural apparatus for buffering and managing the relation with sexual otherness, while creating the illusion of acceptance.

This politics of tolerance is paired up with an ethics of tolerance, which we believe plays an important role in the dynamics of the relationship between normalness and sexual difference. Considerations about fairness, dignity, and justice infuse the politics of tolerance with a sense of direction and with substantive criteria for making decisions at historical junctures, for example when boundaries need to be redrawn or reestablished. It also works as a corrective for the domineering impulses of politics and its practical excesses.

But within the political and ethical discourse of tolerance we find no fundamental ideas, systematic arguments, or discursive devices that can lead to processes of social recognition for sexual diversity. The success of a politics of tolerance can be claimed when the centrality of "normal" sexual self is defended not against the threats of sexual other, but against its own impulses to erase and destroy sexual difference. Tolerance (as a discourse of social and cultural mediation) defends sexual self through the protection it grants to sexual other, not because sexual self understands or cares about sexual other but because it wants to protect the minimum reciprocal foundations for justifying its own existence. The politics of tolerance is predicated on this very basic and primitive notion of reciprocity and on a rationality that dissuades sexual self from erasing and destroying sexual other under the justification of perceived threats.

In this sense, tolerance announces a self-centered, self-referential, and, to a certain extent, a self-contained discourse. At best, a politics and ethics of tolerance can manage and create the institutions for the administration of the relation between "normal" sexual self and sexual difference. But it does very little (if anything) to the structures and patterns of cultural and social interaction that foster and allow for the constant emergence of symbolic and physical violence against sexual difference, against a socially and culturally situated sexual difference that is constantly judged and perceived as threatening to sexual "normalness."

The social and cultural equation that has generated this definition of normal sexual self is restrictive, exclusive, self-centered, and reifies boundaries of difference. As we see it, the problem here is triple. First, normality is defined as a narrow and restrictive set of sexual manifestations. Second, sexual otherness is an event that is seen to occur outside the sphere of normality and thus is associated with deviance and pathology. Third, the boundaries that separate normal and deviant selves are perceived as dichotomous, hermetic, insular, and encapsulating.

We will later (in this paper) come back to discuss further the issues of sexual normality, otherness, and boundaries. For the time being what we want to point out is that the political project of proposing, constructing, and establishing negative sexual rights appears to be currently in a double bind.

There is a need and urgency to create normative mechanisms to protect sexual diversity and the sexual integrity of individuals and groups, as well as to construct norms capable of defending the right to determine one's sexual identity in an unrestricted and autonomous way, and the right to decide how to sexually express, behave, and interact both in the private and the public spheres. This current need and urgency for a protective normative is a call for a politics of tolerance as a possible minimum standard for allowing sexual difference to exist, and for initiating cultural and social processes for the acceptance of sexual diversity. The double bind is that by calling for and supporting a politics of tolerance we might be, at the same time, producing the conditions for a political realignment and normalisation without transforming the structures that generate the violence against sexual diversity. The illusion of acceptance, which a politics of tolerance creates, erodes the sense of need and urgency to address unjust situations, and risks processes where the boundaries of sexual self are redrawn without questioning and challenging the centeredness of heterosexuality. In this way, the creation of protective negative sexual rights would crystallise a "successful" politics of tolerance, yet at the same time it introduces and stabilises a "new" sexual order where heterosexuality is again at the center, but now appears as capable of coexisting with (some) sexual difference. These are the needs, risks, and dangers of the project of negative sexual rights that is solely promoted by a politics of tolerance.

An effective politics of tolerance would be able to generate the normativities to protect sexual difference, while reinstating (a more tolerant) heterosexuality as the central and dominant norm. But, the sources of symbolic and physical violence cannot be resolved until the current definitions of "normal" sexual self are challenged and destabilised and sexual identity is decentred.

Part of the quandary, it seems to us, is that both of these normative processes need to occur within the same cultural context or horizon of meaning. In other words, the same structures of cultural and social relations that are responsible for creating violence against sexual difference will be, at the same time, responsible for denying recognition to sexual diversity as a condition for the construction of comprehensive negative sexual rights. Sexual violence can be regulated and largely contained, and the group and individual effects can be diffused and explained away as discrete and unrelated events by a programmatic unfolding of a politics of tolerance. But under the political dynamics of tolerance, the sources of violence remain fundamentally untouched, because the centeredness of "normal" sexual self (hegemonically masculine heterosexuality) remains unquestioned. A "normal" sexual self can be progressively tolerant of a multiplicity of differences, but insofar as it resides at the center of the social production of sexual meaning this sexual self will have a basic control over the social definition of sexualities. This is part of the cultural privilege and the political power of normalness.

A comprehensive and progressive political project of negative sexual rights promotes with urgency the construction of protective rights, yet understands the limits and, most importantly, the dangers of stopping this critical process within the frame of an ethics and politics of tolerance. Negative rights cannot be a comprehensive and progressive political project until the creation of protective rights have led to a social and critical recognition of sexual diversity, and that is possible (at this historical juncture) by way of challenging, destabilising, and ultimately decentring heterosexuality.

The emergence and consolidation of identity-based social movements in the late twentieth century in many countries around the world have played a crucial and pivotal role for the political project of negative rights. They have allowed for both conceiving the need and urgency of protective rights, and challenging the normality of heterosexuality and the domination of hegemonic masculine identities.

Gay and lesbian first, and then bisexual and transgendered social movements and organisations have reshaped public perceptions of sexualities, but, most importantly, they have reshaped the boundaries that separate private and public sexual life. The eruption of these social movements have placed sexual difference at the center of public demands for recognition, and have forced a redefinition of socially accepted identities, as well as the perceived relation between sexual behaviour and the private sphere.

While the classic second-wave-feminist claim of the "personal is political" encapsulates the social need for reconceptualising what was thought to be personal and consequently to be excluded from the realm of the political, the statement "we are here and we are queer" calls for redefining the (political) presence of sexual difference and thus the boundaries of private and public in regard to alternative sexualities. While feminism took away the exclusivity of the private over the personal, gay and lesbian movements recast the way public sexual expression was conceived.

Before gay and lesbian movements made their political imprint on the public domain, the overt discursive claim was the association of sexual expression and behaviour with the private sphere. Yet, the public domain was controlled by heterosexual and male desire. That is, sexuality was "allowed" to appear in the public realm in so far as it was directed to please heterosexual and hegemonically masculine desire. At the same time, nevertheless, it was thematised as a private issue, as something that could only legitimately occur within the confines of the private. This double discourse of sexual expression and behaviour has been challenged, and a reconfiguration of this private and public split has followed.

But the boundaries of private and public sexual expression and behaviour have been redefined in other ways as well. The private sphere was systematically used as a social and cultural device to cover and hide sexual behaviour that was defined as perverse and deviant. In so far as sexual perversions did not damage anybody, people were "allowed" to engage in perverse and deviant sexualities in the privacy of their lives. Privacy became a mechanism to keep the public sexually "normal" and protected heterosexuality from having to acknowledge other sexualities, behaviours, and expressions as legitimate. Only acceptable sexual manifestations were filtered into the public realm; everything else needed to remain outside the horizon of the public view. The split gave male dominated heterosexuality control over the association that equated public sexuality with legitimate sexuality, keeping other sexualities outside the public realm and confined to illegitimacy, perversion, and pathology. Sexual identity-based social movements challenged, fractured, and forced new reconfigurations of these associations.

Gay, lesbian, bisexual, and transgendered movements brought sexual pathologies, perverse behaviours, and deviant expressions into the public realm of life, forcing everybody to acknowledge their presence and to recognise their pervasiveness. Privacy was no longer enough to contain and confine other sexualities, and to keep them outside the processes of cultural and political legitimation. Furthermore, pathologies, perversions, and deviance were all resignified by the double dynamics of public eruption and the demand for recognition. Categories that named, distinguished, clustered, separated, and marginalised were rendered useless for differentiating the bad from the good, the sick from the healthy, the abnormal from the normal. These movements stepped into the public realm, embraced their sexual difference, and reclaimed it as a source and basis for identity. Not only were these movements refusing to keep deviant sexual behaviours and expressions as part of shadowy lives and illegitimate selves, but they were claiming that the "pathological" was not sexually sick, that the "perverse" was an expression of sexual diversity, and that "deviant" was a product of a narrow definition of normal sexuality. Sexual other was leaving the shadows of privacy and asserting itself in the daylight of the public domain.

This new public assertion of sexual otherness not only disputed the pathologising of sexual difference, but also questioned the currency of sexual normalness. Sexual difference was out in the public; it was here to stay, and it was not going anywhere. The political claim of this new public sexual otherness was for a social and cultural space for constructing sexual identities that could claim, simultaneously, to be legitimate and normal. Out from the prison of pathology and the shadows of privacy, sexual otherness demands a piece of the definition of normal sexual self.

These social movements have opened other spheres, as well, to the possibility of normative transformations. In the challenges they have posed to deeply held conceptions about sexual self and identity, they have been able to threaten the stability of heterosexuality as a model of normalness and to erode cultural strongholds of masculine hegemony. Sexual difference has moved away from criminalised deviance and has been brought back from the dark side of pathology. Additionally, the social and cultural space for the toleration of sexual difference has multiplied, expanded, and grown significantly. These important changes have modified socially acceptable perceptions and definitions of sexual difference, reconfigured the relations between normal and deviant sexual self, and perhaps have been even able to pluralise sexuality. There is no doubt that these changes have positively impacted the lives of many social groups and individuals by carving safeguarded and semi-autonomous crevices within the social and political body for sexual expression, affirmation, and interaction. Yet, as important and significant as these changes have been, they have not been able to decentre heterosexuality.

Sexual identity-based social movements have been very effective in questioning the systematic exclusions that gay, lesbian, bisexual, transgendered, and intersexed people and groups suffer, on a daily basis, from the entitlements and benefits of citizenship. They have been also politically very effective in challenging the claims and the legitimacy of such social and legal exclusions. In effect, their impact has pushed out the boundaries of citizenship, within countries, making the legal set of entitlements more inclusive of sexual difference. But the subject of national law and citizenship continues to be conceived as heterosexual and hegemonically masculine.

In other words, within certain national contexts the expansion of citizenship that has resulted from the political work of these identity based social movements is no doubt important, progressive, and significant. Yet, their critical discourses of heterosexuality are effectively tamed by their need for normalising sexual difference. With the normalisation of sexual difference it is our fear that we might be, at the same time, normalising the critique of heterosexuality, and thus losing the possibility of destabilising and decentring the regime of hegemonically male heterosexual domination, which is (at the end) the reason there is homosexual, bisexual, transgendered, and intersex oppression.

The social and cultural impact that these social movements have had, their political demands and legal achievements, and the effective work of their organisations is what, we believe, makes the project of international human rights for the protection of sexual integrity and the establishment of negative sexual rights a feasible normative project today. At the same time, however, we believe that a progressive, consequential, and critical discourse of the current sexual regime cannot stop with the international institutionalisation of negative sexual rights. From the destabilising forces of current gay, lesbian, bisexual, transgendered, and intersexed social movements we need to create future political horizons capable of decentring heterosexuality and destructuring hegemonic masculinity.

3.   The Push for Positive Sexual Rights

While negative sexual rights are required for protecting the integrity of individuals and groups whose sexual identities, behaviours, and expressions constitute otherness to hegemonically masculine heterosexuality, the political project of positive sexual rights is predicated on the radical nature of sexual otherness, one that cannot be translated into tolerable sexual difference or domesticated by a politics of sexual tolerance. The political project of positive sexual rights seeks ultimately to debunk male hegemony over the practice and discourse of sexuality, and to decentre heterosexuality.

What appears to be morally obvious and seems to soundly justify the political urgency for negative sexual rights rapidly disappears when one ceases to think only of protecting the integrity of sexual difference from the violence and domination impulses of sexual self. It is morally obvious because there is no justification for violence directed towards sexual otherness, and because violence is a gross affront to the humanity of individuals and groups, even when sexual self might interpret the presence of other sexualities as a threat. It is less obvious, however, to argue that what is required is a complete transformation of sexual self and its concurrent regime of sex and gender relations.

The institution of negative sexual rights will serve as effective normative mechanisms for protecting the integrity of sexual difference, but they cannot alone destructure the logic and operation of heterosexism. At best, negative rights can question prejudice and challenge heterosexist behaviours, and perhaps, at some points in time, even demobilise the collective dynamics of sexual intolerance, but they do not have the capacity to change the political arrangements, social relations, and cultural frames that are responsible for these demonstrations of sexual self. In this sense, the ultimate goal of positive sexual rights is to erase the sources that make protective rights such a pressing need today.

While protection is the central idea that organises negative sexual rights, positive sexual rights revolve around the concept of affirmation. On the one hand, they represent a push for the affirmation of sexual diversity, and on the other they designate an affirmation of sexuality as pleasure.[3] Both constitutive parts speak to the need for cultural and social processes of empowerment. They rest on the very basic diagnosis that the current social organisation of sex and gender is structured on two fundamental exclusions: it deprives many individuals and groups from constructing a sexual identity that is socially accepted and celebrated, and simultaneously precludes many from living a sexual life defined by desire and pleasure. Positive sexual rights are seen as normative tools capable of promoting and generating these necessary processes of empowerment and affirmation. Their political aim is to create normatively enforced social spaces that simultaneously foster a complete and thorough recognition of sexual diversity, and encourage living fully gratifying and pleasant sexual lives.

One dimension of positive sexual rights is oriented towards the advancement of full and unrestricted recognition of sexual diversity. These rights recognise, empower, and enable disenfranchised sexual identities, behaviours, and expressions. They are normative enablers of sexual diversity because they grant social and cultural legitimacy to processes of sexual identity construction and manifestations of sexual life that have been historically marginalised. These processes and manifestations have not only been denied full development and unrestricted acceptance within the framework of our dominant regime of sex and gender, but they have also been obligated to subordinate their existence to normalness defined as heterosexuality, and forced to inhabit the world as shadowy and covert subjects that become involved in deviant practices. The entrance and the establishment of a politics of tolerance modify, to be sure, these circumstances of marginality. Yet these modifications have also very clear limits. At best, the marginality of sexual difference gains the new status of subaltern sexualities.

The other dimension of positive sexual rights is oriented towards the creation of universal access to a sexual life filled with joy. These rights advance a full entitlement to sexual pleasure and desire. They normatively promote the social and cultural conditions necessary to live one's own sexuality and engage in sexual relations that respect, embrace, multiply, and diversify sexual pleasure and desire. Historically, the organisation of sex and gender has placed social definitions of sexual pleasure and desire under the control of heterosexism and masculine domination. Here as well, a politics of tolerance modifies conceptions, boundaries, and interactions allowing for new forms of flexible and liberal interpretation of sexual life and sexual practices, but non-heterosexual and alternative sexualities remain, at best, subordinate options.

From the onset, however, we believe that the dimension of sexual rights that affirms pleasure and desire requires normative limits. In our societies and cultures, where domination is intimately intertwined with sexuality and sex, it would be unreasonable and politically naïve to propose positive rights, which promote universal access to sexual pleasure, without normative limits that can prevent the utilisation of sexual pleasure and sex for subjugation and exploitation. We endorse the idea that the affirmation of pleasure and desire needs to be anchored to an ethics of dialogical and relational equality, respect, and reciprocity. As Steven Seidman argues:

> In contrast to a normalising ethic, …a communicative ethic maintains that sex acts are given moral meaning by their communicative context. In other words, the qualities of a sexual desire or act per se cannot be the basis for determining its moral status. Accordingly, the focus of normative evaluation shifts from the sex act to the social exchange. Instead of determining whether a specific act is normal, critical judgment would focus on the moral features of a social exchange; for example, does it involve mutual consent? Are the agents acting responsibly and respectfully? Is there erotic-intimate reciprocity?[4]

This fundamental normative shift moves moral evaluation from the simplicity of judging sexual acts to a more complex judgment that appraises the content of sex as a social relation. Additionally, it also allows us to establish the normative limits that we need for positive sexual rights as affirmation of pleasure and desire.

An ethics of communication builds in the central mechanisms of consent, responsibility, and respect, and consequently (to a large degree) curtails the need for protective or corrective interventions. Yet, because of the current social interlacing of domination and sexuality, we need to explicitly prevent the possibility of affirming sexual pleasure as subjugation and exploitation:

> A communicative sexual ethic suggests that most sexual practices should be viewed as matters of personal or aesthetic not moral choice. It follows that many sexual practices would lose their moral and hence broader social significance. There would be less justification for social intervention beyond regulating behaviour that involves coercion and minors.[5]

Notwithstanding, our current regime of sex and gender has been constructed through an active and systematic process of marginalisation and subordination of sexual otherness. By way of this comprehensive social and cultural process, hegemonically masculine heterosexuality has been placed at the center of this regime and at the top of its hierarchical order. It becomes center to the regime when it is defined as undisputed sexual normality and the model for sexual self. From the center the view of the sexual landscape (so to speak) is not panoramic and horizontal. No, this centeredness has been achieved and is currently defended through domination. Otherness is not only defined as different, but it is at the same time always defined as less and inferior. Abnormal sexualities and sexual perversions describe subjects and conditions that demand "normalisation," not celebration.

The two meanings of positive sexual rights require a politics and ethics that transcend those of tolerance. Additionally, the assertions that these rights normatively encourage and develop announce the initiation of three necessary processes: the subversion of masculine hegemony, the decentring of heterosexuality, and the de-essentialisation of sexual identity. A complete recognition of sexual diversity and a universal access to living sexuality as an affirmation of pleasure create, concurrently, normative platforms for social and cultural changes that relativise and undermine the hegemonic control of masculinity, and that move the destabilisation of heterosexuality a step forward towards its ultimate decentring. It is our hope that these two very central transformations will also open the possibility of unshackling the social processes of sexual identity from essentialist interpretations and experiences.

Of course the question at this point is how would this normative and political project be at all possible? How can we propose such normative changes that, in turn, would stimulate other very profound transformations to our current social regime of sex and gender?

The political project of positive sexual rights is not directly dependent on the normative existence of negative rights, yet it is very difficult to imagine their acknowledgment without the necessary social and cultural conditions for the acceptance of negative rights. In this way, a politics and ethics of tolerance prove a condition for negative rights and a precondition for the political project of positive rights.

What is required for the justification, acceptance, and establishment of negative rights is a politics and ethics of tolerance. Positive rights, however, demand a different political and ethical paradigm. Sexual difference can be protected from the violent impulses of hegemonic sexual self when sexual self realises (through a very simple moral equation) that erasing sexual difference jeopardises its own existence and future. Self does not eliminate other because it erodes the basic reciprocity of boundary containment that assures self to continue existing. Within the paradigm of tolerance self is never compelled, let alone interested, in dealing with or engaging other. Tolerating other is for self a self-serving gesture; it is an action for protecting the privilege of centeredness. Other remains, at best, a mystery. Why would you choose to be other if it is so much better to be self?

Positive sexual rights requires a different paradigm because their political project is precisely about engaging sexual other and sexual otherness, both exterior and interior to oneself. A politics and ethics of recognition is capable of translating and transforming sexual difference into sexual diversity. A sexual self that is forced, better even interested in dealing with and engaging sexual other and sexual otherness has made the first necessary move towards decentredness. By engaging otherness sexual self is able to relativise its position in the social organisation of sex and landscape of sexualities, and gains the possibility of imagining alternative ways of constructing sexual identity and affirming sexual life.

We are not suggesting that the transition from tolerance to recognition would be anything but conflictual. On the contrary, to the extent that tolerance allows for a reconfiguration and a redrawing of boundaries within which sexual difference is allotted spaces of alterity and subaltern existence, and where sexual self remains at the center of the regime of sex and gender, we see no reason why sexual self would give up this renewed legitimacy and more tolerant exercise of power.

What we are suggesting, however, is that sexual self has been forced onto a transitional terrain in which a politics of tolerance overlaps with a politics of recognition, and in which their ethics conflict.

Sexual identity-based social movements emerged and developed in a context where identity politics at large was redefining the dynamics of political mobilisation, the content of political demands, and the objectives of political change. This larger context of contestation gave the struggle for recognition a multiple yet generalised form, and framed the demand as a socially necessary change. The struggles for recognition were not only based on sexuality and gender, but they were also multicultural with claims to ethnicity, race, religion, and nationality, and even to age, as well as to body and physical or mental ability. In this sense, sexual identity-based social movements have greatly benefited from other identity-based movements because they were spared from taking on the political demand for recognition alone. Pushing for a full recognition of multiple and diverse identities, and demanding new forms of inclusion into the body politic, as well as into the national legal frames became a concern of all society, rather than only specific concerns and demands of a segment of society. Recognition, as an end result of multiple processes of inclusion, became a generalised point of convergence and a constant political preoccupation. As Charles Taylor explains,

> The demand for recognition…is given urgency by the supposed links between recognition and identity…The thesis is that our identity is partly shaped by recognition or its absence, often by the misrecognition of others, and so a person or a group of people can suffer real damage, real distortion if the people or society around them mirror back a confining or demeaning or contemptible picture of themselves. Nonrecognition or misrecognition can inflict harm, can be a form of oppression, imprisoning someone in a false, distorted, and reduced mode of being.[6]

Positive rights are a call for creating social and cultural dimensions, spaces, and horizons where new and multiple forms of sexual affirmation are possible. Yet, we see a political project for sexual life and recognition beyond the possibilities of positive rights. While positive rights are possible and, in fact, justified under our current social organisation of sex and gender that in subtle and complex ways intertwines sexuality and power, we believe that ultimately our political goal should be to unlink sexuality from power altogether. Positive rights will multiply forms of sexual affirmation and allow an empowering access to pleasure, but in so far as heterosexuality remains at the center of this multiplicative sexual landscape, and has control over the discourses that articulate sexual self, the social processes of diverse sexual affirmation will remain subaltern.

But the problem of power, we believe, runs even deeper. To what extent have the subtle and complex connections between sex, gender, and power made our sexual identities, behaviours, and expressions dependent on the exercise of specific forms of intimate power and domination? To what extent is the issue of power relations not exterior to the construction of sexual self and sexual other but, in fact, constitutive of the process of sexual identity formation and desire?

These formative, constitutive, and perverse characteristics of power relations over social subjects,[7] justify, in our estimation, the effort of looking beyond the protection of sexual integrity, and the affirmation of sexual diversity and pleasure. At the same time, however, it speaks to the complexity of the task. Separating, or even better liberating sex and sexuality from power would imply necessarily the remaking of sexual self and sexual other, that is, the reconstitution of all sexual selves.

Current definitions and interpretations of normalised sexual identity reveal a sexual self that is not only impoverished, but also quite fragile. It is self-centered, restrictive, and exclusionary, and depends largely on the reification of sexual boundaries and essentialist thought for gaining a sense of security. Sexual "normalness" is not only defined narrowly and within constraining parameters, but it is also highly dependent on the self-serving effects of demonising and debasing sexual otherness. Even when sexual otherness is no longer seen as pathological, perversion remains a shadow and deviance a constant descriptor. Sexual otherness is associated with events that happen or identities that live outside the periphery of normality, leaving very little space (if any at all) for the exploration of otherness within self or the fluid experience of otherness as situational and relational. To protect its fragility, sexual self erects boundaries that separate normal and deviant selves, and that holds at bay the "perverse" influences and temptations of sexual otherness. These boundaries are perceived as dichotomous, and lived as hermetic, insular, and encapsulating of identity.

A politics and ethics of recognition relativise the current social organisation of sex and gender. Sexual normality becomes diffuse because it is no longer the exclusive domain of one form of sexual being and expression. The diversification of sexual acceptance brings into question the use of homogeneity for defining normality. With the diversification of possible sexual selves, normalness becomes heterogeneous, and the conception of normality moves from singular to plural interpretations. There is no longer only one path to sexual development and identity, nor is there only one model to follow or to measure against. Models of sexual being become pluralised by the acceptance and legitimation of sexual diversity.

Recognition also multiplies the horizon of sexual identities and the forms of sexual identification and relations, and with this it erodes the need to use hierarchical thinking to order and organise the worth of sexual manifestations, behaviours, and identities. Sexual otherness is no longer defiled or marginalised, nor is there a need to perceive it as deviant any more because it is not interpreted as a threat to sexual selves. Domination as recourse for identity construction and consolidation appears as increasingly suspicious and unnecessary. In fact, processes of excluding and subjugating sexual other, as ways of affirming sexual self, become not only profoundly delegitimised but actually unwarranted. Sexual other can be sexual self, as well as sexual self can be sexual other within a cultural and social horizon of sexual beings that are irreducibly diverse.

4.   Concluding Remarks

In our view, the political project of sexual rights is possible today because of the (unfulfilled) emancipatory potentials of sexual identity based social movements and also because of a thought transformation that has occurred in social theory and philosophy.

Despite the political limitations of identity-based social movements and their tendency to essentialise identities, they have nevertheless been able to question heterosexism and destabilise (albeit, temporarily) our dominant organisation of sex and gender relations. We can also credit them for having been able to expand citizenship within nations, and to force a new tolerance for sexual difference. But with these processes of institutionalisation their challenges have been flattened and their critique co-opted. However, there is still emancipatory capacity that can be fulfilled by moving from destabilisation to decentring heterosexuality.

In turn, the eruption of postmodern thought and new social theory that has critically engaged the central and multiple challenges that postmodernism has leveled against the project of the Enlightenment, as well as the confluence of different strands of contemporary critical thought like feminism, queer theory, post-structuralism, critical theory, and deconstructionism have all, in our estimation, contributed to a subject decentring of social theory and to a de-essentialising of social identity. In the process, we believe, the emancipatory potentials of a critical Enlightenment project have been renewed.

Throughout this paper, we have argued that the conditions for negative sexual rights are long overdue, and that the possibilities for positive sexual rights are maturing. The social simplicity and cultural obviousness of tolerance is a compelling indication as to how feasible negative sexual rights are today. In turn, the ideas that multiple social differences should be accepted into the landscape of society and that diversity should be fully recognised as a part of social life make positive sexual rights a legitimate, possible, and solid political project to look forward to. Yet, in the construction of these political projects we believe it is crucial to look beyond their normative establishment and set the conditions for unlinking sexuality from power relations and from all forms of domination. An emancipation of this sort might allow for the emergence of a sexual self free from the distortions and the perverse effects of power.

Notes

1. Rosalind Petchesky, "Sexual Rights: Inventing a Concept, Mapping an International Practice," in *Framing the Sexual Subject: The Politics of Gender, Sexuality and Power*, edited by Richard G. Parker, Regina Maria Barbosa, and Peter Aggleton (Berkeley: University of California Press, 2000), 81-103; Geoffrey Robertson, *Crimes Against Humanity: The Struggle for Global Justice* (New York: The New Press, 1999).

2. Axel Honneth, *The Critique of Power: Reflective Stages in a Critical Social Theory* (Cambridge, Massachussetts: The MIT Press, 1991); Michael Kelly, ed., *Critique and Power: Recasting the Foucault/Habermas Debate*. (Cambridge, Massachussetts: The MIT Press, 1994).

3. See Sonia Corrêa and Richard Parker, "Sexuality, Human Rights, and Demographic Thinking: Connections and Disjunctions in a Changing World," manuscript, 2002. Corrêa and Parker attribute the idea of the right to pleasure (as a positive sexual right) to Rosalind Petchesky. It seems to have appeared, for the first time, in a conference paper delivered in Brazil that was later worked as a chapter of a book published in 2000 that was edited by Richard Parker, et al. We heard it for the first time, in 2000, during our discussions in a seminar in Mexico City. See Rosalind P. Petchesky, "Sexual Rights: Inventing a Concept, Mapping an International Practice," in *Framing the Sexual Subject: The Politics of Gender, Sexuality and Power*, edited by Richard G. Parker, Regina Maria Barbosa, and Peter Aggleton (Berkeley: University of California Press, 2000), 81-103.

4. Steven Seidman, "From Identity to Queer Politics: Shifts in Normative Heterosexuality," in *The New Social Theory Reader: Contemporary Debates*, edited by Steven Seidman and Jeffrey C. Alexander, (London: Routledge, 2001), 353-360: 358-359.

5. Seidman, 359.

6. Charles Taylor, *Philosophical Arguments*. (Cambridge, Massachusetts: Harvard University Press, 1995), 225.

7. A central preoccupation of Foucault. See Michel Foucault, *Discipline and Punish: The Birth of the Prison* (New York: Vintage Books, 1977); *Power/Knowledge: Selected Interviews and Other Writings, 1972-1977* (New York: Pantheon Books, 1980); "Disciplinary Power and Subjection," in *Power*, edited by Steven Lukes (Oxford: Blackwell, 1986), 229-242; and *Politics, Philosophy, Culture: Interviews and Other Writings, 1977-1984* (New York: Routledge, 1988).

Select Bibliography

Corrêa, Sonia, and Richard Parker. "Sexuality, Human Rights, and Demographic Thinking: Connections and Disjunctions in a Changing World." Manuscript, 2002.

Foucault, Michel. *Discipline and Punish: The Birth of the Prison*. New York: Vintage Books, 1977.

——. *Power/Knowledge: Selected Interviews and Other Writings, 1972-1977*. New York: Pantheon Books, 1980.

——. "Disciplinary Power and Subjection." In *Power*, edited by Steven Lukes, 229-242. Oxford: Blackwell, 1986.

——. *Politics, Philosophy, Culture: Interviews and Other Writings, 1977-1984*. New York: Routledge, 1988.

Honneth, Axel. *The Critique of Power: Reflective Stages in a Critical Social Theory*. Cambridge, Massachussetts: The MIT Press, 1991.

Kelly, Michael, ed. *Critique and Power: Recasting the Foucault/Habermas Debate*. Cambridge, Massachussetts: The MIT Press, 1994.

Petchesky, Rosalind P. "Sexual Rights: Inventing a Concept, Mapping an International Practice." In *Framing the Sexual Subject: The Politics of Gender, Sexuality, and Power*, edited by Richard G. Parker, Regina Maria Barbosa, and Peter Aggleton, 81-103. Berkeley: University of California Press, 2000.

Robertson, Geoffrey. *Crimes Against Humanity: The Struggle for Global Justice*. New York: The New Press, 1999.

Seidman, Steven. "From Identity to Queer Politics: Shifts in Normative Heterosexuality." In *The New Social Theory Reader: Contemporary Debates*, edited by Steven Seidman and Jeffrey C. Alexander, 353-360. London: Routledge, 2001.

Taylor, Charles. *Philosophical Arguments*. Cambridge, Massachusetts: Harvard University Press, 1995.

International Law, Children's Rights, and Queer Youth

Valerie D. Lehr

Abstract
Queer youth in the United States face an environment dominated by Right-wing assertions that youth are most appropriately not sexual and that parents should exercise control over important decision-making. This paper examines the possibility of creating a counter-discourse, one that is based on understanding youth as able to exercise agency including sexual agency and that sees this as particularly important for citizenship development in contemporary societies. It should also connect U.S. discussions of youth to international human rights discourse, particularly to that found in the Convention on the Rights of the Child, a convention not yet ratified in the U.S. **Key Words:** queer youth, citizenship, human rights, children's rights, youth transitions.

1.   Introduction

One of the most complete analyses of the gay, lesbian, bisexual, transgendered (queer) youth in United States' schools has been completed by Human Rights Watch (HRW).[1] As HRW recognises, the issues that queer youth face can be understood as human rights issues. Further, if we move outside of the focus on schools to explore the pressures that queer youth often experience in their families, the desirability of a human rights agenda for youth generally and queer youth in particular becomes even more compelling. Despite HRW's recognition that international human rights agreements can be an important mechanism for pursuing more equitable and just treatment, most U.S. gay rights organisations do not make arguments that draw from such agreements, nor do they see pursuing the ratification of these agreements as central, or even as a component, of their agendas. Supporting international protections should be a widespread goal of queer activism. In order to most fully protect queer youth, it is also important for activists in the United States to actively pursue ratification of the Convention on the Rights of the Child (CRC).

2.   Youth and Sexual Rights in the United States

Young people enjoy few rights that allow them to define and act on their own when they come into conflict with adult authorities, whether at home or in schools, a (and often *the*) primary institution in many youth's lives. Sexual rights, then, are virtually non-existent, making it difficult for young people to gain the information necessary to establish a sexual identity with intention and purpose. Queer youth activist Colleen Donovan sums this up:

> As a youth activist, I have seen the systematic devaluation of young people's ideas, thoughts, dreams, musings, and inspirations. Discounted as immature, irresponsible, and ignorant, youth have few rights in this society, and as we have seen with the recent spate of "parental rights" bills, even those few are tenuous. As youth within the queer movement, we challenge the ageist system with our very existence.[2]

This challenge comes from the assertion that youth can, and maybe even should, have a chosen, agential sexual identity. Ironically, although in most states sixteen year olds may be able to consent to sexual relations, most will attend schools that either stress abstinence until marriage or that use the $138 million appropriated in 2004 by the federal government to fund abstinence-until-marriage-only sexuality education. In most states homosexuality is either invisible or virtually invisible within sex education other than when it is portrayed negatively. The impetus for such policies has come from the Religious Right, which, as Judith Levine simply puts it, "has all but won the sex education wars."[3] At the same time, the Right has focused on asserting the power of parents to make decisions for their children and to be responsible for the decisions of their children, often including abortion, a discourse that also has some currency in Great Britain.

As I've detailed elsewhere,[4] the power of parental rights in the United States, combined with the denial of voice to young people in public spaces such as schools, creates a lethal combination for many queer youth, one that results in a paucity of safe spaces for these young people to explore sexuality/gender. The regime of parental power, which has only been strengthened by the Bush administration, means that young people who wish to assert a sexual or gender identity in opposition to parental desires are highly vulnerable to unwanted psychiatric treatment, homelessness, and schooling in religious institutions that may define queerness as a sin. Vocal parental groups mobilised by the Right have created an environment in which most public schools are unwilling (or fiscally unable) to provide an education that encourages youth to develop into decision-makers with a sense of efficacy to affect their environment, either sexuality or socially.

Kitzinger argues, however, that the counter to a culture with widespread abuse of children, whether sexual or otherwise, must be not the reinforcement of childhood through parental rights, but its deconstruction: "Children's need for protection (by adults, from adults) or their need for assertive self-defense strategies would be substantially reduced if they had more access to social, economic, and political resources."[5] For young people who try to leave their parental homes, the increasing provision of services through religious social service organisations allowed to discriminate makes the situation even more complex.[6] Without access to services in supportive environments, queer youth are likely to continue to suffer from higher suicide rates, higher school drop out rates, higher homelessness rates, and greater frequency of diseases such as AIDS than other youth. Without a definition of youth as sexual agents, queer adults will continue to be discouraged from providing necessary support to youth by charges that they are recruiting young people who lack the maturity to make sexual decisions. Again, Donovan's analysis is insightful: "Heteropatriarchy is a powerful tool that uses scare tactics to separate generations under the myth of recruitment. It is meant to threaten adult mentors, resources, or support."[7]

Hope for access to greater resources and power for youth, however, is not great. It is consistent that the Bush administration is hostile to the concept of children's rights generally and the Convention on the Rights of the Child in particular.[8] Given the power of the Religious Right in America, it is not surprising that even Democratic administrations are unlikely to advocate either the sexual/democratic rights of youth or any international mechanisms that might call U.S. anxiety about youth and/or sexuality into question. It was, for example, the Clinton administration that encouraged Surgeon General Joycelyn Elders to resign in the wake of her comment that perhaps masturbation should be discussed in schools. The United States, then, lacks a persuasive discourse with any potential to further youth power in relation to sexuality, or citizenship rights more generally. Theorists of youth cultures suggest that such Conservative approaches fail to meet the needs of most youth or their parents, and that many parents are also quite aware of this. Nonetheless, the lack of a coherent counter-discourse, or even much attention to youth issues outside of the Right, makes this failure continue to be experienced as the failure of individual young people and their parents. In suggesting the foundations for a counter-narrative, I first want to turn to the work of theorists of youth transitions, who recognise both the power of economic structures to constrain youth and the social forces that enable at least some people to define themselves as creative agents despite these forces.

3.   Theorising Post-Modern Youth Transitions and Citizenship

As consumption and education credentials have become more central to economically developed countries, the role of youth in these societies has changed. In literature on youth informed by political economy and cultural studies, a key question involves the extent to which social structures limit agency, and in particular, the ways by which youth are increasingly excluded from meaningful citizenship as a result of de-industrialisation. A number of studies on youth, citizenship, and transition suggest that young people want to exercise agency, that they want to have responsibility, that they are capable of what Ule and Rener term "individualized identity,"[9] but that the risks of failure are increasingly taken on by the individual, with the structural forces that make the definition of self increasingly remote from the consciousness of young people. Despite neo-liberal ideology, structural forces remain powerful, from those that mandate that youth remain in educational systems for longer periods of time, and that see the lack of desire to do so as a personal failure, to the increased dependence on adults fostered by this need for credentialing, to the reliance of many capitalist industries on the purchasing power of youth and young adults. One result of these demands on youth, Ule and Rener note, may be a increased tendency for young people to define themselves not in relation to "grandiose values that draw on powerful ideologies (politics, religion, national bonds)," but rather in relation to "more individualized values situated closer to personal experience (material and social security, friendship and interpersonal relations, a healthy environment, the quality of everyday life, and so on)."[10] This broad point is illustrated not only by Ule and Rener's data on youth in the Czech Republic, but also in Jacobsson and Hebert's discussion of animal rights activists in Sweden, youth who see activism connected to personal commitments as more important than activism within traditional political formations.[11] When the subcultures that youth create are taken seriously, Guidikova and Siurala suggest, it becomes apparent that "it is not young people who refuse responsibility, but adult society which denies them opportunities for participation."[12] Many governments respond by developing programs to reintegrate youth into job markets or educational programs or developing initiatives intended to bring young people's voice more thoroughly into the public realm. Alternatively, governments can respond, as Sharon Stephens indicates has been the case in the United State and Great Britain, by seeing the need for greater control of children.[13]

Though the different impact of these changes on males and females is considered in this literature, sexuality/gender identity is much less present. In one attempt to link sexuality and these changes, Bob Coles writes:

> A number of authors have also emphasised the importance of gaining a steady boyfriend or girlfriend as a signifier of becoming regarded as adult. They have also recognised that in areas of high employment, partnership with a man in full-time employment is important to young women.[14]

Though the first sentence leaves open the possibility that one can be queer and "adult," the second sentence suggests that for many young women, such an option may be economically unwise. What Adrienne Rich termed "compulsory heterosexuality" may be even more compelling in a more challenging environment, yet those focusing on these economic dynamics do not explore this possibility. Authors who explore the increased dependence of youth on parents do not explore the possibility that increased dependence could be experienced in vastly different ways by queer youth and those who identify with hegemonic gender and sex norms.

Part of the literature on structural change and youth highlights how youth engage in identity formation in light of postmodern realities. Rattansi and Phoenix discuss this in their review of European approaches to youth identity and implications for citizenship in democracies. They suggest the literature has highlighted identity as constructed within particular social circumstance, and as relational, multiple, and always undergoing change. Identities are very much a product of social structures and individual agency. Yet, despite quoting work that indicates the importance of social institutions in constructing "stable heterosexual relationships (especially for girls) and other forms of appropriate behavior," their conclusion reverts to the centrality of class, gender, and "race" for the multiple identities of youth.[15] In her discussion of this essay, Griffin argues bringing sexuality to the center of analysis is critical because it is so deeply connected to how the concept of youth is constructed:

> Issues of sexuality, and especially adult panics over adolescent sexuality, have been long central to the treatment of youth. Relations of gender and sexuality-as well as race and class-have collided in the debate over "teen pregnancy" and "adolescent sexuality" for example.[16]

In the end, she notes, our understanding of citizenship and its development requires that we see youth as involved in production, consumption, and reproduction. Without understanding how their decision-making is influenced by both global forces that restrict and expand possibilities and local forces that play the same dual role, in relation to each of these spheres, our notion of citizenship and youth will remain too constricted.

The more common invisibility of sexuality from the literature on identity and citizenship is puzzling. As Griffin observes, since adolescence is seen to resolve around puberty and the onset of sexual agency,[17] it seems that sexuality would be very present. At the same time the increased emphasis on marketing to youth has made the sexuality of young people a powerful public presence. Further, with the delay in decision-making about the role that they will play in production, the question of sexuality seems to be an area where the potential for agency remains powerful at younger age. Given the extent to which family and relationship decisions have expanded, to a point where marriage really is optional in a number of European countries, it would seem that considering how young people develop the capacities necessary to enact different forms of family and relationship ethically would, in fact, concern those interested in youth and citizenship. Finally, the increased dependence on parents and the power of peer relationships can create real difficulties for young people who are defining their sexualities in opposition to hegemonic norms and parental norms. This is particularly a problem in the United States, since parental power remains so strong and many youth continue to lack access (other than electronically) to peer groups supportive of greater sexual freedom. Thus, the structural conditions of late modernity, though opening up the possibility for increased sexual agency, also increasingly put youth in a position where their failure to enact sexual identity may be internalised as their own failure, rather than understood in social and political terms. Ule and Rener see the dominant social forces as leading to two possibilities:

> Our conclusions about the individualisation of youth in modern developed societies indicate that young people react extremely ambivalently to the contradictions of the globalisation process and post-industrial modernisation. They oscillate between two possibilities which both require various forms of expression. The first possibility is psycho-social demoralization, the second is the development of "altruistic individualism," that is, social sensibility and responsibility in connection with personal satisfaction and personal lifestyles.[18]

This description is suggestive of the two paths that queer youth often take: either organising locally to demand recognition or feeling alienated and/or depressed. Human Rights Watch describes these two possibilities:

> One counselor we interviewed expressed concern that girls rarely excelled once they were publicly identified as lesbian. Boys were sometimes able to find a niche for themselves in the drama club, as a band major, or even as the class clown to survive, but girls rarely, if ever, seemed to find such a niche for themselves....Lesbians who can prevail against the sexism and homophobia they face report feeling empowered. Alix M. told us that it took her three years to get the courage to start a small gay-straight alliance in her school. Faced with deepening depression and painful feelings of isolation,

she turned to the Internet to get information on how to start a gay-straight alliance." The result of her activism is that she has become a "stronger individual able to conquer her fears."[19]

The challenge for gay organisations is to work to create conditions that might help young people to develop altruistic individualism.

In the United States, this requires a broader focus on youth as citizens and on the rights of young people, something that is more advanced in Europe, a number of authors suggest, because the CRC has been taken more seriously and has begun to prompt significant reflection about what it means to recognise the capacities of young people, and therefore, the citizenship of youth. In the United States, questions of youth and agency have come to focus more on getting (middle-class) young people to perform community service as a mechanism to involvement in civil society, rather than encouraging youth participation in a manner that might encourage the expression of voice in the present. This is a perspective in which sexuality is made invisible, and not an approach to youth engagement likely to be of benefit to sexual minority youth. In concluding, I will review writing about how the Convention is forwarding dialogue in Europe, while suggesting that this success, particularly in the U.K., indicates that the United States needs a discourse that links young people to the development of identity not as future citizens, but as current contributors to society.

4. Prioritising the International Convention on the Rights of the Child

In commenting on the CRC, Levesque notes that, in general, it would maintain the importance of the parent-child relationship in ways consistent with United States law. He continues: "The Convention, however, goes one step further. The Convention calls for States to take on the revolutionary obligation to ensure that parent's recognise and ensure their children's rights."[20] Central to this change, is view that the "child is human being, not the germ of a human being."[21]   While the CRC identifies the family as the ideal location for raising children, it ensures that the child's voice be heard, while also demanding that the State work to ensure that the best interests of the child are provided, even by the family.

The CRC can potentially address many of the needs of LGBTQ youth. In part this is the case because the Convention articulates *both* the civil and political rights of children and youth, and the social and economic rights of young people. It is exactly this combination that young LGBTQ youth need: civil and political rights mean that their definition of their evolving sexual/gender identity must be taken seriously by the adults and institutions that are so central to their lives, while guaranteeing social and economic rights means that those whose parents are unwilling to accept their gender/sexual identity must be provided with alternatives. Under the Convention, the State has a meaningful obligation, enforceable by law, to provide resources for them.[22] For those young people who are regularly subject to violence in schools, the Convention would demand the State protect their individual personality rights by addressing the violence and mandating that the state make an effort to continue to provide educational opportunity.[23] In general, a broad reading of the CRC and scientific research, might suggest that since sexual identity is defined by young people around the age of fourteen and there is significant evidence that fourteen year olds are generally approaching maturity as decision-makers,[24] recognising the "evolving capacities" of youth means that parents and the state must begin recognise the sexual choices that young people make and create conditions that allow them to explore and express these choices safely.

I've suggested a fairly liberal interpretation of what the CRC might be read to require. There are a number of realities that limit this optimistic picture. In considering whether ratification of the treaty and enforcement should be a priority for those concerned with LGBTQ youth, one must ask if there is there evidence that international human rights law can be an effective mechanism for increasing the rights of queer people. Evidence on this question is mixed, but international human rights bodies do in fact see sexuality as a realm in which human rights provisions are applicable. In relation to the Human Rights Committee's actions,[25] Eric Heinze reports:

> In its more recent comment on individual State reports, the Committee has cited ill-treatment of homosexuals as raising concerns about violations of the Covenant. In view of its expansive interpretation of the scope of protected categories, there is good reason to believe that the Committee will be generally willing to include sexual orientation as a protected category.[26]

Although the Committee's decisions are "highly persuasive," they "are not binding in international law."[27] Nevertheless, they at least move forward the discussion of how gay men and lesbians might be protected within international human rights. The United Nations Human Rights Commission[28] has also given attention to anti-homosexual discrimination.[29] Additionally, the U.N. is recognising the issues facing transgendered people.[30]

Heinze, however, is not optimistic about the potential of international organisations to force member states to see anti-gay/lesbian discrimination as a violation of human rights, suggesting that gay rights are defined as a Western imposition on other countries.[31] He cites the Fourth World Conference in Beijing's Declaration and Platform for Action, which does not include sexual orientation, as evidence that lesbians and gays will not win human rights protections. Wilson, however, is more hopeful, suggesting that although activists may not have won all that they desired at Beijing, what they achieved is an improvement over past meetings:

> In the end, the term *sexual orientation* was not included in the Program for Action. However paragraph 96 addresses women's right to make sexual decisions free from coercion, discrimination, and violence and presents a strong point for future organising around the U.N.[32]

Petchesky contextualises the Beijing discussions and the final platform noting that the conservative outcome resulted from a Conservative, Vatican-led backlash against the more progressive discussions at the 1994 International Conference on Population and Development in Cairo, a conference that resulted in the first human rights document to recognise "'a satisfying and safe sex life' as an affirmative goal."[33] Further, the document "urges governments to provide adolescents with a full array of sexual services and education 'to enable them to deal in a positive and responsible way with their sexuality.'"[34] This is directly connected to the response in Beijing:

> In Beijing itself, the fundamentalist campaign against "gender" and "sexual rights" fronted as a crusade on behalf of "parental rights"; its real targets were clearly the sexuality of all unmarried adolescents and lesbian sexuality.[35]

The challenge, then, as Petchesky and Cervantes-Carson and Citeroni recognise, is to develop an international human rights framework that can challenge such fundamentalism by asserting positive sexual rights.[36]

The ability to use effectively the language of parental rights in international human rights discussions is connected to a second concern: even countries that are making progress in hearing the voice of children may not yet be able to recognise that fourteen year olds should have sexual rights. In discussing the importance of the establishment of the Children's Rights Commissioner in Flemish Belgium, Ankie Vanfekerckhove notes:

> One proposal, which triggered heated debate, was the suggestion that the age of consent be lowered from sixteen to fourteen. The proposal was never enacted

> since the majority of adults consider young people
> unable to handle their own sexuality under the age of
> sixteen. (Needless to say, not a single young person took
> part in this debate.)[37]

She comments on the irony of this situation: "Children are considered to be competent to commit crimes at fourteen years of age, but are judged incapable of developing, exploring, and experimenting with their own sexuality."[38] Importantly, recognition of children's rights has prompted such a debate.

If developing an identity is not simply a process of claiming an essentialist sense of self, then exploration of the possibilities for sexual expression and family expression is a central component of constructing a self. This is particularly important in the public realm of the school because of the power that families and the media have to reinforce hegemonic norms. Doing this is a way that furthers "recognition of sexual diversity" and that forwards "the creation of universal access to a sexual life filled with joy," then, must be the goal.[39] The broad strokes of the convention provide such a possibility. The danger in putting forward an approach that grows out of human rights is that rights tend to focus on the individual, rather than fostering social equality.[40] Despite this, the Convention offers a possibility for beginning to take seriously the social and economic rights that young people need to be more free as sexual beings. Without the ability to develop relationships that matter from a relatively age, young people are vulnerable not just to the beliefs and resources of their communities, but even more to those of their parents. To have no freedom in relation to these relationships is to be deprived of the opportunity to reflexively define oneself, and, in the end, to not develop the capacity of autonomy that one needs to be a democratic citizen. Thus, gay organisations have an interest in focusing on developing not simply essentialist sexual identities, but democracy; those interested in fostering democracy should have an interest in sexual freedom; and both need to understand youth (both the concept and the real people) as of central importance.

I want to illustrate the potential of the CRC by highlighting how European countries are translating human rights strategies into frameworks for empowering youth. In his introduction to *The New Handbook of Children's Rights,* Bob Franklin points out that although child poverty rates, school exclusion rates, and imprisonment rates remain unacceptably high in the U.K., particularly for African-Caribbean children, there have, nonetheless, "been significant developments in children's rights," since 1995. Importantly, and at least in part because of the U.K.'s ratification of the CRC, children's rights are on the political agenda.[41] Focusing on the contradictions between government policy (whether Conservative or the Labour Party) and the Convention, Deena Haydon argues the U.K. needs to take seriously the right of children to information about sexuality, regardless of parental wishes. Prohibiting children from decision-making, "contravenes the right of children to express their views in all matters affecting them and to have their views taken seriously."[42] She suggests that the government remains committed to this perspective because it is adults who have the power to define "maturity," and therefore, to determine what rights are appropriate at any given moment in a young person's life.[43] However, such interpretations are not acceptable to the Human Rights Commission, thus the government hears a counter voice.

Tony Jeffs' analysis is suggestive of the ways that calling the construction of childhood and youth into question might provide a foundation for queer activists to work much more broadly to create an alternative discourse. Jeffs argues that to provide youth with real voice, as he suggests the recognition of children's rights demands, calls into question much about the dominant educational paradigm in Great Britain. British schools, he argues, have made some progress in recognising the need to address bullying and the exclusion of African-Caribbean students as a human rights problem.[44] In both instances, this is moving further that U.S. schools have managed. Nonetheless, if young people have no serious voice in the curriculum, mandatory attendance laws lead to conditions that challenge, rather than encourage, democratic ideals. Rarely today, Jeffs notes, are schools "places where civilized or cultured persons of any age would want to linger."[45] Mandatory attendance laws are particularly a threat, Leck notes, to students whose sexual expression is denied.[46]

Educators do not lack models of democratically informed schools that encourage young people to define and discuss topics that are of interest to them. Schools that do provide students with a voice in curricular matters find that students are interested in, and able to discuss in a mature way, issues that are linked to sexuality.[47] The best chance for countering the image of youth as unable to make important decisions, such as those about their own sexuality, is to provide them with the opportunity to develop their abilities and their autonomy by discussing these issues and making decisions that matter.[48] Such experiences help youth to be active participants in democracy. Although some adults are skeptical on this point, real experiences in decision-making lead to greater adult confidence in youth as decision-makers.[49] Those attempting to understand and counter bullying understand that reforms short of major structural changes intended to develop more participatory, democratic, and less isolated spaces where youth and adults can interact more equally, will not succeed. Duncan and Lesko each note the extent to which age segregation plays a role in sexual bullying.[50] This is not to say that peer relationships will not remain important for youth, but to suggest that models of development that are, in Lesko's words, recursive rather than cumulative and one way need to guide our thinking about educational environments. Such a model makes the learning process between adults and youth more intergenerational by recognising that youth have much to contribute to society, even as they receive the support necessary to develop their knowledge and perspectives. Providing space for queer youth to challenge peers and work with adults is critical to the development of both safe schools and a democratic citizenry that includes youth.

The CRC, I believe, provides a perspective in line with what Lesko advocates. Often developed countries use it to try to push less developed countries to pay attention to issues such as child labour and forced marriages, yet it may be equally important in encouraging these countries to explore and take seriously their own relationship to youth. Gay organisations in the United States might reframe their own interactions with young people by fully recognising the full range of opportunities that youth require to be the sexual human beings whom they wish to be. In her introduction to *Revolutionary Voices,* Margot Kelly Rodriguez challenges queer adults to recognise the full range of institutional forces, including schools and mainstream gay politics, which make it difficult for queer youth to feel part of the present. [51] *Revolutionary Voices* indicates that such alienation does not always lead to greater alienation disengagement; it can lead to new forms of public engagement. But the latter requires an open enough and supportive enough society, in terms of economic, social, and political rights, that young people can develop into altruistic individuals. The difficult task for adults is to challenge cultural definitions and institutional structures to encourage the multiple voices of young people, while not containing them to our own ends. Despite the limits of human rights frameworks, the almost complete lack of rights discourse concerning youth in the U.S., combined with the power that Human Rights language has in some European countries to provide a language for critique and action, leads me to conclude that adults concerned with youth need to demand that the United States recognise broadly the importance of international human rights and the CRC. Further, queer organisations internationally need to engage in global battles for *both* sexual freedom and rights and youth freedom and rights.

Notes

1. Human Rights Watch, *Hatred in the Hallways* (New York: Human Rights Watch, 2001).

2. Colleen K. Donovan, "On Diversity," in *Revolutionary Voices: A Multicultural Queer Anthology*, ed. Amy Sonnie (Los Angeles: Alyson Books, 2000), 205..

3. Judith Levine, *Harmful to Minors: The Perils of Protecting Children from* Sex (Thunder Mouth Books, 2003), 91.

4. Valerie Lehr, "Parental Rights As If Queer Youth Mattered," presented at the Annual Meetings of the American Political Science Association, 2002, Boston, MA. < http://it.stlawu.edu/~vleh/APSA%202002%20--final.pdf> (3 October 2004).

5. Jenny Kitzinger, "Who Are You Kidding? Children, Power, and the Struggle Against Sexual Abuse," in *Constructing and Reconstructing Childhood*, eds. A. James and A. Prout (London: Falmer, 1990), 184.

6. Human Rights Watch reports the story of Anika P., who "was rejected by several facilities [for homeless youth] which are run by religious organisations because they are allowed to discriminate against transgender youth" (Human Rights Watch, 61).

7. Donovan, 206.

8. See Bob Franklin, "Children's Rights: An Introduction," in *The New Handbook of Children's Rights*, ed. Bob Franklin (London: Routledge, 2002), 15-42.

9. Mirjana Ule and Tanja Rener, "The Deconstruction of Youth," in *Transitions of Youth Citizenship in Europe: Culture, Subculture, and Identity*, eds. Andy Furlong and Irena Guidikova (Strasbourg: Council of Europe Publishing, 2001)

10. Ibid, 284.

11. Kerstin Jacobsson. and Niels Hebert, "Disobedient Citizens: Young Animal Rights Activists in Sweden," in *Transitions of Youth Citizenship in Europe: Culture, Subculture, and Identity*, eds. Andy Furlong and Irena Guidikova (Strasbourg: Council of Europe Publishing, 2001), 17-40.

12. Irena Guidikova and Lasse Siurala, "Introduction: A Weird, Wired, and Winsome Generation," in *Transitions of Youth Citizenship in Europe: Culture, Subculture, and Identity*, eds. Andy Furlong and Irena Guidikova, (Strasbourg: Council of Europe Publishing, 2001), 10.

13. Sharon Stephens, "Introduction: Children and the Politics of Culture in 'Late Capitalism,'" in Children and the Politics of Culture, ed. Sharon Stephens (Princeton: Princeton University Press, 1995), 28.

14. Bob Coles, "Vulnerable Youth and Processes of Social Exclusion," in *Youth, Citizenship and Social Change in a European Context*, ed. J. Bynner, L. Chisolm and A. Furlong, (Aldershot: Ashgate Publishing, 1997), 72.

15. Ali Rattansi and Ann Phoenix, "Rethinking Youth Identities: Modernist and Postmodernist Frameworks," in *Youth, Citizenship, and*

Social Change in a European Context, eds. J. Bynner, L. Chisolm and A. Furlong (Aldershot: Ashgate Publishing, 1997), 143.

16. Christine Griffin. "Youth Research and Identities: Same as it Ever Was?" in *Youth, Citizenship and Social Change in a European Context*, eds. J. Bynner, L. Chisolm, and A. Furlong (Aldershot: Ashgate Publishing, 1997), 164.

17. Ibid.,162.

18. Ule and Rener, 285.

19. Human Rights Watch, 54-5.

20. Roger J. R. Levesque, "The Internationalization of Children's Human Rights: Too Radical for American Adolescents." *Connecticut Journal of International Law* 9 (1994), 243.

21. A. Lopakta, quoted in Rochelle D. Jackson,"The War Over Children's Rights." *Buffalo Human Rights Law Review* 5 (1999), 236.

22. Jackson, 238.

23. Human Rights Watch.

24 Rhonda Gay Hartman, "Adolescent Autonomy: Clarifying an Ageless Conundrum," *Hastings Law Journal* 51 (2000).

25. The Human Rights Committee enforces for the International Covenant on Civil and Political Rights.

26. Eric Heinze, "Sexual Orientation and International Law." *Michigan Journal of International Law.* 22 (2001), 293.

27. Ibid .

28. There are a number of different United Nations bodies responsible for promoting human rights. The Human Rights Commission is separate from the Human Rights Committee. See Ibid., 293.

29. International Gay and Lesbian Human Rights Commission, "U.N. Human Rights Commission Opens Doors to Sexual Minorities," *International Gay and Lesbian Human Rights Commission.* 2001a <www.iglhrc.org/news/press/pr_020411.html> (3 August 2002).

30. International Gay and Lesbian Human Rights Commission, "U.N. Rep Meets with Transgender Activists," *International Gay and Lesbian Human Rights Commission.* 2001b. < ww.iglhrc.org/news/press/pr_010629.html> (3 August 2002).

31. Heinze, 305-309.

32. Ara Wilson, "Lesbian Visibility and Sexual Rights at Beijing," *Signs* 22 (1996).

33. Rosalind Petchesky, "Sexual Rights: Inventing a Concept, Mapping an International Practice," in *Sexual Identities, Queer Politics*, ed. Mark Blasius (Princeton, NJ: Princeton University Press, 2001), 121.

34. Ibid., 121.

35. Ibid., 123.

36. Ibid., and Alejandro Cervantes-Carson and Traci Citeroni, "Sexualities, Human Rights, and the Decentering of Heterosexuality." Chapter , this volume, 2005.

37. Ankie Vandekerckhove, "A Commissioner for Children's Rights in the Flemish Community in Belgium," in *The New Handbook of Children's Rights*, ed. Bob Franklin (London: Routledge, 2002), 363.

38. Ibid., 363.

39. Cervantes-Carson and Citeroni.

40. See Momin Rahman, *Sexuality and Democracy* (Edinburgh: Edinburgh University Press, 2000) and Petchesky.

41. Franklin, 6.

42. Deena Haydon, "Children's Rights to Sex and Sexuality Education," in *The New Handbook of Children's Rights*, ed. Bob Franklin (London: Routledge, 2002), 191.

43. Ibid.,192.

44. Tony Jeffs, "Schooling, Education, and Children's Rights," in *The New Handbook of Children's Rights*, ed. Bob Franklin (London: Routledge, 2002), 45-6.

45. Ibid.,55-6.

46. Glorianne M. Leck, "Heterosexual or Homosexual? Reconsidering Binary Narratives on Sexual Identities in Urban Schools," *Education and Urban Society*, 32 (2000), 324-48.

47. Donald Sehr, *Education for Public Democracy* (Albany, NY: SUNY Press, 1997).

48. See Hartman.

49. Franklin, 23.

50. Neil Duncan, *Sexual Bullying: Gender Conflict and Pupil Culture in Secondary Schools* (London: Routledge, 1999) and Nancy Lesko, *Act Your Age: A Cultural Construction of Adolescence* (New York: Routledge Falmer, 2001).

51. Margot Kelley Rodriguez, "'We are the Ones We Have Been Waiting For,'" in *Revolutionary Voices: A Multicultural Queer Youth Anthology*, ed. Amy Sonnie (Los Angeles: Alyson Books, 2000), xxi-xxvi.

Select Bibliography

Alan Guttmacher Institute. "State Policies in Brief." *Alan Guttmacher Institute.* 1 May 2004 (3 October 2004). <http://www.siecus.org/policy/states/AGI_Chart.pdf>

Cervantes-Carson, Alejandro and Tracy Citeroni. "Sexualities, Human Rights, and the Decentering of Heterosexuality." Chapter in this volume.

Coles, Bob. "Vulnerable Youth and Processes of Social Exclusion." In *Youth, Citizenship and Social Change in a European Context*, edited by J. Bynner, L. Chisolm and A. Furlong, 69-88. Aldershot: Ashgate Publishing, 1997.

Donovan, Colleen K. "On Diversity." In *Revolutionary Voices: A Multicultural Queer Youth Anthology*, edited by Amy Sonnie, 205-07. Los Angeles: Alyson Books.

Duncan, Neil. *Sexual Bullying: Gender Conflict and Pupil Culture in Secondary Schools*. London: Routledge, 1999.

Franklin, Bob. "Children's Rights: An Introduction." In *The New Handbook of Children's Rights*, edited by Bob Franklin, 15-42. London: Routledge, 2002.

Griffin, Christine. "Youth Research and Identities: Same as it Ever Was?" In *Youth, Citizenship and Social Change in a European Context*, edited by J. Bynner, L. Chisolm, and A. Furlong, 157-68. Aldershot: Ashgate Publishing, 1997.

Guidikova, Irena. and Siurala, L. "Introduction: a Weird, Wired, and Winsome Generation." In *Transitions of Youth Citizenship in Europe: Culture, Subculture, and Identity*, edited by Andy Furlong and Irena Guidikova, 5-16. Strasbourg: Council of Europe Publishing, 2001.

Hartman, Rhonda Gay. "Adolescent Autonomy: Clarifying an Ageless Conundrum." *Hastings Law Journal* 51 (2000): 1265-362.

Haydon, Deena. "Children's Rights to Sex and Sexuality Education." In *The New Handbook of Children's Rights*, edited by Bob Franklin, 182-95. London: Routledge, 2002.

Heinze, Eric. "Sexual Orientation and International Law." *Michigan Journal of International Law* 22 (2001): 283-309.

Human Rights Watch. *Hatred in the Hallways: Violence and Discrimination against Lesbian, Gay, Bisexual, Transgender Students in U.S. Schools*. New York: Human Rights Watch, 2001.

International Gay and Lesbian Human Rights Commission. (2001a). "UN Human Rights Commission Opens Doors to Sexual Minorities." *International Gay and Lesbian Human Rights Commission*. <www.iglhrc.org/news/press/pr_020411.html> (3 August 2002).

International Gay and Lesbian Human Rights Commission. (2001b). "UN Rep Meets with Transgender Activists." *International Gay and Lesbian Human Rights Commission*. < www.iglhrc.org/news/press/pr_010629.html> (3 August 2002).

Jackson, Rochelle. D. "The War Over Children's Rights." *Buffalo Human Rights Law Review* 5 (1999): 223-51.

Jacobsson, K. and N. Hebert. (2001), "Disobedient Citizens: Young Animal Rights Activists in Sweden." In *Transitions of Youth Citizenship in Europe: Culture, Subculture, and Identity*, edited by Andy Furlong and Irena Guidikova, 17-40. Strasbourg: Council of Europe Publishing, 2001.

Jeffs, Tony. "Schooling, Education, and Children's Rights." In *The New Handbook of Children's Rights.* edited by Bob Franklin, 45-59. London: Routledge, 2002.

Kitzinger, Jenny. "Who Are You Kidding?: Children, Power and the Struggle Against Sexual Abuse." In. *Constructing and Reconstructing Childhood,* edited by Allison James and Alan Prout, 165-89. London: Falmer Press, 1990.

Leck, Glorianne M., "Heterosexual or Homosexual? Reconsidering Binary Narratives on Sexual Identities in Urban Schools." *Education and Urban Society* 32 (2000): 324-48.

Lehr, Valerie. "Parental Rights as if Queer Youth Mattered." Presented at the Annual Convention of the American Political Science Association. Boston, MA, 2002. < http://it.stlawu.edu/~vleh/APSA%202002%20--final.pdf.> (3 October 2004).

Lesko, Nancy. *Act Your Age: A Cultural Construction of Adolescence.* New York: Routledge Falmer, 2001.

Levesque, Roger J. R. "The Internationalization of Children's Human Rights: Too Radical for American Adolescents." *Connecticut Journal of International Law* 9 (1994): 236-93.

Levine, Judith. *Harmful to Minors: The Perils of Protecting Children from Sex.* New York: Thunder's Mouth Press, 2003.

Petchesky, R. "Sexual Rights: Inventing a Concept, Mapping an International Practice." In *Sexual Identities, Queer Politics,* edited by Mark Blasius, 118-40. Princeton, NJ: Princeton University Press, 2001.

Rahman, Momin. *Sexuality and Democracy.* Edinburgh: Edinburgh University Press, 2000.

Rattsani, Ali and Ann Pheonix. "Rethinking Youth Identities: Modernist and Postmodernist Frameworks." In *Youth, Citizenship and Social Change in a European Context*, edited by J. Bynner, L. Chisolm and A. Furlong, 121-50. Aldershot: Ashgate Publishing, 1997.

Rodriguez, Margot Kelley. "'We are the Ones We Have Been Waiting For.'" In *Revolutionary Voices: A Multicultural Queer Youth Anthology*, edited by Amy. Sonnie, xxi-xxvi. Los Angeles: Alyson Books, 2000.

Sehr, Donald T. *Education for Public Democracy.* Albany, NY: SUNY Press, 1997.

Stephens, Sharon. "Introduction: Children and the Politics of Culture in "Late Capitalism." In *Children and the Politics of Culture,* edited by Sharon Stephens, 3-48. Princeton: Princeton University Press, 1995.

Ule, Mirjana and Tanja Rener. "The Deconstruction of Youth." In *Transitions of Youth Citizenship in Europe: Culture, Subculture, and Identity*, edited by Andy Furlong and Irena Guidikova, 271-288. Strasbourg: Council of Europe Publishing, 2001.

Vandekerckhove, Ankie. "A Commissioner for Children's Rights in the Flemish Community in Belgium." In *The New Handbook of Children's Rights*, edited by Bob Franklin, 362-73. London: Routledge, 2002.

Wilson, Ara. "Lesbian Visibility and Sexual Rights at Beijing." *Signs* 22 (1996): 214-18.

Acting Like a Professional:
Identity Dilemmas for Gay Men

Nick Rumens

Abstract
   The purpose of this chapter is to explore the discursive nature of how gay men make sense of themselves at one and the same time as professionals and gay men within the workplace. Ideas of professionalism and the ideal of being professional are set out within these pages as discursive resources that can be made use of by gay men handling identity issues in relation to sexuality, work, and normality. I use a Foucauldian influenced approach to understanding how identities are discursively constituted to examine how ten openly gay men working in one National Health Services (NHS) Trust in the U.K. draw on available discourses to (re)interpret who they are and manage the tensions arising from how co-workers might seek to fix their identities in terms of sexuality.[1] I take as the object of central investigation, the normalising effects of discourses which determine who and what is viewed as *normal* and acceptable in the workplace. I argue that the attribution of being normal may be accomplished through professionalism. As a mechanism for the operation of normalising processes, professionalism especially articulates and reinforces specific gender conventional displays of masculinity among gay men. **Key Words:** gay men, professionalism, normality, masculinities, sexual identities, work, discourse, resistance, workplace inclusion.

1.   Introduction: Gay Men, Sexuality, and Organisation

   In order to understand how sexuality is implicated in the process of professionalism it is important to briefly sketch out the current status of the literature concerning gay men, sexuality, and organisation. Recent scholarship within this field suggests that the vocational concerns for gay men might have changed from being less about evading the suspicion of homosexuality and more about satisfying the aspiration to be seen as normal, and thus equal to heterosexual co-workers. Certainly, within the thin body of literature concerning gay men's experiences in organisations, homophobia and discrimination are no longer the principal objects of empirical enquiry. This has given rise to the consideration of new perspectives on familiar themes in the organisational lives of gay men. For example, studies about gay male identity formation and management strategies developed in the 1980s and the following decade often documented how coming out in many workplaces was tantamount to career suicide.[2] More recently, the same topic has been investigated using a number of different viewpoints that have helped us to understand the identity work required of gay men committed to the project of being out and staying out in contemporary business environments.[3] This in itself relates to a number of broader issues including professionalism which pose questions for the study of, and how we might come to comprehend how gay men utilise ideas of professionalism.

David Shallenberger's study of the professional lives of twelve American gay men conveyed an important message: "it is possible to be [openly] gay and a successful professional."[4] Equally significant was that the study reminded us about the identity dilemmas of openly gay male professionals in organisations, dilemmas associated with managing the discursive interconnections between private notions of self-identification and ascribed (social) identities. Thus, the interrelationship between self-identify and social identities can be particularly problematic for gay men seeking to identify as professional given the powerful homophobic discourses that have associated male homosexuality with death, disease and waste. As Jill Humphrey argues in her study of gay men and lesbians employed within U.K. public sector organisations, "vilification reaches its zenith precisely at the point when lesbians and gay men become qualified as public service professionals."[5] The implication is that much of the time gay men are likely to spend negotiating their identities in ways that draw upon discursive resources to counter the notion of the male homosexual as an intensely sexualised category that could be worryingly camouflaged by the projection of a professional identity.

2.   Gay Men, Professionalism, and Normalisation

While David Shallenberger and Jill Humphrey make important contributions to thinking through connections between gay sexualities and professionalism, they ignore the gendered dimension to professionalism. Saying such is to recognise at a theoretical level that being professional is a contingent form of identity work that is also coded in terms of masculine ideals of conduct and appearance. The feminist poststructuralist inspired work of Stephen Whitehead and Deborah Kerfoot has shown how professionalism is overlaid with masculinities and the consequences for those wo/men seeking ontological security as professionals and man/agers in the workplace.[6] While such scholarship and more generally, research currently produced by pro-feminist researchers has rendered visible men and masculinities as objects of critical examination, the discussion of gay men within these debates is neglected. Taking a step towards addressing this omission I offer an empirical level examination of how gay men may relate to the ideal of being professional, which is viewed as being mutually interconstitutive of heterosexual based versions of masculinity. Following this line of pro/feminist thinking, I position masculinity and professionalism within the same frame, but to serve a different end. Whereas pro-feminist researchers have used this frame to demonstrate how certain (masculine) behaviours are privileged within the workplace, I extend its application to explore the consequences for gay men. As Kerfoot asserts that professionalism "privileges the masculine as an instrumental, purposive-rational mode of being in the world" of work, often to the detriment of some wo/men, it may hold open opportunities for new inclusivities for gay men.[7] Here, I suggest that professionalism as a discursive resource for the construction of a professional identity may also operate as an important site for the attribution of a normal gay identity. In order for this perspective on the professionalism to have purchase, it needs to be located and understood in the larger context of sociological discussion concerning what it means for gay men to be regarded as normal, good citizens deserving of social and organisational inclusion. Such debates are necessary to take into account for they have a significant relevance to how gay men might use professionalism to counter the attempts of co-worker to fasten their identities in terms of sexuality.

As I have suggested earlier, contemporary debates concerning gay men within organisations are less about the way in which the corporate closet acts as an organising principle in their work lives, and more about the ways in which openly gay men are seeking to pursue and enjoy rewarding work careers. This is not to refute the existence or downplay the inimical effects of contemporary work closets and homophobias for gay men. Moreover, it is to provoke consideration of the observation made by Steven Seidman that within the U.S. a discourse is gaining currency that positions gay men and lesbians as normal. This is to suggest that they are the "psychological and moral equal of the heterosexual."[8] The concept of the normal gay is intimately bound up with the heteronormative notion of citizenship. A review of the commentary regarding how citizenship has been constituted in largely heterosexual terms and the subsequent emergence of the idea of the normal gay/lesbian is beyond the scope of this chapter. What is important to take notice of is that scholars outside of the U.S. are exploring the notion of the normalisation of select gay identities.

Diane Richardson's recent discussion of the themes of citizenship, gay sexualities, and normality is especially noteworthy in that respect.[9] Richardson, a British sociologist, raises a number of questions concerning how normality may be attributed to gay men and lesbians and draws upon Steven Seidman's study of the lives of American gay men and lesbians work to that effect. As Seidman puts it, in the current context of living beyond the closet, the "normal gay is expected to be gender conventional, link sex to love and a marriage-like relationship, defend family values, personify economic individualism, and display national pride."[10] It follows that a number of sites potentially exist where normalising processes may occur. The crucial point to make at this stage is that the workplace may be read as one such site. In my view, a locale where discourses of normalisation shape the generation and take up of subject positions by gay male workers. Significant, too, is that questions surrounding the effects of these normalising processes for gay employees have received little empirical investigation. Thus, following this research trajectory in parallel with a line of enquiry concerning the relationship between professionalism and gay sexualities permits an exploration of one aspect of the notion of being openly gay and professional that is situated within the relationship between organisationally reinforced modes of professional engagement among organisational members and masculinities. The key concern of my own study is to present insights into how professionalism is a form of regulation of the self that especially articulates and reinforces specific gender conventional displays of masculinity among gay men.

3.   Research Methodology

The research methods for my wider study into the vocational experiences of gay men working in the NHS included in-depth qualitative interviews. These took place over a ten-month period after constructing a sample and adopting a purposive sampling framework in conjunction with a snowball technique to accrue participants. The men ranged in age from twenty to forty-eight, identified as white, able-bodied, and "out" as gay men to co-workers within their roles as managers, hospital doctors, call centre workers, and administrators. The aim of the interviewing process was twofold. One was to acquire a qualitative account of how the men perceived themselves at work and the discursive practices they engaged in to that effect. Second was to analyse the intersections between competing discourses to understand how the men constructed or resisted the engineering of "normal" gay identities in relation to work. Extracts taken from some of the ten interviews that took place are presented here under the pseudonyms the respondents self-selected.

4.   Public/Private Gay Selves: Professional and Sexual Selves

The vocational concerns of the gay men reported in my own study can be broadly summarised as a concern with pursuing the status of normality. In much of the men's talk concerning their experiences of work beyond the corporate closet, many of the men spoke about wishing to be identified by co-workers as "normal" and "ordinary," which in the words of one male paramedic (Gordon), was about aiming "to blend in" within the "straight" workforce. By emphasising the importance of being "normal" in this way, most of the men participated in the (re)production of a normalising discourse embedded within professionalism. That professionalism, read by all of the men as constituted by a set of job attributes such as possessing expert knowledge, technical competence, as well as conducting and constituting oneself in an appropriate manner, should be connected to normality is notable. It signifies a claim to the identity of the normal gay in a way that utilises the notion of professionalism as a micro-level identity practice through which identity conflicts can then be negotiated and managed. Significant, too, was that not all the men in the study were members of established professions such as Medicine. However, something more is happening here that goes beyond the observation that non-professionals may deploy the label of professional along side their professional counterparts. In relation to the chief concerns of this study, the gay men caught up in the discourse of professionalism were at one and the same time, constructing themselves as economically valuable and gender conventional according to a set of particularised masculine behavioural displays. However, I wish to guard against using the data to present an over easy identification with professionalism. Staking claim to identities, be they professional, sexual, or gendered, is marked by inequality.

In order to secure a sense of self as professional many of the men articulated how they established, in the words of one man (Dion, clinician) "clear deep blue water" between professionalism and sexuality. For this cohort, sexuality was deemed to be a "personal" matter and so by default, rendered irrelevant to most co-workers. This was striking in the talk of one participant employed as a senior hospital doctor (Ryan), who remarked: "I'm a professional who just happens to be gay." What Ryan exemplifies here is a prioritisation of a core work identity, compounded further by his belief that there "is no space for sexuality in your professionalism." Ryan's bald assertion of professionalism, together with many of the other men's understandings of being professional, is premised on the notion of the existence of a neat division between the public and private. Historically, the split between the public and private has been characterised as one where male homosexuality, as a sexualised category, is cordoned off within the private. However, such understandings of the public-private dualism are no longer tenable. For example, Katie Deverell's study of gay male AIDS/HIV workers underscores the tense relationship between professionalism, read by Deverell as an "identity rather than a set of job attributes", and sexuality in organisation.[11] The gay men in Deverell's study had a "professional concern defined in terms of sex and sexuality…and [were] often employed on the basis of their own sexuality."[12] Thus, the gay men crossed and violated conventional boundaries and understandings of professionalism and public-private selves.

From Deverell's study it is clear that sexuality occupied an ambiguous position between the public and the private. However, such alternative readings of the public-private dynamic do not automatically undermine traditional demarcations between the private and the public. As in the case of Ryan, the separation of professionalism from sexuality, mapped onto the public-private dichotomy is fundamental to maintaining a professional identity. Of interest here, is that the professional self-presentations of men such as Ryan in the public domain, shape the specific form that expressions of gender take in their conversations about work. For example, Ryan spoke with some sense of pride about investing in his career to the point of describing himself as a "workaholic." In doing so, Ryan constructs his professional self as one who is willing to whatever to become "top dog" within the medical profession. Other men, including Dion and Gordon also spoke about working "ludicrously hard" to effect bottom line "results" so as to eventually reach the pinnacle of their professions. In all, these men are participating in the (re)production of a normalising discourse that mirrors self-interest and careerism that accords closely to a traditional competitive masculinity. However, a feature of this discursive engagement, highlighted in the work of Deborah Kerfoot and David Knights, is that it creates the illusion of a unitary and coherent sense of self.[13] This is problematic, particularly where the presentation of the self artificially separates the public from the private: "I'm Ryan the doctor first, then Ryan the gay man second"; for it tends to muffle self-doubt and disturb the expression of insecurities concerning the construction of individual subjectivity. For those men seeking mastery over the public and private selves to match the ideals of what constitutes an acceptable professional identity, must tirelessly engage in an unending endeavour of reconstituting the professional self in accordance with masculinist priorities.

5.   Staying Out as a Professional

Analysis of the study data revealed that most of the men saw their sexuality as one option among a range of identity options. For most, the workplace was the site where personal investment in a professional work based identity was given primacy over investment in sexual identities. As I have suggested earlier, it may be possible to understand this in the context of the normalisation of gay identities at an institutional level. To do so, according to Diane Richardson, gives rise to a number of questions concerning the importance gay people attach to sexual identities. In relation to the study data one perspective might be the efforts of some of the men to "blend in" and render themselves indistinguishable from heterosexual co-workers, involves the desexualisation of sexual identity. In other words, the decoupling of sex from (male) homosexuality in favour of emphasising gender conventionality through professionalism underpins the process of engineering a normalised gay identity in the work place.

One possible end point might be that sexual identity is seen less of a (sexualised) threat to the heterosexual order of society and more of an acceptable social identity.

However, it is important not to assume that the normalisation of gay identities is both monolithic, applies equally to, and practised the same way by all gay men. For example, some men might be more adept than others at projecting a gender conventional identity in a range of work situations. Stating such is to recognise especially, that identity artistry involved in the desexualisation of gay sexualities is constituted through performance. Judith Butler expresses it as such in her much studied and cited work, suggesting that identity is both fabricated and performed. Indeed, this analysis is extended to gender which is similarly conceptualised by Butler as "an 'act,' as it were, which is both intentional and performative, where 'performative' suggests a dramatic and contingent construction of meaning."[14] This is to come to understand the discontinuous nature of the men's performances as they engage in and within discourses of sexual and gender difference. In this section then, the aim is twofold. First, I wish to demonstrate how constructions of the self can be undertaken by (heterosexual) others in the presence and absence of the (gay male) subject and the deleterious effects of doing so. Second, I explore some of the anxieties associated with the performance of professionalism in order to stay out as such to work peers.

While the self can be fashioned in a deliberate and conscious manner within various work contexts the self can also be constructed by others. Even those who endeavoured to appear professional, and thus normal, were aware of how this sense of self is created in, and constitutive of, certain work locales. Some work settings were not as accepting or even tolerant of gay men, as Carl (supervisor) pointed out: "there are quite a few homophobes in the call centre and some of them I have to manage." Maintaining a negotiated sense of self as a well credentialed "health information professional" was sometimes problematic. As Carl illustrated:

> There was a time when one of the call handlers referred
> a difficult call to me by shouting out in the call centre,
> "the caller wants to know how to produce a semen
> sample, that's your area of expertise." They thought it
> was a joke but I knew it was homophobic.

As this excerpt shows, subjects cannot always position themselves unproblematically at the junction between discourses of professionalism and sexual difference. These intersecting discourses, which contain within them understandings of professionalism and gay sexualities, can befog the presentation of the professional self. Such incidents remind us that a homophobic discourse about male homosexuality being associated with disease, perversion and waste, still exerts influence over how gay men are understood.

Equally vexing, is the notion that others can undertake the construction of the self in the absence of the subject. Indeed, Judith Butler writes, "consider the situation in which one is named without knowing that one is named."[15] The infinite ways in which the self might be manufactured within the imaginations of others is a compelling, if not haunting, thought. With regard to this idea, one gay man (Tom, administrator) expressed it thus: "I know people probably think I'm the randy old queen who sits behind a computer all day typing." He went on to suggest that his sexuality had been the subject of interest on the part of those "straight" co-workers who would, in the main, see gay sexualities as "abnormal." Friends in the workplace had informed Tom of how he had been identified as such by one particular male heterosexual co-worker. As Tom explained: "it made me feel uncomfortable…and inadequate and I was aware of the agendas going around in his head even if he never voiced them in front of me." Together, these examples indicate that the attainment of professional identity is ephemeral and fragile, being either bolstered or, undercut by a complex set of perceptions of self held by subjects and others. Here I wish to emphasise that while a professional identity may be constructed through performance, it does not imply that being a professional, or indeed being a gay man, are roles the individual can slip in and out of effortlessly. As I now turn to examine, the men did not suggest to me that such identities were played out in a frivolous manner with little care for their performance.

When asked the question about what counts as acceptable professional conduct in the workplace, two men employed as hospital doctors, responded by outlining what it did not encompass. Common and striking to both descriptions was the rejection of "camp." Described by the two men as "acting like a woman" and "being overtly feminine," camp was seen to be the antithesis to a dominant type of heterosexual based masculinity reinscribed through the behaviours that compose what it is to be a professional hospital doctor. In the main, these men talked about how they cultivated a professional sense of self in line with hegemonic values of clinical rationality in which the deployment of a cool and "detached bedside manner," along with "clinical competence" and "expert medical knowledge," is privileged. Such knowledge and technical expertise affords these men, to use Ryan's words, a "top dog relationship over peers" or, to borrow the words of sociologist Robert Connell, a form of "technically-based dominance over workers."[16] Either way, the stark type of masculinity ingrained in this portrait of professionalism is one that elevates rationality above all other skills and personal attributes.

Both men reported they knew camp gay men employed on the hospital wards and criticised them for presenting as "effeminate poofs." As one doctor (Tony) said: "patients don't expect to see camp gay men on the wards, let alone have them look after them…I've seen some patients look oddly at one camp gay nurse…I'm sure it made them feel uncomfortable." Another interviewee, Gordon (paramedic) echoed this sentiment: "camp may be funny but it isn't professional…it gives the impression you're not good at your job." Yet, in the rush to expel camp or the feminine from the canon of professional behaviours, Tony later admitted, albeit tentatively, that he thought the use of camp was permissible in certain work situations. He said, "with the female nurses I am camp sometimes…but when I am, I'm only acting…just to have a laugh." Here, Tony constructs himself as a person who is apprehensive with the performance of camp as a form of non-professional behaviour. Eager to accentuate the theatricality of his camp "act" he went on to reassert and essentialise his "straight acting" features as ones that are both "normal" and "natural traits." Tony's reification of his masculinity may be seen as an identity strategy deployed as a response to the ambiguity that surrounds the performance of camp. The use of camp by gay and heterosexual men to elicit laughter among hetero/homosexual audiences has according to Richard Dyer, a lengthy history not least of all within popular culture.[17] But it is not always easy to discern whether heterosexual audiences in laughing at camp performances enacted by gay men, are laughing at or with them. For Tony, the worry of being construed purely as an object of ridicule is countered to some extent by associating with a heterosexual based masculine identity using an essentialist vocabulary.

Yet, as Judith Butler famously argued, gender is a copy of a copy that has no original.[18] This anti-essentialist notion has subversive potential for undermining social and organisational arrangements that are normatively heterosexual. However, Tony's imprisonment of camp within a mode of aestheticism extinguishes any subversive promise held in the performance itself. As Butler has shown, camp as a queer manifestation offers a destabilising perspective that can at one and the same time, provoke heteronormative gender roles and codes of visibility as well as challenge the prevailing ideology produced by the white, straight male, middle class elite. In fact, even Tony alluded to the *naughtiness* of camp in the workplace, understanding it as something that would be "frowned upon" by his male heterosexual co-workers and clinical superiors especially. In the end, the display of camp is regarded as a slippage in the presentation of professional self. Knowledge about how he might be misidentified by his heterosexual male co-workers was reason enough for Tony to remain diligent about regulating the presentation of self.

6.   What Being the "Normal (Professional) Gay" Means: Towards Inclusion?

So far, the performances of professionalism presented in this study lend themselves to being read as insights into how the interviewees, as men, prop up dominant professional practices that privilege a narrow version of masculinity. However, a few of the men appeared to resist the notion of the professional ideal as one being exclusively and conjointly, interconstitutive of a heterosexual based masculinity. This is not to say that these men abandoned altogether the construction of a professional sense of self that demonstrated a commitment to gender conventionality. It is to suggest that some identity strategies were utilised by the men that gave primacy to their sexual identity in certain situations to secure workplace rewards. This was prominent in the relationships where gay men reported to female line managers. To illustrate Ciaran (training manager) described his relationship with his female line manager as such:

> Using facets of my sexuality to my advantage is very much what I'm about and when I want something from my boss I talk about nice things...she loves the whole thing about gay men...she doesn't get that with the other straight managers...so we talk about fabrics and the colour of the office and I tend to get what I want.

Here, sexuality is being mobilised as a resource for the gay professional to cultivate, in Ciaran's words, a "closer...and mutually beneficial relationship" with his line manager. The exchange of "sage-like wisdom" on matters such as "fashion" and "men" for "organisational favours" such as "promised promotion" may not upon first inspection, endorse traditional notions of what constitutes professional conduct.

In one respect, dominant discourses of professionalism have sought to fence off professionalism from sexuality. Yet, the data ruptures a simple polarisation of professionalism and sexuality. When asked if his female boss saw him as professional, Ciaran was quick to reply in the affirmative:

> we have an understanding and respect of each other as professionals, so the gay thing is not an issue. ...If anything, it helps us to work together because we have common ground to talk about things like men and fashion.

Present here is the attempt on Ciaran's part to establish a deeper human connection that engenders mutuality. Using sexuality as a discursive resource to foster and profit from the informal aspects of his relationship with Fiona marks Ciaran out from the other men in the study, as an unconventional political agent. As Deborah Kerfoot asserts, those who desire to appear professional "both operate within and recreate the organization as a political entity."[19] That sexuality may be used as a resource to get past organisational gate-keepers in order to get to the top, is not a new idea. Feminist researchers such as Cynthia Cockburn have suggested that heterosexuality is available to men, though not exclusively, as a resource for exploitation and (re)producing patriarchal relations in the workplace.[20] However, little attention has been given to understanding sexuality as a resource on hand to gay men to advance their position and status within organisations. Thus, in extending Kerfoot's conception of the professional as organisational politician, is to recognise that gay sexualities and genders are characterised by principles of performance, and that such performances may pocket workplace rewards.

However, this is not to argue that such performances are the sole property of individuals. To do so would amount to an unproblematic conception of the ownership of such cultural performances. Moreover, I wish to highlight the transient nature and unpredictable outcomes of such performances. While Ciaran might provide for Fiona that view of the Other as one that is entertaining and subsequently rewarded for its diversionary appeal, it is characterised by contextual contingency. Ciaran told me that it might be difficult to deploy his sexuality in the same way within homosocial arrangements among "straight men" or within a line management relationship with either, a "straight" or "gay boss." Furthermore, Ciaran may use his sexuality to manoeuvre Fiona into certain ways of thinking about the allocation of organisational rewards, but he does so, confining sexuality to safe outlets of expression. The situational construction of sexual identity in the exchanges between Fiona and Ciaran are stripped of any connotation to sexual activity. As Ciaran said, "we don't do sex…it's the one thing we don't talk about." De-sexualising gay sexuality within his relationship with Fiona seemed important to Ciaran, as to do otherwise would be to "sully" the relationship's "professional" core. So, while the study findings point up how male gay sexualities harbour the potential for gay men to secure allies in the workplace, they also remind us that the success with which such resources are utilised depends in part, on the degree to which gay sexualities are recognised and appeal to the interests of potential supporters. Thus, one key issue arising from this line of argument regards the impact of these identity expressions for countering hegemonic representations of masculinity and claiming new ways of being in the world of work.

One perspective might be that professionalism offers gay men new inclusivities within masculine practices and behaviours that have become synonymous with the professional ideal. In such gendered terms, openly gay men are furnished with opportunities to demonstrate their professional conduct and economic value. As Morgan, an IT Manager proclaimed, "I can be out and proud so to speak, and show that I can add value to the Trust." Another interviewee (Dion) employed in a clinical governance role felt positive about working in an environment where there is "no overriding interest in your sexuality, just in your ability to do the job and deliver results." In such organisational settings where questions regarding economic outputs are frequently being asked, there is perhaps, the chance for gay men to approach their work lives in a manner that enables them to undergird their identities as active producers (rather than consumers) of work outputs. Individual concerns about quantifying work performance and productivity and the attendant behaviours such concerns evoke, projects an intensely masculine image. Certainly, study data goes some way to support the viewpoint that the work lives of some of the men resemble those of their heterosexual co-workers. This is to suggest, that identity building in relation to sexuality is as Seidman puts it, treated more like a "thread" where other identities are constituted as the heart of self-definition. After all, as Seidman goes on to say, rather wryly, the advantage for gay persons "claiming a heterosexual identity is that it confers real social and cultural privileges."[21]

While this might be the case, claiming workplace rewards and privileges is by no means straightforward or without cost. Even where being gay is apparently seen in positive terms, gay sexualities may become marginalised or even trivialised. Arguably, while treating gay sexuality as an identity thread may achieve some minority rights and possible inclusiveness within organisations, it does not dismantle heterosexual dominance. Indeed, it could be said that the (re)production of normalising discourses of professionalism undertaken by a number of the men shores up the heteronormavitity of organisation. Identity acts that demonstrate gender conventionality may amount to a form of collusion, which reinforces heteronormative ways of behaving, of which the successful performance bestows professionalism and also normality. The very possibility, that dominant heterosexual groups may gift normality to some gay men, suggests that a normal gay identity is no less insecure.

7.   Conclusion

In this chapter, I have endeavoured to explore how the notion of professionalism as a discursive site for the construction of a normal gay identity at work takes on new and intriguing meanings that may well problematise traditional approaches to understanding professionalism.

Sexuality is deeply implicated in the process of professional boundary making, and, yet, seldom is this explored in the sociology of professionalism. I have taken a step towards contributing to the scholarly work that is beginning to fill this lacuna in the literature. Within these pages I have explored some of the issues that arise from consideration of the idea that some workplaces may well permit greater flexibility in how gay identities are constructed. This leads me to an important point: that is, to steer attention to the conditional nature of the often tacit workplace arrangements whereby gay men may seek to identify as professional and, thus, be recognised as normal and equal to their heterosexual co-workers. For example, I have maintained that traditional understandings of the public-private split, where sexuality is quarantined within the private sphere, no longer appear stable or relevant. One implication associated with viewing gay men as the same as their straight co-workers is that gay men may occupy the public world of work with greater prominence. However, as the study data has shown, levels of visibility of male gayness may be more apparent in some work locales over others. Indeed, the men's talk revealed how some cling to traditional processes of professional boundary making even if such distinctions between professionalism and sexuality might be deemed artificial. One argument might be that professionalism as a site for normalising gay male identities by emphasising gender conventionality produces an acceptable public face of male homosexuality that gay men must match. While the men may identify as being openly gay at work, some at least remain ever watchful of the presentation of public self that adheres to a familiar logic in terms of regulating public (professional) and private (sexual) selves.

The study contributes to existing knowledge about how professional and gay are not uniform identity categories in the way they are practised and experienced at work. The men may take up these identity options but they cannot do so with absolute freedom. Indeed, access to identities is sutured by inequality and those individuals who seek to appear normal make choices to appear as such within the constraints imposed by social norms and rules. Therefore, under the conditions of cultural production ordered by the concept of heteronormativity, the new public face of the normal gay man is an unmitigated heteronormative invention. As Steven Seidman reminds us, while the emergence of the normal gay may be worth celebrating for the cultural privileges it may confer onto some gay men, it is important to recognise that it does not herald the demise of heterosexual dominance. Set against this argument questions concerning the nature of the relationship between gay men and their heteronormative work sites are brought into sharper relief. In the context of the gay men there is some evidence of collusion with heteronormative practices. Acts of collusion are mostly likely to reside in how the men discursively procure the status of normality in terms of sameness. However, these collusive practices that contribute to (re)producing sexual inequalities in the workplace also serve to validate the identity of some gay men within particular work locales. In this respect they might be clearly seen as worth sustaining. This study has illustrated some of the contradictory and paradoxical situations that exist for gay men positioned with and in an instrumental relationship to heteronormativity. In (re)creating the professional self, the gay men are making use of available discourses to (re)interpret who they are and who they might be within the world of work. Thus, it is important for future studies of the organisational experiences of gay men to explore the conditions that exist across a myriad of work sites under which the discursive construction of the normal, gay professional may be enacted or resisted.

Notes

1. The notion of discourse being employed within these pages is a Foucauldian one, in which discourse is viewed as a connected - but sometimes incoherent - set of ideas, expressions and statements which together, constitute a way of understanding and engaging within the social world. Discourses may be drawn upon by individuals to shape subject positions, subjectivities and craft identities.

2. James Woods and John Lucas, *The Corporate Closet: The Professional Lives of Gay Men in America* (New York: The Free Press, 1993).

3. Jill Humphrey, "Organizing Sexualities, Organized Inequalities: Lesbians and Gay Men in the Public Service Occupations," *Gender, Work and Organization* 6 (1999): 119-142.

4. David Shallenberger, "Professional and Openly Gay: A Narrative Study of the Experience," *Journal of Management Inquiry* 3 (1994): 119-142.

5. Humphrey, p. 135.

6. Deborah Kerfoot, "Managing the 'Professional' Man," in *Managing Professional Identities: Knowledge, Performativity and the 'New' Professional*, eds. Mike Dent and Stephen Whitehead (London: Routledge, 2001), 81-95.

7. Kerfoot, p. 92.

8. Steven Seidman, *Beyond the Closet: The Transformation of Gay and Lesbian Life* (New York, London: Routledge, 2002), 133.

9. Diane Richardson, "Locating Sexualities: From Here to Normality," *Sexualities* 7 (2004): 391-411.

10. Seidman, p. 14.

11. Katie Deverell, *Sex, Work, and Professionalism: Working in HIV/AIDS* (London: Routledge, 2001), xiv.

12. Deverell, p. xiii.

13. Deborah Kerfoot and David Knights, "Managing Masculinity in Contemporary Organizational Life: A 'Man'agerial Project," *Organization* 5 (1998): 7-26.

14. Judith Butler, *Gender Trouble: Feminism and the Subversion of Identity* (New York: Routledge, 1990), 139.

15. Judith Butler, *Excitable Speech: A Politics of the Performative* (London: Routledge, 1997), 30-1.

16. Robert Connell, *Gender and Power: Society, the Person, and Sexual Politics* (Cambridge: Polity, 1987), 181.

17. Richard Dyer, *The Culture of Queers* (London: Routledge, 2001).

18. Butler, 1990.

19. Kerfoot, p. 87.

20. Cynthia Cockburn, *In the Way of Women: Men's Resistance to Sex Equality in Organizations* (London: Macmillan, 1991).

21. Seidman, p. 12.

Select Bibliography

Butler, Judith. *Excitable Speech: A Politics of the Performative*. London: Routledge, 1997.

Butler, Judith. *Gender Trouble: Feminism and the Subversion of Identity*. New York: Routledge, 1990.

Connell, Robert. *Gender and Power: Society, the Person, and Sexual Politics*. Cambridge: Polity, 1987.

Deverell, Katie. *Sex, Work, and Professionalism: Working in HIV/AIDS*. London: Routledge, 2001.

Humphrey, Jill. "Organizing Sexualities, Organized Inequalities: Lesbians and Gay Men in the Public Service Occupations." *Gender, Work and Organization* 6 (1999): 119-142.

Kerfoot, Deborah. "Managing the 'Professional' Man." In *Managing Professional Identities: Knowledge, Performativity and the 'New' Professional*, edited by Mike Dent and Stephen Whitehead, 81-95. London: Routledge, 2001.

Kerfoot, Deborah and David Knights. "Managing Masculinity in Contemporary Organizational Life: A 'Man'agerial Project." *Organization* 5 (1998): 7-26.

Richardson, Diane. "Locating Sexualities: From Here to Normality." *Sexualities* 7 (2004): 391-411.

Seidman, Steven. *Beyond the Closet: The Transformation of Gay and Lesbian Life*. New York, London: Routledge, 2002.

Shallenberger, David. "Professional and Openly Gay: A Narrative Study of the Experience." *Journal of Management Inquiry* 3 (1994): 119-142.

Woods, James and John Lucas, *The Corporate Closet: The Professional Lives of Gay Men in America.* New York: The Free Press, 1993.

How Big is Your God?
Queer Christian Social Movements

Jodi O'Brien

Abstract
        This paper is based on a more comprehensive ethnographic project in which I develop the thesis that the contradictions between Christianity and homosexuality are the driving tensions in the formulation of a historically specific expression of queer religiosity. The emergence and proliferation of a uniquely queer Christianity can be considered as a form of social movement taking place within the pews. This movement is being shaped by the presence of lesbian and gay members and the contradictions their presence forces on their congregations. Particular discursive strategies emerge as congregations struggle to manage these contradictions and to articulate "open and affirming" statements of inclusion for lesbian and gay members. These strategies reflect a re-orientation on the meaning of Christianity as "love and community." When put into practice, this theological position serves as a motivation for many congregations to become activists for unexpected political causes such as same-sex marriage. **Key Words:** Christianity, homosexuality, social activism.

1.   Introduction

        Amidst the current clamour surrounding the politics of "gay marriage" another battle for cultural inclusion and belonging is garnering less public attention, but, arguably, is implicated in widespread and significant social change. This battle is not being waged in courtrooms, congressional halls, or voting polls; it is taking shape within the pews of Christian houses of worship. For more than a decade, mainstream Christian denominations have been engaged in considerable conflict over the participation of lesbian and gay members.[1] Congregations are wrestling with difficult questions of inclusion and its theological and organisational implications. The literature on this tension *within* congregations and on the related tensions between congregations and denominations is scant. Media and political discourse that present Christianity in dichotomous terms further eclipse the significance of this groundswell of social activism: good Christians are anti-gay; gays are anti-Christian. My intent in this paper is to problematise this conception by describing the widespread phenomenon of mainstream Christian congregations that support lesbian and gay ministry and members.

A. Queer Christian Identities

Who are queer Christians and why do they want to belong to religious organisations that treat them as outcasts? This question underlies much of the current literature on religion and homosexuality. One presumed, uncritical, and uninformed answer is that queer Christians are somehow misguided and tortured souls who have not managed to throw off the cloak of shame and oppression. Those who attempt to provide a more critical explanation of lesbian and gay involvement in Christian organisations, suggest that religion is one of the "last citadels" of gay oppression.[2] From this perspective, the struggle for inclusion is viewed a final step toward attaining cultural and political acceptance. In this literature, lesbian and gay Christian involvement is interpreted as a form of political expression whereby queers are taking on traditional homophobia by acting from within. The problem with this interpretation is that it presumes an "oppositional consciousness"[3] that conflates outcomes (religious reform) with motivation and presumes a motivation (desire to reform) that is not necessarily reflective of the actual experiences of lesbian and gay Christians.

In a previous study, I sought to understand the experiences of lesbian and gay Christians and how they make sense of the seeming contradiction between being Christian and queer.[4] My ethnographic research suggests that there are several stages of awareness and articulation that occur before any form of "oppositional consciousness" develops among lesbian and gay Christians. What is most significant for these individuals is the contradiction itself. "Living the contradiction" is a commonly understood experience among lesbian and gay Christians. Queer Christian self-articulation is forged through attempts to grapple with this contradiction, or what is known as the "gay predicament."[5] According to this predicament, religion is a primary system of meaning, a basis for addressing big questions about life, meaning, and purpose. In traditional Christian narratives, the homosexual is irretrievably cast off from this system of meaning. Reconciliation, which is a stage in the articulation of a queer Christian identity, involves the recognition of this tension as a *raison d'etre* or the basis for making sense of and organising one's life, and a recognition of homosexuality as a gift from God. This gift that also signifies the queer Christian's particular "cross to bear" and as such, is strongly resonant with general Christian ideals of martyrdom and sacrifice.

Queer Christian identity involves a transformation whereby the discourse of shame and silence is replaced with a discourse of pride and expression – a shift from "irredeemable problem" to "path of redemption" for the Church itself. Accordingly, queer Christians issue a challenge to fellow congregants to accept them and thereby accept *all* that God has created. In so doing, the challenge is for Christians generally to acknowledge God's unconditional love by demonstrating their own unqualified support for homosexual members. Queer Christians see themselves as "better Christians – indeed, better persons, as a consequence of this struggle."[6] They believe that they are a kind of crucible through which other members and the church as a whole will forge a more loving institution. In other words, they see their contradictory presence as good for the church. In this regard, they consider themselves to be both modern day Christian soldiers and sacrificial lambs.

The emergence and proliferation of a queer Christian identity and consciousness is historically unique and should be understood within the context in which it is developing. Specifically, in this case, the motivation for participation should be understood in terms of the homosexual Christian's desire for self-understanding in Christian terms and for reintegration into a system of meaning from which he or she has been cast off.[7] Similarly, the emergence of a queer Christian social movement can be usefully understood within the framework of attempts by religious congregations to make sense of the contradictions and tensions revealed in the presence of lesbian and gay members. The fullness of the phenomenon that some have referred to as the "queering of Christianity" is best understood in terms of separate, but mutually constitutive fields of relations: individual, community, organisational, and ideological. In the following comments, I offer a description of contemporary congregational communities and their responses to the growing presence of openly gay members. I then discuss some of the historically unique implications of the proliferation of queer Christianity. I conclude with a consideration of the radical and/or conserving implications of such a movement and a few notes on the emergence of a new Christian "left."

It is not my intent to provide a definitive record of queer Christian social movements, or to elaborate social movement theories as they are currently written. Rather, my intent is to remind readers of the significance of religion as a basis for social meaning and community activism and to complicate a troublingly simplistic set of ideas about religious tolerance, activism and the implications for the public arena.[8]

2.   Congregations as Communities

Congregations are a form of community wherein members seek meaning, belonging and a sense of engagement and purpose. To this extent, congregational dynamics, like all community dynamics, reflect the complex and often contradictory sensibilities of the collective membership. At the same time, congregations are situated in organisational structures that transcend the everyday relations of community participants. In this regard, congregations are beholden to theological doctrines and organisational procedures that reflect a top-down governance process. Catholicism and the various Protestant denominations differ greatly in the formal degree by which congregations are allowed to chart their own course. They differ still more in the degree of informal articulation by which congregations actually steer the course. One implication of this is that there is often tension between specific congregations and the organisational denomination. These tensions are significant in shaping religious discourse. To this end, congregations serve as a kind of grass roots social movement reflecting the commitments and values of the congregation, which may be in conflict with the denomination.

Both denominational and congregational responses to the question of homosexuality have been more complicated than is commonly recognised. As Cadge points out in a survey analysis, mainline Protestant denominations have been formally debating aspects of homosexuality since 1966, a fact largely ignored even in many specific congregations.[9] In the past two decades, the development of Christian AIDS ministries, and debates about gay marriage ceremonies and clergy "coming out" have heightened the recognition of a lesbian and gay presence in Christian congregations. These various events have sparked tremendous controversy and upheaval. The turmoil has been exacerbated by the formal actions of some denominational organisations (e.g., Baptists and Methodists most recently) denouncing congregational acceptance of lesbian and gay members and clergy, and the increasing support of anti-gay activities by some religious organisations. Congregations began to solidify around these issues and, in some cases, have been galvanised in response to anti-gay activities. For instance, one Seattle area church, in a congregational letter announcing its unanimous vote to become "open and affirming" notes that the final impetus for this vote was a visit to the city by the anti-gay activist, Fred Phelps. In a gleeful aside to his parishioners, the pastor writes in his letter, "Psst...don't tell Fred Phelps that his presence here only served to solidify our support of becoming Open and Affirming on this Lord's Day."[10]

Numerous Christian congregations throughout British Columbia, Great Britain and the United States have issued formal statements of "inclusion and affirmation" of lesbian and gay members.[11] The issuance of such a statement marks the group as a "reconciling congregation." Cadge traces the model for "reconciling congregations" to a 1978 program ("More Light") launched in a Presbyterian congregation. The term "reconciling congregation" comes from a discussion among United Methodists in 1982. The aim of some of the early "reconciling congregations" was to serve as a "bridge" to assist congregations in crossing from an emphasis on "morality to "ministry." By 2000, an umbrella organisation, Reconciling Networks, was created and listed 176 congregations at the time of inception.[12]

In most cases formal statements of inclusion and acceptance evolve only after considerable debate among congregants. Many members may leave a parish or congregation because of its actions on behalf of lesbian and gay members (for example, performing marriage ceremonies, the revealed presence of gay clergy and the issuance of formal inclusive statements). Equally significant, but less often discussed, are those who leave a congregation because of its intolerance toward lesbian and gay members. In my research, I have encountered many heterosexual Catholics and Protestants who had explicitly sought out 'open and affirming' churches after experiencing a "crisis of faith" in observing the intolerance of their previous congregations. One recent development is the increasing polarisation of Christian denominations around the issue of gay inclusion. For some churchgoers, an "open and affirming" marquee is a positive indicator that the church also espouses other "liberal values." It is possible that "open and affirming" has become a kind of trope signifying the practice of other religious commitments and values. A consequence of the proliferation of "reconciling congregations" and related congregational debates has been a tremendous demographic shuffling among churchgoers in recent years. Congregants leave one church in search of either more "traditional" or more "progressive" alternatives. Accordingly, some observers note that religious narratives and practices are beginning to reflect more extreme "progressive" or "traditional" positions with less and less emphasis on the so-called comfortable middle that characterised the "McChurches" of the eighties.

Religious scholars posited the 1980s rise in church participation among the middle class as a form of "lifestyle accessorising." Upwardly mobile aspiring families selected congregations that enhanced their general class standing. Roof called the phenomenon a "spiritual marketplace" in which the baby boomer generation "shopped" for religious congregations that provided comfortable and non-controversial forms of community without requiring much in the form of commitment or sacrifice from its members.[13] Accordingly, individuals select congregations that reflect personal beliefs and values. The marketplace model implies that people will tend to gravitate toward religious communities that support personal commitments and, conversely, leave when these commitments are threatened.

In the marketplace of churches, the first wave of congregations that become "open and affirming" share a profile that includes existing anchors in active, social justice oriented service. Many of these churches already had prison ministries, poverty and immigration missions, a legacy of involvement in the civil rights movement, and, more recently, AIDS ministries. High levels of commitment among members in these service-oriented congregations may indicate a search for church as a form of fulfilment and not just a "club" that conveys community standing and prestige. Interestingly, many of the congregations most opposed to lesbian and gay membership have similar "service-oriented" profiles. Official congregational positions on lesbian and gay presence (as well as abortion and, more recently, sexuality education) have become the wedge issues that divide these congregations even within denominations. In consequence, individuals are leaving and/or joining different churches in response to the congregational conversations about homosexuality.[14]

B. Who are the "Progressive Parishioners?"

Progressive parishioners tend to be middle to upper middle class and have college degrees. Though not limited exclusively to urban areas, most reconciling congregations are found in areas known to be relatively "liberal."[15] In my own studies of "open and affirming" congregations located along the west coasts of the U.S. and Canada I was initially struck with the "average white, middle-classness" of the membership...and the prevalence of heterosexuality. The first congregation I became involved with (in Seattle) had only two or three gay members as far as I could tell (and as confirmed by other members). In this case, the membership consisted mostly of 40-75 year old white, middle-class, heterosexual professionals. In 1998 (when I first met them), this congregation was embroiled in a nationally headlined battle with its Baptist denominational leaders over the recent issuance of a formal "open and affirming" statement. Baptist denominational administrators had threatened to revoke the church's charter if they did not retract the statement. The members refused to budge. I was more than a little curious about the motivations underlying this vociferous show of support for lesbian and gay Baptists, especially in a congregation that didn't seem to have many.

As I came to know the members at this Seattle area Baptist church and those engaged in similar battles in Methodist and Presbyterian congregations in the same region, a profile emerged. Many of these individuals had come of age politically during the civil rights moment. Several talked enthusiastically about their participation in voter registration and other activities during this tumultuous period. For these members, exclusion of lesbian and gay members from their chosen place of worship was akin to segregation. In personal and collective discussions with me, many members expressed dismay and outrage in response to what they perceived to be increasingly intolerant attitudes taken by some religious leaders toward lesbian and gay Christians. For these congregants, such exclusion was "just wrong."

In particular, two things, personal affiliation with lesbian and gay Christians, and a growing anti-gay sentiment in several religious communities, seemed to galvanise these members in their support of lesbian and gay members. Many members know someone who is lesbian or gay, who attends services regularly, participates in congregational activities and may even hold lay leadership positions in the church. In many instances, individual congregants seem content to worship side by side with lesbian and gay members and "not make a big deal about it." This quasi, "don't ask, don't tell" practice has been increasingly difficult to maintain in recent years. Paradoxically, the shattering of silence often comes in reaction to decrees made by religious officials that are perceived by individuals and congregants as "outrageously hypocritical." For instance, in 1996 following a General Conference, the United Methodists declared that clergy could not perform lesbian and gay commitment ceremonies. One year later, Methodist minister Jimmy Creech challenged the decree by performing ceremonies. He was tried and found "not guilty" on a technicality, but later, after performing yet more ceremonies, was retried and found "guilty" and defrocked. Not long afterward, another Methodist minister was tried and sanctioned for publicly "coming out" to his congregation. These events and similar episodes in the mid to late 1990s received enough national media attention to assume that most congregations were aware of the proceedings.

Events such as these generate a split between local congregations and administrative denominations. In response, congregations often convene formal meetings to consider whether to take an official position on the presence of lesbian and gay members. Deliberation and the generation of a formal position in response to perceived social injustices is a common and organised procedure in many Protestant congregations. Unlike the tight, top-down theocracies of Catholicism and Mormonism, Protestant congregants expect some semblance of public discussion and debate to occur at the congregational level with regard to important community issues. These discussions reveal the intensity of the conflict many members experience in reaction to the presence of lesbian and gay members.

B. The "Word" or the "Deed"

The deliberations that lead to the articulation of "open and affirming" policies are long and difficult processes. For most congregations, the process takes from 18 months to three years and many congregants leave the community during this time. Two themes are prevalent in the discussions: personal connection and definitions of Christianity as an expression of God's love. In these discussions the initial conversation is very general and the tension revolves around the contradiction between concerns for social justice and the inhumanity of exclusion versus "God's word" on homosexuality as an "abominable sin." Members struggle to find rhetorical solutions to this seemingly irreconcilable contradiction. I observed several instances where conversation broke down entirely around this point. Members left meetings frustrated, exhausted, and, frequently, "demoralised."

Intriguingly, in the attempts to grapple with this frustrating demoralisation, congregants often take a more personal tack. This tack is expressed in narratives about lesbian and gay members they know personally. Members will share stories about the faith of a particular gay member or the dedication and service of a lesbian Christian. Invariably, this particular conversation converges around the collective wonderment of how/why God would exclude such good people from His plan. This is also the point at which the split between "accepting" and "non-accepting" members begins to take shape explicitly as each side seeks to "convince" the other. Non-accepting members tend to emphasise the point that there is room in theology to "love the sinner but hate the sin." They don't wish to exclude lesbian and gay members, but see no reason why these "obvious sinners" should be *formally* supported in their "deviant lifestyles." This particular point is the button that sets off a "crisis of faith" for many, eventually accepting, members.

The following quote from a 68-year-old Baptist congregant captures the sentiment of many on this point:

> Who am I to judge? I listen to all of you claiming to know God's mind. I don't know God's mind. I just know that He told us to love one another. I'm trying to know God's heart. My own heart is telling me that I sit with these people every week and they're not so different from me…probably a lot more faithful even, some of 'em. And when I hear some leader saying 'these people are the good people and those people are the bad people and you should smite them,' well, that makes my heart sick. I don't think God meant for this kind of heartsickness. It turns us against one another. It's hate.

In interviews, members told me repeatedly that they viewed the presence of lesbian gay members and the occasion of the congregational discussions as an "opportunity to examine my own commitment to Christianity." This narrative was prominent in the collective discussions and was even referred to in some settings as "a test." The presence of lesbian and gay members and the call to action on their behalf is seen by many congregational supporters as an opportunity to "live God's unconditional love."

This discursive strategy turns the discussion away from difficult and intractable discussions about God's intended "word" on homosexuality and resets the focus on the expression of God's love through deed. Ultimately, congregations that adopt "open and affirming" policies make a collective transition whereby they reconcile the contradictions of Christianity and homosexuality with the idea that "God is love." Accordingly, God's churches should embody and reflect that universal and unconditional love. In this manner, "open and affirming" congregations do not see themselves as being merely tolerant; they see themselves as having "reconciled" a contradiction that enables them to practice God's intent more fully and widely. There is a strong stream of activism in this discourse: members must "reconcile" their congregation to the fullness of God's love, they must actively fight against those who would diminish some of God's children; they must take a stance.

This congregational transformation parallels a similar transformation among individual lesbian and gay Christians in the formation of a queer Christian identity. A defining moment in this transformation is the redefining of one's homosexuality from "sin" to "a gift from god." The gift comes in the form of a "call to action" whereby lesbian and gay Christians see themselves as charged with the task of "reforming" an institution that has shrunk away from the full meaning of God's love. Similarly, gay affirming congregants view themselves as modern day warriors battling to break the oppressive bands of institutions that no longer represent the fullness of God. To attain this goal, these congregations seek to support and affirm "the *full* participation of *all* who profess faith in Christ."[16] Deliberations regarding homosexuality that are framed in terms of God's unconditional love" tip the equation toward rendering God as an expression of agreement and affirmation among a collective body united in spirit and intent rather than as an anthropomorphic figure handing down his particular rules for all to obey. In short, "god" becomes the extent of the community's expression of love. The larger the reach of the group's love, the bigger their god.

3.   Emergence and Proliferation of a Collective Queer Christianity

What are the organisational and ideological consequences of a lesbian and gay presence in mainstream Christianity? I have suggested that lesbian and gay Christians and many Christian congregations are articulating a historically specific queer religiosity in their attempts to resolve the predicament of homosexual exclusion. What are the larger implications of these emerging discourses of "reconciliation" and transformation? Reconciling and queer Christian theologies resituate and redefine the parameters for discussions of sexuality and morality. Regardless of one's views on the matter, the conversation is different as a consequence of acknowledging homosexuality. The proliferation of a "gay liberation theology" wherein homosexuality is seen as a "gift from God" has led leading many congregations to re-examine what the meaning of theology as a "living guide" that reflects its times.

A. Queer Christian Resources

Ten years ago, lesbian and gay Christians struggling with their identities and congregations struggling with questions of inclusion had few resources from which to draw alternative information. In the past decade, a vast array of queer Christian websites and literature has emerged. These resources include a literature that attempts to define and authorise a "specifically gay, lesbian, or queer 'spirituality' as an alternative to the restrictions of 'organised religion.'"[17] There are websites such as lesbianchristians.com and books with titles like *Religion is a Queer Thing: A Guide to Christian Faith for Lesbian, Gay, Bisexual and Transgendered People* and *Coming Out While Staying In* that are intended explicitly to assist the queer Christian who wishes to maintain connections to mainstream Christianity. Several schools of ministry and theology now have either LGBT centres or host LGBT conferences and forums.

Online technology is a central factor in the proliferation of shared queer Christian narratives and the cohering of a culture. Online communication operates as an information dispensing mechanism that traverses geographical boundaries to make resources widely available. It also functions as a site for meeting and interacting with like-minded others; in this case, fellow queer Christians who now have an opportunity to formulate and perform variations on queer Christian identities. Online merchandise marketing can be used as a kind of indicator of cultural development and/or social movement status. In this case, the availability of queer Christian themed products available for purchase is staggering.

B. Discursive Themes

Discursive strategies centred around the theme "God is love" were used to foment lesbian and gay inclusion in the first "reconciling" congregations. The past decade has seen the emergence of a critical mass of "open and affirming" congregations. One implication of this development has been the articulation of additional themes whereby aspects of traditional Christianity are elaborated, re-emphasised, or reinterpreted to facilitate queer Christian narratives. Three themes in particular occur repeatedly in queer Christian literature, on websites and in congregational conversations.

1. "Jesus Was a Liberal"

The first theme focuses on the notion that "Jesus was a liberal." This discursive tact emphasises Jesus' work with the poor, the outcast and the downtrodden. One popular on-line magazine (whosoever.org) publishes a series titled: "Lepers, Loons, and Losers: The Outcasts of the Gospels." In each installment, author Tom Yeshua retells a familiar biblical story (for example, the Lepers) and emphasises Jesus' love for and service to these "social outcasts." He concludes each episode with a discussion intended to convince the reader that "see, the bible really is gay friendly." The stories are also noteworthy in the twin themes of struggle and redemption as re-interpreted to apply to queer Christians. After having chronicled the ways in which lepers were cast out as "unclean," Yeshua concludes:

> Why we were created lesbian, gay, bisexual or transgender, will rightfully remain secure in the mind and wisdom of the Almighty God. It is not for us to know, only to embrace, to grow, to share with others what we have learned through our struggles, our painful defeats and glorious victories. We are among the outcasts of society, left by the roadside. But it is exactly from that vantage point that we can see Jesus first as he walks along.[18]

In addition to frequent references to Jesus' special acceptance of the outsider, another variation on the theme of Jesus as a liberal is expressed through an increasingly widespread queer Christian slogan: "religion should unify, not divide." Contemporary queer Christian authors are quick to make associations between the "evils" of current governments and religious organisations that are divisive in their attempts to "rally the membership into hate-mongering." This is not something Jesus would do. The play on words uttered by U.S. president Bush is also a reference to the associations between the Bush administration and ultra-conservative evangelical Christians, a group that many Christians are eager to disassociate themselves from.

2. "Journey of Acceptance"

Another common theme emphasises the "born again" Christian idea of "journey and transformation." Queer Christians struggling to reconcile the contradictions in their lives are counselled to treat the process as a journey and to focus on self-acceptance. One self-help book for queer Christians (and there are more than a few) admonishes: "you cannot accept Jesus into your heart until you accept yourself – as you are –

gay." Struggling individuals are told to use the "serenity prayer" as a source of inspiration and self-acceptance. This discourse is especially prominent among members of ex-gay ministries who, recently, have begun to back away from attempts to help gays and lesbians become "un-gay" and are focusing now on helping them toward "acceptance" within a Christian framework. Jeremy Marks, the founding director of one prominent "ex-gay" ministry, Courage (based in the U.K.), states that queer liberation theologies have given him a basis for reinterpreting his mission. He hopes now, instead of trying to change gays and lesbians to "be something other than what God made us to be," to assist both straight and gay Christians on the "path to acceptance."[19]

The journey of acceptance figures prominently in the Evangelical gay group, Good News, described in Scott Thumma's ethnography.[20] In similar fashion, this group has prepared literature and related resources to help its members find the path to self-acceptance. This acceptance is seen as a first and crucial step toward blazing a path of pride and presence among other Christians.

3. "Humor is the Master's Tool"

Queer Christian writers and spokespeople remind one another regularly to "turn the other cheek" and to use humor and education to combat the enemy. Indeed, in my own review of this literature, I've noticed a pronounced effort at a humorous and educational tone. Articles such as "Spiritual Romance: An Adam and Steve Love Story" use humour to help lesbian and gay Christians grapple with their concerns about same-sex sexuality. Perhaps most striking however, is the wit employed to challenge and reframe anti-gay political and cultural expressions. For instance, in response to the chatter about cartoon character, SpongeBob's reputed homosexuality, one lesbian pastor took the opportunity to compare this pressing social issue ("the biology of sea sponges") with other aspects of Focus on the Family politics. Using oceanographic metaphors, she reminds her readers of the necessity of "staying on the high ground and away from Dobson's tidal wave in injustice."[21]

The explicit use of humor and education as tools in a struggle for recognition and dignity is especially noteworthy in comparison to anti-gay Christian rhetoric. Christians who participate in anti-gay movements tend to see themselves as persecuted. They often employ discourses of persecution and self-protection to justify their activities.[22] In contrast to queer Christians, there is little humour and even less tolerance in the defining literatures and conversations of anti-gay Christians. Two very different images of god and Jesus emerge from these distinctive positions: queer Christians tend to portray "Jesus as teacher and minister to those in need," whereas anti-gay Christians (who are usually fearful of being persecuted by more than just lesbians and gays) adopt a Christian warrior strategy. According to this strategy, they are protecting themselves from *intrusion* by the wicked and by those who seek to destroy what God intends for them to have. In this light, they see their anti-gay activities (including church burnings and bombings) not so much as *attacks on* but as *protection against invaders.*

As I will elaborate below, the distinctive discourses and tones have significant implications for the re-emergence of "Christian left" and those who count themselves as allies in this movement.

4.   Queer Christian Social Movements

To this point I have suggested that congregations grappling with questions of lesbian and gay inclusion in the early to mid 1990s did so amidst considerable turmoil and conflict. Individual members experienced "crises of faith" as they attempted to reconcile doctrinal statements against homosexuality with their own positive knowledge of lesbian and gay members and/or their discomfort with the practice of exclusion in the name of Christianity. Congregations that eventually developed statements of "inclusion and affirmation" did so only after many months, years even, of "listening, dialogue, and discernment" – a process often fraught with bitter dispute and frustrating contradictions. Successful transformation, by which I mean the congregation's ability to reach agreement toward inclusion, required the generation of narratives that enabled congregants to reinterpret Christianity in a manner that reconciled the contradictions. In the ensuing years, the discourses that have emerged from these congregational debates reflect these tensions and contradictions. They also parallel similar processes undertaken by individual lesbian and gay Christians as they attempt wrestle with the contradictions of their own predicaments. The resulting discursive themes use these contradictions and tensions as a framework in making the theological claim for full acceptance and participation, including ordination of lesbian and gay ministry. The result is an emerging queer Christianity that has hallmark characteristics in terms of scriptural interpretation and religious practices. Accordingly, homosexuality is viewed as a kind of crucible or challenge issued to members and religious institutions to practice the fullness of god's love. This particular expression of Christianity is finding traction among more liberal or "progressive" Christians generally. In recent years, Christian congregations and alliances have taken up gay causes under the banner of Christian social justice. These pockets of social movement are worth critical analysis in terms of both the kinds of alliances being formed ("strange bedfellows") and the social values and commitments being promoted by these groups. In the following discussion, I use same-sex marriage as a site of exploration for this analysis.

A. "A Calling to Speak Out"

Scholars of social movements and collective action have repeatedly noted the power of religious organisations in fomenting social change. For example, Christian churches are credited as the organising force behind a successful civil rights movement. The reasons for effective social action among religious groups include shared beliefs and values among members, shared sense of organisational legitimacy, and strong sense of belonging to something larger than the individual. In other words, participants view the group (and related causes) as highly meaningful and are committed in heart as well as mind. Additionally, churches have well formulated lines of communication and structures of authority that help in the mobilisation of resources.

Recently, much attention has been given to the increasing presence of an extreme Christian right in public and political forums. Observers note that the high level of commitment among these Christians combined with effective organising strategies makes the "liberal left" seem even more wishy washy and ineffective in its bid for political influence. Much less attention has been given to the (re)emergence of a liberal Christian "left." The activities of these Christians are beginning to show up on the political radar in collective actions undertaken on behalf of unexpected issues such as same-sex marriage. Observers and participants alike note that the galvanising forces in this emerging collective action include: "extreme, hate driven evangelism," the state's attempts to implicate faith communities in political agendas, and current issues such as same-sex marriage, sex education, and abortion rights.

A majority of individuals who consider themselves evangelical Christians are distraught at the actions being taken in the name of evangelism. Many report that they feel the actions of a small, but vocal minority are misrepresenting both the values and commitments of members and the appropriate focus for the lord's work. As one evangelical minister writes, "we have a few bad seeds playing into the hands of politicians."[23] Members of other Protestant religions are actively working to distance themselves from "extreme evangelicals." Moderate evangelicals and other Protestants have become more unified recently in their collective denouncement of the current Bush administration's use of faith communities to support questionable causes. For example, the administration's attempt to halt the removal of a feeding tube in the case of Terry Shiavo was a subject of considerable discussion on Christian talk radio. Talk show hosts and most guests were loudly and often angrily united in their fury at the administration, especially Tom Delay, for "misusing" Christianity as "justification" for hegemonic posturing.

Same-sex marriage has become a talking and action point for many Christian communities. Onlookers expect to see Christians leading the opposition, but may be surprised to learn that some of the most coherent support is also being organised under the auspices of religious groups. Several states now have coalitions of religious groups working explicitly to promote "marriage equality." In the state of Washington, a group called "Puget Sound Religious Coalition for Marriage Equality" holds regular rallies, makes appearances in Congress and provides advocacy workshops. This coalition is considered by lesbian and gay activists in the Pacific Northwest to be perhaps the single most effective advocacy group working on the same-sex marriage.

Why all this effort among self-described straight, Christians? The coalition was founded by a group of area clergy who represent Baptists, Methodists, Presbyterians, Unitarians, and Congregationalists. Founding members also include a Muslim cleric and a Jewish rabbi. Included in the coalition's "rally packets" (available online) is a sample newsletter that participants are encouraged to personalise and distribute to their congregations. The newsletter explains why, as believers in God, members should take up the "urgent and worthy cause" of marriage equality. As proclaimed in the letter (and also the coalitions website banner): "The Church is an agent of divine love and justice – we have a calling to speak out."[24]

For the participants in this religious coalition, engagement in advocacy work for marriage equality is one way to "demonstrate commitment to the lord's work." Individual motivations are complex, but the collective discursive motivation in this instance of active Christian support for same-sex marriage is founded in a belief that God's work requires members to be responsive to the issues of the times. As Christians of faith, "we must speak out against injustice." There is more than a little irony in the observation that the basis for the injustice that these groups are speaking out against is also rooted in Christian ideology. Same-sex marriage foes have certainly used Christianity as an effective rhetorical framework in the attempts to "save marriage." Both sides see themselves as engaged in the work of the lord and it is this common belief in the necessity of such work that impels high levels of activism on both sides. Secular observers often refer to same-sex marriage as a "culture war." Given the active and highly articulated participation of Christian groups on both sides of the issue, it might be more accurate to refer to this as a religious war.

B. Strange Bedfellows

There are several factors responsible for the re-emergence or renewed social action of a Christian left. The inclusion of lesbian and gay members in religious congregations and, more recently, the coalescing effects of the fight for marriage equality, are one set of issues that have garnered the attention and resources of "progressive" Christian activists.[25] The most apparent reasons why this particular issue has become a rallying point for "speaking out" include organised reaction to what is perceived as "hate mongering" among the extreme Christian right. Many congregations, fresh from the challenges of deliberating policies of "inclusion and affirmation" view the debates on marriage equality as a compelling battleground for practising "divine love and agency." This particular fight enables them to put newly articulated ideologies into practice. Marriage ceremonies also have a marked history for Christian clergy. Since the 1970s, the performance of religious ceremonies for same-sex couples has been a matter of heated discussion and earnest discernment among clergy and, in several highly publicised cases, a kind of "line in the sand" drawn between ministers willing to perform such ceremonies and the administrative bodies of their respective denominations. The issue is definitely a lightening rod.

In addition to the various reasons that make same-sex marriage a compelling cause for mostly straight identified "progressive" Christians, especially those worshipping in "open and affirming congregations," the presence of an LGBT Christian community is making itself increasingly known. In England, for example, LGBT Christians are the largest lesbian and gay activist group on record.[26] Among this group, for reasons explained below, same-sex marriage is a particularly significant symbol toward full recognition of the blessings that god intends all his children to enjoy.

The Christian "movement" for marriage equality is a convergence of different paths and interests even among self-identified Christians. Some of these diverse reasons include the feeling among queer identified Christians of a special "mission" or "calling." Among the straight-identified faithful, this is a call to action on behalf of divine work of the lord. Simply the civil rights aspect of the issue compels some. Several observers have posited the notion of marriage equality as the civil rights *cause celebre* of the new century. Others participants claim to be less certain about the "rightness" of same-sex marriage, but are compelled, ultimately, to take action against the "hate-mongering" among a few bad seeds who are perceived to be misrepresenting "the rest of the good evangelicals."

In addition to the various motivations and underlying values among Christians fighting on behalf of lesbian and gay justice, the movement is gaining momentum as less active and/or non-Christians join the ranks. Large numbers of individual non-Christians who "want to make a difference" are joining groups such as the Puget Sound Religious Coalition because they see such groups as *the* most effective in their organising strategies. Lesbian and gay activist leaders echo similar notions. One director of a national gay and lesbian task force recently confided that she was encouraging LGBT community groups to align with religious coalitions largely because these groups "have the most amazing resources – including media tips, advocacy packets and lists of talking points."

Thus, while manifesting the appearance of being united in cause, this particular social movement is populated with some seemingly strange bedfellows. The mix grows more intriguing still as politicians recognise the strength of a galvanised constituency and begin to play to their interests. It's too soon to tell what the consequences of such alliances will be. Similar alliances of equally unexpected partners are forming in opposition to same-sex marriage and other LGBT justice concerns. One likely outcome is the de-centring of stereotypes – both Christian and queer – that is already occurring as such a diverse group of people join ranks to fight the same cause. The active presence of Christian leadership in this movement, and its accompanying rhetoric of motive, does beg the question is this movement ultimately "radical" or "conservative?" I address this question and related implications of a queer Christian social movement by way of conclusion.

5.   Concluding Observations

What are some of the likely outcomes of a movement that uses a Christian rhetoric of motivation in support of lesbian and gay causes?

A. The Radical Implications of Queer Theology

Earlier in this paper and in previous work, I have suggested that the discursive strategies used to reconcile the contradictions of Christianity and homosexuality result in a particularly queer form of religious expression. This queer religiosity has radical implications in the transfiguring of an anthropomorphic god into a manifestation of a collective expression of love and the articulated will of the body operating under this mantle of love. This emerging form of gay liberation theology is already being used as a framework for congregations that are taking a stance against denominational administrations in questions of lesbian and gay inclusion. Thus, a queer theology can be said to be radical in its approach both to the image of god and in response to structures of authority in religious institutions. In making the decision to become "inclusive and affirming" congregations emphasise an equation whereby God = love and Christianity = community. This can be interpreted as a radical departure from an equation wherein god = a literal interpretation of scripture and Christianity = the accepted authority for that interpretation. Some observers have likened the movement among "reconciling congregations" to early forms of Christianity and its emphasis on communal values.

As this form of expression takes shape, leaders are stressing the *agency* associated with Christian values of love and harmony. These values must be "practised." Accordingly, it is possible to imagine a refashioning of a *Christian citizen identity* – an identity that is forged through processes of contradiction played out in the public sphere in response to the "urgent and worthwhile" causes of the day. By engaging actively in the fight against injustices, the Christian citizen demonstrates a willingness to do god's work. In this regard, activism on behalf of homosexuality is similar to other social justice interests that have long been the hallmark of many Christian groups. What is different, arguably radically so, is the necessity of reinterpreting and reincorporating a class of people that has been explicitly outcast in order to do the work of justice. This is radical doctrinal alteration.

B. Sexuality

One consequence of congregational deliberations about homosexuality has been more explicit conversations about sexuality generally. While participating in one such deliberative discussion with a Baptist congregation, I was startled one day when one of the women present shouted suddenly, "The problem isn't *homosexuality,* it's sexuality period. Sexuality is really just a big problem for the church and that's what we should be talking about!" After chewing on this idea for a while, this particular group decided to launch a series of "Sunday School talks" on sexuality. They invited various speakers to address a variety of topics, one of which was "Women and Sexuality." Following this particular talk, in which this group of mostly over fifty women had learned some basic feminist ideas about the history of men as sexual agents and women as sexual servants, one woman chuckled and said with glee, "There's going to be some interesting fights in some of our bedrooms tonight." Five years later, this congregation now sponsors a regular sexuality lecture series with speakers invited from around the world. They host an active forum on adolescent sexuality education and family planning and are strong opponents against "abstinence only" education.

Similar activities have emerged in many congregations to the extent that it is reasonable to conclude that more complicated conversations about sexuality are taking place in religious settings. I am not suggesting that considerations of lesbian and gay inclusion are the only factor in launching more critical discussions of sexuality in churches, but my observations suggest that these considerations do open up lines of discourse that allow for more complicated views on the topic. The most radically oriented aspects of these discussions concern sexuality education, especially the need for communities to take more responsibility in teaching young people about the relationship between sexuality, emotion and relationships, and women's sexual agency. Ironically, homosexuality may be a catalyst for these conversations, but when it comes to talk about same-sex relationships and sexuality, the silence is still deafening.

C. Marriage and Forms of Relationships

There is an intriguing (albeit familiar) absence of sexual referents in talk about same-sex relationships. Queer Christian literature and supportive congregations are careful to use terms such as "marriage equality" and "same-gender-loving-communities." Articles written as relationship guides for gay Christians use phrases such as "spiritual romance," which is defined as "monogamous, loving companionship intensified through sexual union." Such definitions are consistent with traditional Christian marriage guidelines that emphasise the desirability of containing sexual expression within marriage. A focus on the specific reasons that Christian groups have articulated regarding the "rightness" of same-sex marriage is instructive in thinking about the implications of this particular social movement. Many groups have articulated a "faith statement" similar to the one below:

> Love is a universal constant spoken of in all religions. To restrict the right of any couple to express their vows of love and form families through marriages or unions is an unconscionable violation of religious freedom. We believe that the government should never act to impose the beliefs of some religions upon others.
>
> We oppose any effort to change the Constitution of the United States to enshrine discrimination into law. We believe that doing so infringes upon the rights of the individual states to regulate marriages. We further believe that, should such an amendment pass, it would violate the spirit of freedom for all people that the founders of our nation instilled in us.
>
> We must speak out. We have participated or officiated in unions and marriages of same-sex couples, some of us for many years, and have been profoundly moved by the sincere desire for tradition and stability within these families. We have seen how these unions have benefited and built community.[27]

The rhetoric is interesting both in the interplay of religion and state and in the image of marriage and its value in society. This group, as do many others, frame their activism in terms of the need to keep the state out of religious choices. At the same time, they use a rhetoric of state granted individual rights as a rallying point for claims of injustice. What I find particularly noteworthy in the context of this essay is the emphasis on the desirability of marriage as something that is good for both individuals and communities. Detailed reading of various "faith statements" indicates a discursive strategy whereby marriage is seen as an earthly institution that brings stability to individual families and, subsequently, serves as a bridge of stability and prosperity between the family and other social institutions. In this conception, marriage is indeed the bedrock of society and *anyone,* gay or straight, who is willing to "take on the burdens and responsibilities" of marriage should be allowed to do so *because it will stabilise and strengthen society.* According to the Christian rationale, marriage serves not only to stabilise society, but also to stabilise individual desires and faith by containing them through commitment to a single partner.

This traditional formulation can be seen as radical only to the extent that it extends union to same gendered partners. Indeed, given the primacy of gender as a form of social organisation, there is a strong radical component to this equation, especially in the recognition of the bonds of support and companionship that are affirmed through recognition of same-sex unions. At the same time, it is likely that this particular conception will lead to increasing exclusion of those who cannot and will not marry in a traditional manner. Feminist scholars have already made a strong case for the problems of vesting so many primary benefits and assurances in traditional marriage, especially to the extent that marriage is an extension of the welfare state (and used thereby to police and sanction female sexuality in particular). Suffice it to say here that there is a kind of bittersweet quality in observing Christians fighting so valiantly for the rights of a group that has, historically, been so vilified within Christianity as evil. Watching this complexly wrought movement is a reminder of the ways in which Christians too, as a group, are frequently dismissed and misrepresented through stereotypes. At the same time – and especially given the level or resources and organisation that Christian activists are able to employ on behalf of the causes they choose to pursue – we should be cautious about the content of what is being "won" on behalf of lesbian and gays. As Nancy Polikoff reminds us, traditional marriage "is a coercive institution that creates insiders and outsiders symbolically and by conferring benefits [unequally]."[28] The various rationales made by Christian organisations in defence of same-sex marriage give every indication that traditional forms remain the only form on offer. Lesbian and gay families are being invited to take part by having their unions recognised and blessed within the context of a "welcoming, nurturing community." But the terms and implications of this Christian acceptance have yet to be critically assessed.

D. Totems and Anti-Totems: The Power of Religiosity

Religion captures both the hearts and minds of its members. It provides a coherent system of meaning from which to address significant questions such the meaning and purpose of life (and death). In analysing religious based activism, a useful distinction can be made between attempts to shore up and expand the religion itself and the *practice* of religious belief through collective action. In terms of the latter, collective action on behalf of a particular cause or group can be viewed in terms of both instrumental political action and expressive collective ritual. Scholars have noted that both activities are necessary in supporting and maintaining the collective consciousness. Ritual expression relies on totemic symbols to focus the energies of participants and to coalesce this energy into the experience of collective synergy. In short, totems are a basis for collective rallying. Some observers have speculated that in the absence of meaningful collective symbolism, for instance when the collective sentiment is waning and religiosity is losing its pull, a focus on the "outsider" or "other" functions as a kind of "anti-totem" that can be used to galvanise support. In this regard, homosexuality (along with abortion) can be viewed as a form of anti-totem being used by some Christian organisations as a basis for fomenting religious support and expanding religious presence. Anti-totems elicit fear, suspicion and hate, all of which are powerful drivers in collective action. In contrast, the homosexual as represented in "open and affirming" congregations and religious coalitions for marriage equality can be viewed as a totem or symbol of the downtrodden, or cast off member of society who deserves god's love and recognition. The distinctive discursive strategies used by Christian "extremists" and "progressive" Christians in activism related to gay social justice can be usefully interpreted in terms of anti-totem versus totem frameworks. The former relies on narratives of persecution, scarcity and erosion of traditional institutions, the latter focuses on the mantle of God's love and its extension through acts of divine agency on behalf of others. In both cases, the homosexual signifies a kind of totem pole around which participants rally to re-experience and renew religious commitments. In looking toward the future and trying to ascertain some of the implications of this intense, complex and often polarising basis of collective action, I wonder about the implications of the queer as a *site* of worship (versus as a participant in the process of worship). I also wonder about the relative power and sustainability of anti-totems (based as they are on a rhetoric of hate and exclusion) versus totems crafted out of a rhetoric of love and inclusion. Does one or the other have a stronger pull on the hearts and habits of those who heed the rallying cry? If so, what does this kind of heartfelt action, undertaken in the name of God, portend?

Notes

1. In this paper I use the phrase "lesbian and gay" because it is the most accurate description of the group about which I am writing. The term lesbian/gay/bisexual/transgendered (LGBT) is politically strategic and meaningful, but often not descriptively accurate in specific cases.

2. Keith Hartmann, *Congregations in Conflict* (New Brunswick, New Jersey: Rutgers University Press, 1996).

3. Jane Mansbridge, "The Making of Oppositional Consciousness," in *Oppositional Consciousness: The Subjective Roots of Social Protest,* eds. Jane Mansbridge and Aldon Morris. (Chicago: University of Chicago Press, 2001), 1-16.

4. Jodi O'Brien, "Wrestling the Angel of Contradiction: Queer Christian Identities," in *Culture and Religion,* Vol 5. (2004): 179-201.

5. Ibid., 184.

6. Ibid., 189.

7. Ibid., 197.

8. The comments in the paper are based on an ethnographic study I began in 1998 and continuing to the present. This study includes participant observation with seven Protestant congregations located in the western United States and British Columbia, 67 interviews and sustained contact with members of these congregations as well as members of lesbian and gay Christian groups, Affirmation and Dignity. Unless otherwise noted, all expressions written in quotes are taken from this study. Because this essay is intended as *suggestive* of a general trend, I do not identify individual quotes and congregations unless directly relevant.

9. Wendy Cadge, "Vital Conflicts: The Mainline Denominations Debate Homosexuality," in *The Quiet Hand of God: Faith-Based Activism and the Public Role of Mainline Protestantism,* eds. Robert Wuthnow and John H. Evans (Berkeley: University of California Press, 2002), 265-86.

10. O'Brien, 2004, 195.

11. Various denominations have different names for lesbian and gay supportive congregations including Open and Affirming/O&A (Disciples), Open and Affirming/ONA (United Church of Christ), Reconciling Congregations (United Methodist Church) and More Light (Presbyterian Church), Welcoming (American Baptist Church), and Reconciling in Christ (Evangelical Lutheran Church in America). In this paper I use variations on these specific names to address the general phenomenon.

12. Wendy Cadge, "Reconciling Congregations Bridging Gay and Straight Communities," in *Gay Religion,* eds. Scott Thumma and Edward R. Gray (Walnut Creek, CA: AltaMira Press, 2004), 31-46.

13. Wade Clark Roof, *Spiritual Marketplace: Baby Boomers and the Remaking of American Religion* (Princeton, New Jersey: Rutgers University Press, 1999).

14. See Scott Thumma, "'Open and Affirming' of Growth? The Challenge of Liberal LGBT-Supportive Congregational Growth," *A Quarter Century of Congregational Studies*, ed. Robert Ratcliff (Oxford: Abingdon Press, forthcoming), n.p., for a discussion of the demographics of membership in response to congregational debates on homosexuality.

15. Nancy T. Ammerman, *Congregations and Community* (New Brunswick, New Jersey: Rutgers University Press, 1997).

16. Seattle First Christian Church (Disciples of Christ) "Statement of Inclusion and Affirmation," (2000).

17. Gary David Comstock, *Que(e)rying Religion: A Critical Anthology* (New York: Continuum Books, 1997), 11.

18. Tom Yeshua, "Lepers Loon and Losers: The Outcasts of the Gospels, Part 2: Roadside Lepers" (2004). http://www.whosoever.org/v8i4/yeshua.shtml.

19. Evangelicals Concerned, "Conservative Leader No Longer Changes Gay People," July10, 2004.
http://www.ecwr.org/aboutus/New_Ex-gay_Leader_Speaks_july10.htm.

20. Scott Thumma, "Negotiating a Religious Identity: The Case of the Gay Evangelical," in *Gay Religion,* eds. Scott Thumma and Edward R. Gray (Walnut Creek, CA: AltaMira Press, 2004).

21. Rev. Peggy R. Gaylord, "Help Get SpongeBob Out of Hot Water!" March, 2005. http://www.whosoever.org/phprint.php.

22. Tom Linneman, *Weathering Change: Gays, Lesbians, Christian Conservatives and Everyday Hostilities* (New York: New York University Press, 2003).

23. Gaylord.

24. Religious Coalition for Equality. See website, <http:www.religious coalition-wa.org>.

25. Other "liberal" Christian issues of concern include sexuality education and the poverty. See, for instance, Jim Wallis, *God's Politics: Why the Right Gets It Wrong and the Left Doesn't Get It* (San Francisco: Harper Books, 2005) for an intriguing commentary on the escalation of poverty under the Bush administration and why Christians should care.

26. S. Gill, *The Lesbian and Gay Christian Movement: Campaigning for Justice, Truth and Love* (London: Cassell, 1997).

27. Religious Coalition for Equality, "Statement of Faith-based Support for Same-Sex Marriage." <http:www.religious coalition-wa.org/statement.htm>.

28. Nancy Polikoff, "Why Lesbians and Gay Men Should Read Martha Fineman," *Journal of Gender Social Policy and the Law,* 8 (American University, 2000),167-176. See also, Jodi O'Brien, "Seeking Normal: Considering Same-Sex Marriage," *Seattle Journal for Social Justice,* 2 (Seattle University, 2004):459-473.

Select Bibliography

Ammerman, Nancy T. *Congregations and Community.* New Brunswick, New Jersey: Rutgers University Press, 1997.

Cadge, Wendy. "Vital Conflicts: The Mainline Denominations Debate Homosexuality." In *The Quiet Hand of God: Faith-Based Activism and the Public Role of Mainline Protestantism,* edited by Robert Wuthnow and John H. Evans, 265-86. Berkeley: University of California Press, 2002.

———. "Reconciling Congregations Bridging Gay and Straight Communities." In *Gay Religion,* edited Scott Thumma and Edward R. Gray, 31-46. Walnut Creek, CA: AltaMira Press, 2004.

Comstock, Gary David. *Que(e)rying Religion: A Critical Anthology.* New York: Continuum Books, 1997.

Gaylord, Rev. Peggy R. Gaylord. "Help Get SpongeBob Out of Hot Water!" March, 2005. http://www.whosoever.org/phprint.php.

Gill, S. *The Lesbian and Gay Christian Movement: Campaigning for Justice,Truth and Love.* London: Cassell, 1997.

Hartmann, Keith. *Congregations in Conflict.* New Brunswick, New Jersey: Rutgers University Press, 1996.

Linneman, Tom. *Weathering Change: Gays, Lesbians, Christian Conservatives and Everyday Hostilities.* New York: New York University Press, 2003.

Mansbridge, Jane. "The Making of Oppositional Consciousness." In *Oppositional Consciousness: The Subjective Roots of Social Protest,* edited by Jane Mansbridge and Aldon Morris, 1-16. Chicago: University of Chicago Press, 2001.

O'Brien, Jodi. "Wrestling the Angel of Contradiction: Queer Christian Identities." *Culture and Religion,* Vol 5 (2004): 179-201.

———. "Seeking Normal: Considering Same-Sex Marriage," *Seattle Journal for Social Justice,* 2 (Seattle University, 2004): 459-473.

Polikoff, Nancy. "Why Lesbians and Gay Men Should Read Martha Fineman," *Journal of Gender Social Policy and the Law,* 8 (American University, 2000):167-176.

Roof, Wade Clark. *Spiritual Marketplace: Baby Boomers and the Remaking of American Religion.* Princeton, New Jersey: Rutgers University Press, 1999.

Thumma, Scott. "Negotiating a Religious Identity: The Case of the Gay Evangelical." In *Gay Religion,* edited by Scott Thumma and Edward R. Gray, 67-82. Walnut Creek, CA: AltaMira Press, 2004.

——. "'Open and Affirming' of Growth? The Challenge of Liberal LGBT-Supportive Congregational Growth." *A Quarter Century of Congregational Studies*, edited by Robert Ratcliff, n.p. Oxford: Abingdon Press, forthcoming.

Wallis, Jim. *God's Politics: Why the Right Gets It Wrong and the Left Doesn't Get It.* San Francisco: Harper Books, 2005.

Yeshua, Tom. "Lepers Loon and Losers: The Outcasts of the Gospels, Part 2: Roadside Lepers" *Whosoever* 2004. http://www.whosoever.org/v8i4/yeshua.shtml.

Notes on Contributors

Tovi Bibring is Ph.D. student in the Department of French in Bar Ilan University, Israel. Her thesis is entitled "Eroticism and Danger: Desire, Transgressions, and Adventurous Ladies in the *Lais* of Marie de France." Her translation into Hebrew of Marie's *Lais* and *Fables* is forthcoming.

Margaret Sönser Breen is Associate Professor of English and Women's Studies at the University of Connecticut, where she specialises in lesbian and gay literature and gender studies. Recent edited collections include *Butler Matters: Judith Butler's Impact on Feminist and Queer Studies* (2005), which she co-edited with Warren J. Blumenfeld, and *Minding Evil: Explorations of Human Iniquity* (2005).

Julia Bruggemann is an Associate Professor of History at DePauw University in Greencastle, Indiana where she teaches courses in German and European history, women's history, and Russian history. She is currently finishing a book manuscript on prostitution in Hamburg during the nineteenth century.

Alejandro Cervantes-Carson is Assistant Professor of Sociology at Mary Washington College. Born in Mexico City, he studied both in Mexico and the United States, obtaining a Ph.D. in sociology from the University of Texas, at Austin. His primary areas of interest and research are the sociology of intimacy, political sociology, social justice and inequality, and Latin America. He has written articles on gender, sexuality, human rights, population policies and reproductive rights, and democracy and social justice. He is currently writing a book on sexual rights and the decentering of heterosexuality, and is part of a research team studying a transnational community that connects northern Virginia, U.S., and southern Puebla, Mexico.

Tracy Citeroni is Associate Professor of Sociology at Mary Washington College in Fredericksburg, Virginia. Recipient of a pre-dissertation fellowship from the Social Science Research Council, she earned her Ph.D. in sociology at the University of Texas at Austin. Citeroni specialises in the sociology of health, aging, gender and the body. She has published in the area of gender and sexuality and has presented numerous conference papers on such topics as life histories of older women in Mexico, a conceptual critique of interdependence in aging research, and life history as an act of deliberative democracy. She is currently at work on a long-term collaborative research project investigating transnational communities of Mexicans in the United States.

Susanne Dodillet works as a Ph.D. student and university teacher in History of Ideas at the University of Göteborg in Sweden. Her dissertation is a comparative study of current German and Swedish prostitution policies and their history.

Ed Green completed an undergraduate degree in Ancient and Medieval History at the University of New England, Australia. He then went to teach in a country High School for two years. Subsequently, he "went bush" to run the family sheep property of some 16,000 acres in North Western NSW for the next eighteen years. During this time he learnt to fly planes and was involved in many aspects of the life of his community. He came to have a thorough experiential knowledge of rural life, its mores, morals, mood and mind. It was during this time that Ed also gained a Master of Letters degree, with Distinction, with a thesis on the experience of friendship in the life of the twelfth century English Cistercian monk – Aelred of Rievaulx. In the early 1990s, Ed left his work on the land to look to a new life-phase and career. It was at this stage that he became interested in the issue of youth suicide, particularly as it related to young men living in rural areas. His early research began to focus on the issues that faced young gay men living in the countryside, and that initial interest has now evolved into a more thorough study leading [hopefully] to a Ph.D. Ed has had his academic work published in texts and training manuals and has given a number of papers at national and international conferences. Ed works as a Senior Policy Officer with the Higher Education Unit in the NSW Department of Education and Training.

Dr. Karoline Gritzner is Lecturer in Theatre Studies in the Department of Theatre, Film and Television Studies at the University of Wales, Aberystwyth (UK). Her research interests include contemporary British and Irish Drama, Modern European Theatre, Gender and Sexuality, Aesthetics and Critical Theory. She organised a symposium on "Theatrical Aesthetics of Eroticism and Death" at Aberystwyth University in 2004. Forthcoming publications include "The Fading of the Subject in Sarah Kane's Later Work," in Daniel Meyer-Dinkgräfe, ed., *Consciousness, Theatre, Literature and the Arts* (Cambridge Scholars Press, 2005).

Katerina Kitsi-Mitakou is Assistant Professor in the School of English, Aristotle University of Thessaloniki. She holds an M.A. in Theatre Studies from Leeds University, UK, and a Ph.D. in English Literature from Aristotle University of Thessaloniki. Her teaching and research interests focus on Realism, Modernism, and the English novel, as well as on feminist and body theory. Her book *Feminist Readings of the Body in Virginia Woolf's Novels* was published in Thessaloniki in 1997. She has co-edited the 2003 issue of *GRAMMA: Journal of Theory and Criticism* ("Wrestling Bodies"), as well as a collection of essays entitled *The Flesh Made Text Made Flesh* (New York: Peter Lang), which is expected to appear in 2006. She is currently working on Enlightenment sexualities and Defoe's novels.

Valerie D. Lehr is Professor of Government and Gender Studies at St. Lawrence University. Her research and teaching focuses on gay/lesbian/queer politics, the politics of the family, and youth and politics. Publications include *Queer Family Values,* "Framing an Alternative Rhetoric: How 'Family Values' Harms the Left," in *Fundamental Differences: Feminists Challenge the Right*, edited by Cynthia Burack and Jyl Josephson and "Relationship Rights for a Queer Society." In *Child, Family, and State*, edited by Stephen Macedo and Iris Marion Young.

Jodi O'Brien is Professor of Sociology at Seattle University. She teaches and writes in the areas of sexualities, religion, inqualities, and social psychology. Her work focuses on the cultural politics of transgressive identities and communities. Her recent books include *The Production of Reality* and *Social Prisms: Reflections of Everyday Myths and Paradoxes*, both published by Sage, and *Everyday Inequalities*, published by Blackwell.

Dr. Shalmalee Palekar is an early career researcher who works in the areas of literary/cultural, feminist and postcolonial studies. She has taught in Indian and Australian universities and is currently a Visiting Fellow at the Centre for Asia-Pacific Social Transformation Studies (CAPSTRANS), University of Wollongong, where her research focuses on representations of women's sexualities in Indian cinemas. Along with being an academic, she writes, acts, and performs professionally with three women and a cello, collectively called "Funkier Than Alice."

Fiona Peters is Senior Lecturer in Cultural Studies at Bath Spa University. Her teaching is mainly in the area of History of Ideas, Cultural Theory and Psychoanalysis. Her specialist teaching includes courses on Representations of Evil and Wickedness, Culture and Barbarism and Feminism and Psychoanalysis. She has recently completed a Ph.D. on anxiety, waiting and lack of desire in the work of the Crime Fiction writer Patricia Highsmith. Recent publications include works on Evil, Monsters, and Monstrosity and a re-evaluation of the concept of the gaze.

Serena Petrella is a Ph.D. candidate in sociology at Carleton University, in Ottawa, Canada. She specialises in theories on the governance of citizens in Neo-Liberal democracies, and on social theories of sexual development, identity and desire.

Nick Rumens is a Lecturer in Human Resource Management at Southampton Institute, where he specialises in the study of diversity and inequalities in the workplace and more broadly, teaches aspects of organisational behaviour and the study of managers and their work practices. He is also a Ph.D. candidate at Keele University and is currently working on a research project that explores the linkages between professionalism, masculinities, and sexualities in public sector organisations. In addition, his research and publication interests include workplace friendships and forms of intimacy in organisations, diversity management, and emotion in corporate settings. Nick is publishing in the field of organisational theory that includes international journals such as Management Learning.

Robert D. Tobin, Professor of German at Whitman College in Walla Walla, Washington, is a 2004-5 Rockefeller Fellow at the Program for the Study of Sexuality, Gender, Health and Human Rights at Columbia University, where he is completing a book on the emergence of modern discourses of sexuality in nineteenth-century German-speaking central Europe. He is the author of *Warm Brothers: Queer Theory and the Age of Goethe* (2000) and *Doctor's Orders: Goethe and Enlightenment Medicine* (2001).

Barbara Wagner holds a doctorate in Art History and is volunteer at the Staatliche Kunsthalle in Baden-Baden, Germany, and involved with curating exhibitions on contemporary art. Her research interests include the representation of body images and gender identities in the art of twentieth- and twenty-first century. She recently published an essay on Claude Cahun and Suzanne Malherbe, lesbian artists who actively took part in the resistance during World War II on the Channel Island Jersey. The article appeared in *Ariadne* 47 (May 2005).